THE
THEOPHRASTAN
CHARACTER

LONDON : GEOFFREY CUMBERLEDGE
OXFORD UNIVERSITY PRESS

THE
THEOPHRASTAN
CHARACTER

IN ENGLAND

TO

1642

BENJAMIN BOYCE

WITH THE ASSISTANCE OF NOTES BY
CHESTER NOYES GREENOUGH

HARVARD UNIVERSITY PRESS
CAMBRIDGE, MASSACHUSETTS
1947

TO

D. M. G. B.

PREFACE

Students of English literature may be glad to know something more about the Character. As a literary form giving easy hospitality not only to humorous and acute observation of human nature but also to wit, imagination, and as nice shaping as any pattern of prose, the Character delighted a generation reared in the humane tradition, and it may still give pleasure. What has been attempted in the following pages is not an enticing display of Theophrastan dishes (though the Character lends itself naturally to anthologists), but a study of the literary progress and especially the technique of the form in the years before the Civil Wars shook the aging culture of England and, incidentally, turned to the hard use of national controversy the small art of the Character. The study begins necessarily with Theophrastus. It comes to an end in 1642, perhaps somewhat arbitrarily. Yet in the period of fifty years after 1592 a literary species had its full growth. What came later, the sketches of the pamphleteers, historians, and periodical writers, of Butler and Dryden and Addison and Johnson and Thackeray—this is another story, a sequel in which Theophrastus becomes almost a minor figure. The first story must come first.

At the time of his death in 1938 Professor Chester Noyes Greenough, whose interest in Character-writing was well known, had assembled an extensive bibliography and index of Characters and had laid out a plan for a comprehensive history of the Character in English literature. Happily the bibliography was almost in final form; it has been edited and seen through the press by J. Milton French (*A Bibliography of the Theophrastan Character in English*, Cambridge: Harvard University Press, 1947). Of the history, unfortunately, only a few paragraphs of an introductory section were written, and though a great body of miscellaneous notes had accumulated, they indicate that most of the matter of the discussion was to come from Mr. Greenough's well-stocked mind. When in very generous fashion Mrs. Greenough suggested that I take the notes to do with as I could, I supposed that I should have the benefit of his fine feeling for literature and his gift of phrase. Instead I have found the notes chiefly—and immeasurably—useful as a guide for reading, in secondary material as well as in the Characters themselves. The jottings on Hall, Overbury, and Earle, however, went beyond bibliography into biography and analysis. Many another note served to suggest a line of attack, and I have made one or two levies upon Mr. Greenough's unpublished Harvard dissertation on Character-writing. Those who remember Mr. Greenough's lectures will be sorry to learn that not a sentence in the book came from his pen. The principal point at which I have departed from the implications of his outline (other than in a free modification of the order and dimensions of his scheme) is that of definition. Mr. Greenough's tendency, proper in a pioneer, was inclusive and broad; mine, whether properly or not, has been, in view of the work of Gwendolen Murphy, Richard Aldington, D. Nichol Smith, W. J. Paylor, E. N. S. Thompson, E. C. Baldwin, Harold Osborne, and others, exclusive and analytical. To keep the discussion within bounds I have usually related things to the model of Theophrastus and to the three best English Character-writers, Hall, Overbury, and Earle. Although I am no longer able to say of many pages whether more of the responsibility is Mr. Greenough's or mine, the critical judgments, though of course shaped by the impression Mr. Greenough's lectures on the Character made on me some years before I began the study, are in a more immediate sense largely my own.

In the quotation of early texts my practice has been to use

u and *v* in the modern way and to fill out contractions. The
spelling of the titles of individual Characters has regularly been
modernized. Unless otherwise specified, the place of publication of books mentioned is London.

Scattered among the notes in Mr. Greenough's boxes were
communications of many helpful varieties from his colleagues
at Harvard and elsewhere and also from his students. I share
the gratitude he unquestionably felt for such aid. In the proper
places I have acknowledged several particular debts, but there
are probably others that have gone unrecorded. The presence
among the notes of many in Mrs. Greenough's hand attest part
of the help she gave, especially in the British Museum and the
Huntington Library. For myself I must express thanks also
to Mr. Karl Pfitzer, Mr. Joseph Scott, and Mr. Bary Wingersky
for assistance in matters Greek and Latin; to Miss Audra Royse
for unfailing care in the preparation of the typescript; to the
staffs of the Harvard and Huntington libraries for innumerable
kindnesses; to Professor William A. Jackson for permission
to quote from manuscripts in the Houghton Library; and, most
of all, to Mrs. Greenough and Professors Douglas Bush, William H. Irving, and Hyder E. Rollins for a critical reading of
the entire manuscript. My greatest debt, other than that
recorded in the title page, is inscribed in the dedication.

B. B.

The University of Nebraska
December 18, 1946

CONTENTS

THE
THEOPHRASTAN
CHARACTER

I
THE
CHARACTERS
OF
THEOPHRASTUS

Virtue is not loved enough nor vice sufficiently detested because both are not seen. The Character, said Joseph Hall, strips both naked, with nothing left them but bare presence to plead for affection. Sir Thomas Overbury or one of the "learned Gentlemen his friends" defined the Character as wit's descant on any plainsong, a definition we might illustrate with Overbury's describing an "Affected Traveler" as one who "hath taken paines to bee ridiculous, and hath seen more then he hath perceived" or with John Earle's identification of a "Plain Country Fellow" as one who manures his ground well but lets himself lie fallow and untilled. But there was more to the seventeenth-century Character than epigram. The whole figure had to be built around a kernel, leaf upon leaf artfully chosen and judiciously placed, keeping always the same center but perpetually turning the thing around for a view from another side. The method, though not difficult, was important, and epigram was a last elegance, the gilt upon the carving, which not everyone could achieve and which no one should use continuously. The originator of the method and the artist who employed it with so acute a sense of design that he did not need the tint of ingenious phrasing was the Greek, Theophrastus.

The Characters were written by Theophrastus, whose real name was Tyrtamus,[1] somewhere near the year 319 B. C. when

---

[1] Most of our information about Theophrastus comes from Diogenes Laertius (V, 36-57), who as he lived in the third century after Christ can hardly be an infallible authority. Many of the doubtful points are considered in Octave Navarre's *Caractères de Théophraste Commentaire* (Paris, 1924).

3

tear - T - mus .

he was about fifty. A universal genius, he contained in one person the man of affairs, the speaker of pithy sentences, the devoted pupil (first of Plato, then of Aristotle), the splendid teacher (drawing as many as two thousand students to his lectures), the head of a school (he succeeded his master in the Peripatetic Academy); and he wrote treatises on botany, rhetoric, mathematics, love, epilepsy, physics, comedy, the sea, animals that bite or gnaw, mines, winds, music, smells, astronomy, politics, dizziness, and innumerable other subjects. The little set of Characters, thirty in number, are full of the most exact knowledge, seemingly, of the habits of common types of men, types not restricted to Athens though Athens is frequently mentioned in their description. Just where this contribution to knowledge belongs—in the department of rhetoric or ethics or politics or psychology or dinner-table recreation—has been seriously canvassed. Isaac Casaubon and Joseph Hall were very much drawn to the statement in the dedicatory proem that Theophrastus described good kinds of men as well as the bad. But only the Characters of bad types have survived, and modern scholars have doubted the authenticity of the proem. Devoted to the memory of Theophrastus and also to the cause of religion and morality, Hall worked out a way of presenting admirable types. But frail and wicked men are always more interesting. It is the Characters of bad types that flourished in the seventeenth century, and it is the method of Theophrastus with which the long line of Character-books started out. The technique of Theophrastus, then, we must first examine. Though no one followed it exactly (seventeenth-century taste was too baroque for that), no one produced a genuine, finished Character-book until Theophastus' method was brought to attention.

Of varying length but all brief (averaging perhaps three hundred words in a literal English translation), the Characters

4

of Theophrastus attempt to sketch the typical manifestations in human nature of some one quality of character. To the modern reader the aspects of character chosen may sometimes seem rather more psychological than moral; as a result, Theophrastus often strikes one as being merely an amused observer of men rather than a moralist or reformer. Certainly the spirit of comedy lurks in his pages. But if we adopt the Aristotelian doctrine, as of course Theophrastus did, that virtue is a mean between two extremes of conduct and that the extremes are vices (though not, indeed, all equally reprehensible), we shall see the propriety in the label given these pieces by Diogenes Laertius— *Ethical Characters* (ἠθικοὶ χαρακτῆρες). Whether rhetorical or ethical or in a sense botanical, Theophrastus' sketches of the Flatterer, stuffing his cloak in his mouth to choke his laughter at a stale jest; of the Garrulous Man, babbling of what he had for supper and of who set up the largest torch four months ago and of the weather and his vomiting yesterday and what poor men we are; of the Distrustful Man, happily protecting himself from universal dishonesty; of the Pettily Proud Man, strutting before his wife—these and others retain an uncanny, laughable, and captivating truth.

The method in each of these pieces is first to name the moral quality or habit and then very briefly to define it: thus, "Grumbling . . . is an undue complaining of one's lot"; "Garrulity is the delivering of talk that is irrelevant, or long and unconsidered." After the definition comes the main development, the list of actions and speeches that are typical of a victim of the quality under consideration.[2] The picture is built up entirely of details of what

---

[2] In the Greek, the word defined in each first sentence is an abstract noun, a feminine in *-ia*. Then in the second sentence a masculine noun naming the type of man that corresponds to the abstract quality starts off the list of typical actions. One formula appears repeatedly in the second sentence of each sketch: the described man "is one who" or he

5

the man does or says, usually in apparently random order, as
seen or heard by an impersonal observer. Although Theophrastus allows the reader some opportunity to read between
the lines, he refrains from explicit statement either of what the
character thinks or of what Theophrastus thinks of the character.[3] The language is simple; and almost nothing appears that could be labeled wit. The Character of "Petty
Pride" (ΜΙΚΡΟΦΙΛΟΤΙΜΙΑΣ), one of the best, will serve to
illustrate the ordinary method as well as the kind of merit one
may look for in the Characters.

> Petty Pride will seem to be a vulgar appetite for dis-
> tinction; and the Pettily-proud man of a kind that when
> he is invited out to dine must needs find place to dine next
> the host; and that will take his son off to Delphi to cut his
> first hair. Nothing will please him but his lackey shall be
> a blackamoor. When he pays a pound of silver he has them
> pay it in new coin. He is apt, this man, if he keep a pet
> jackdaw, to buy a little ladder and make a little bronze
> shield for that jackdaw to wear while he hops up and down
> upon the ladder. Should he sacrifice an ox, the scalp or
> frontlet is nailed up, heavily garlanded, over against the
> entrance of his house, so that all that come in may see
> it is an ox he has sacrificed. When he goes in procession
> with the other knights, his man may take all the rest of
> his gear away home for him, but he puts on the cloak and

"is such a man as would," and so on. On another question of phrasing
see *The Characters of Theophrastus*, edited and translated by J. M.
Edmonds (Loeb Classical Library, 1929), p. 4. R. C. Jebb and J. E. Sandys
in their edition (ΘΕΟΦΡΑΣΤΟΥ ΧΑΡΑΚΤΗΡΕΣ *The Characters of
Theophrastus*, 1909) alter the usual order of the Characters for the sake
of putting the sketches of related types together, and they translate the abstract nouns of the titles as if they named a possessor of the abstract
quality.

[3]Modern scholars consider the general, moralizing sentences at the
end of Characters I, II, III, VI, VIII, XXVII, and XXIX to be late additions,
perhaps Byzantine. Cf. Navarre, pp. XXIII-XXV, and Edmonds' notes on
those Characters.

makes his round of the market-place in his spurs. Should his Melitean lap-dog die, he will make him a tomb and set up on it a stone to say "Branch of Melitè." Should he have cause to dedicate a bronze finger or toe in the temple of Asclepius, he is sure to polish it, wreathe it, and anoint it, every day. This man, it is plain, will contrive it with his fellow-magistrates that it be he that shall proclaim the sacrifice to the people; and providing himself a clean coat and setting a wreath on his head, will stand forth and say "The Magistrates have performed the rites of the Milk-Feast, Athenians, in honour of the Mother of the Gods; the sacrifice is propitious, and do you accept the blessing." This done he will away home and tell his wife what a great success he has had.[4]

"Petty Pride" represents the majority of the Characters in that it deals with a moral type. But there are four other sketches —a circumstance of some interest in connection with seventeenth-century English Characters—which may properly be considered to be sketches of social and professional types. "Flattery"(II) as Theophrastus presents it belongs with many sketches in Menander and Terence, Martial and Juvenal, of the notorious professional parasite. "Boorishness" (IV) gives us not just a crude nature but crudity as seen in a rustic. The contrasted pair of political types in "Oligarchy" (XXVI) and "Friendship with Rascals" (XXIX) go beyond a bent of character to an official alignment in public life. Although the latter (XXIX) was apparently not included in editions of Theophrastus until 1798,[5] the other three sketches would suggest to an inventive imitator the possible extension of the genre outside the narrow limit of moral classes to the picturing of social, professional, and national ones.

---

[4] Edmonds' translation.
[5] In the edition of Goez published at Nuremberg. Cf. Jebb-Sandys *Theophrastus*, p. 166.

"Petty Pride" also exemplifies the usual building-up of the Characters by many concrete but independent actions and spoken words, enumerated is if without plan. But Theophrastus departed from this routine also. "Cowardice" (xxv) consists not of an accumulated, unordered list of varieties of cowardly behaviour but rather of two graphic little scenes—the coward at sea in a storm, and the cowardly gentleman in a battle on land. In three other Characters—"Garrulity" (iii), "Newsmaking" (viii), and "Backbiting" (xxviii)—action is largely abandoned in favor of speech. "Garrulity," which consists of one unbroken monologue from the Garrulous Man seated beside an unfortunate stranger, is a vivid skit.

At first glance all the Characters seem, in Jebb's words, "to consider a quality as embodied in a representative man," but Jebb noticed that one Character, "Ill-breeding" (or, in his rendering, "The Unpleasant Man"), impresses the reader as being composed of unsorted and unanalyzed details. More recently Mr. Edmonds has remarked, in the introduction to his edition of Theophrastus, that in the traditional ordering of the Characters in the manuscripts an artistic development can be traced from the earlier, "sketchier" ones to the later, more complete pieces, from those that represent "Anyone" to those of "Somebody." But the difference is not, I think, one of degree, as Mr. Edmonds seems to imply, but one of kind, and the more successful—that is, more vivid and individual—pictures are not all at the end. The less completely realized types—"Dissembling" (i), "Willful Disreputableness" (vi), "Tactlessness" (xii), "Officiousness" (xiii), "Stupidity" (xiv), "Ill-breeding" (xx)—differ from the more vivid Characters in that the vivid ones present a man of a certain type (the flatterer, for instance) in several characteristic actions, whereas the less effective Characters present actions of a certain type (acts of dissembling, for

8

instance) in several men who may not be all alike except in possessing this one quality. The result in the vivid Characters is a good focus, a real picture, as if in making a Hiroshige print the craftsman had superimposed the various plates of colored ink properly; but in a piece like "Dissembling" or "Ill-breeding" it is as if the several printings had been unaccountably taken from a number of similar but not identical designs, so that the result is not one figure clearly done in full tones but several figures all just faintly outlined. Theophrastus' "Flattery" or "Petty Pride" stays in the memory as a unit not because both are more complete than "Dissembling" or "Ill-breeding" but because they are more descriptive and less theoretical—in a word, because they are pictures of a type of man whereas the latter are more nearly essays on certain kinds of actions. The distinction may not be conspicuous in Theophrastus but in the English writers it sometimes is.

When one evaluates the artistic merits of the *Characters* one must admit that their data of conduct and conversation lack subtlety. Yet Theophrastus could differentiate contiguous types —for example, "Garrulity" and "Loquacity"—nicely. He is not bookish; his descriptions in their basic material are probable, permanent, and universal, as if by the direction of his master he proposed to write poetry, not history. The combination of generality and individuality, the representing of a class through the lively picturing of a man whom we can see—Theophrastus is "very good" in this, as Jebb says. And if some of the Characters are better than others, the very nature of the material creates them so. "Petty Pride" is an excellent piece because vanity is a quality that can show, and in extreme cases does show, in all that we see of a man—his dress, his remarks to his wife, his choice of pets and his burial of them, his mannerisms on a public platform—whereas a propensity toward dissembling or tactlessness does not cry out so loudly to the passer-by. Furthermore, modern notions of psychology lead us to look beyond dissembling or "willful disreputableness," which we might term secondary features, to the primary impulses that produce them. The Aristotelian-Theophrastan morality was simpler and perhaps more logical than ours. But even so, when Theophrastus treated a secondary quality not in a diffuse essay but in a focus such as one finds in "Arrogance" and "Affability," the picture still satisfies in spite of the fourth-century Athenian costuming. And in such pieces as "Arrogance," "Petty Pride," and "Meanness" (xxx) the life of one type of man in the midst of his family, with his friends, on the street, in the house, at the sacrifices, is so beautifully painted in, that a moral temperament and a dramatic biography are compressed into one small artistic *objet*.

II
THE
CHARACTER
AND
CLASSICAL RHETORIC

1. THEOPHRASTUS AND ARISTOTLE

How did Theophrastus, a philosopher and teacher and scientist, happen to write his *Characters?* The answer to this question cannot be final, but it must be pursued none the less, for it will lead our discussion in the important direction of Aristotle and the equally important direction of rhetorical theory and teaching, from classical Athens to Jacobean London and Cambridge. The various theories about the origin of the *Characters*—whether they were matched with Characters of virtues in some longer collection, or were a part of a work by Theophrastus on ethics or politics or even poetics, or were composed specifically to illustrate Aristotle's ethical doctrines—are discussed by Jebb and Edmonds. The suggestion that the *Characters* were written in a light mood to entertain a group of friends or pupils is attractive.[1] It would account for the numerous resemblances between these pieces and the *Rhetoric* and *Nicomachean Ethics* of Aristotle. As Jebb has pointed out, some of the Characters appear to be a methodical illustrating of the pronouncements of Artistotle on moral character (ἦθος) and the emotions (πάθος). "Petty Pride," for example, brilliantly amplifies one species of the moral character described by Aristotle

---

[1] See the Jebb-Sandys and Edmonds Introductions. G. Pasquali, "Sui 'Caratteri' di Teofrasto" (*Rassegna Italiana di Lingue e Letterature Classiche,* I [1918], 73-79), argues that the Characters, too unfinished to have been regarded by Theophrastus as suitable for publication, were probably used in his teaching—maybe, of ethics.

in the *Ethics* (IV, iii [1125a]) under the general heading of the Vain (χαῦνοι); it also seems to demonstrate how a foolish man may pervert a truth, in this case the Aristotelian dictum that "unique possessions are the nobler."[2] A more remote, stylistic resemblance can be seen between the list of skeptical and non-committal rejoinders at the end of "Dissembling" and the cautious "maybe" and "perhaps" of old folk as analyzed in the *Rhetoric* (II, xiii). In general the *Characters* seem to be the *jeux d'esprit* of a man who observed life shrewdly but whose ways of thinking were so habitually along Aristotelian lines that, pedagogue as he was, he kept a good deal of schoolroom logic even in his jokes.

Most serious students of the Character have observed that Aristotle anticipated the writing of his favorite pupil by composing some similar sketches himself. Best known are those in Book IV of the *Ethics*, where, in order to clarify and enliven his exposition of the several virtues that exist between the several pairs of opposed extremes or vices, Aristotle draws pictures of the Magnificent Man and the Great-minded Man. In mentioning the vicious aberrations he touches briefly on several of the moral qualities which Theophrastus developed into Characters and writes a sentence of suggestive concrete detail about the Rich Man of Vulgar Profusion (IV, ii [1123a]) that could easily be passed off as a fragment of a lost Character on that subject by Theophrastus. In the *Rhetoric* after describing in general terms the various emotions in pairs (anger and mildness, fear and boldness, pity and indignation, and so on), Aristotle proceeds to list the typical actions, motives, and passions of, respectively, young men, old men, men in their prime, well-born men, rich men, men

---

[2]*The Rhetoric of Aristotle*, translated by Sir Richard C. Jebb and edited by J. E. Sandys (Cambridge, 1909), p. 39 (*Rhetoric* I, ix). The footnotes in the Jebb-Sandys *Theophrastus* analyze parallels between the Characters and the *Nicomachean Ethics*.

of power, and men of good fortune.[3] These descriptions, though more objective than the sketch of the Magnificent Man, are still somewhat subjective and hypothetical. Such passages and, even more truly, those in the *Ethics* are disquisitions, not Characters. They are more philosophical and in some cases more thorough and more complete than the compositions of Theophrastus; they mostly eschew humor and present only a modicum of concrete detail about dress and action and speech; and, most significantly, they investigate causes and explain emotions, interrupting the description at any moment with a generalization. Compression, a stellar virtue of the Character form, Aristotle lacks.

But, as one might expect of a philosopher, Theophrastus kept close to the theory of his teacher, if not, in these works, to his practice. The theory we must notice. First, there was the doctrine of the mean, already mentioned, according to which one may see three states or degrees in respect to any moral quality and according to which also one may pick out three types of people, the central virtuous type and the two extremes of excess and defect. Theophrastus left us pictures only of the extremes, the vices, but the implication of the sketches is that a normal, admirable character is possible.[4] In one case, by drawing an excess of friendliness in "Flattery" and a defect in "Surliness," Theophrastus makes it easy for the reader to conceive of the virtuous mean as Aristotle describes it in the fourth book of the *Ethics* (IV, vi [1127a]). Such a doctrine of morality, fixed yet actually

---

[3]II, xii-xvii.

[4]Because we shall have to talk about virtue or virtuous character a good deal and because the definition of the phrase is complicated by modern disagreements in psychological and philosophical theories, it may be useful here to recall that Aristotle's notion was (*Nicomachean Ethics*, II, i) that we are furnished by nature with certain capacities for moral development but that virtuous character comes only by acts of working that produce the fixed habit of such conduct. Aristotle, needless to say, believed in the freedom of the will.

relative, inevitably kept one's mind busy distinguishing the too little and the too much. G. S. Gordon in an illuminating essay[5] describes Theophrastus' *Characters* as an "artistic by-product" of such necessary, recurrent defining. "Aristotle had exhibited the method in his *Ethics*, and handed over the results to the rhetoricians in his *Rhetoric*; it was the part of his successors to keep the application up to date, since social terms are always changing their meaning. . . . Eudemus and Theophrastus are busy at it [the game of distinguishing moral qualities and types] in the age of Alexander, and all the imitators of Theophrastus up to Philodemus of Gadara, in the age of Cicero and Caesar."

Another familiar idea of Aristotle's, significant for our subject, requires of the poet (as distinguished from the historian) that his creations of character should be true to life by being true to type and consistent, each person speaking and behaving in a fashion probable for his kind of character—that, in a word, he should be universal.[6] No art, says Aristotle, considers the particular; "thus the medical art considers, not what is wholesome for Sokrates or Kallias, but what is so for a certain sort of man or a certain class. This is characteristic of an Art, whereas particulars are infinite and cannot be known. Hence Rhetoric, too, will consider, not what is probable to the individual . . . but what is probable to a given class."[7]

A third idea, less familiar than the other two and requiring a more detailed explanation, connects Aristotle and the theory of Character-writing. A speaker, says Aristotle, must manage to appear to his audience to possess intelligence, virtue, and good will.[8] The first two of these qualities are aspects of moral

---

[5]"Theophrastus and his Imitators," in *English Literature and the Classics* (Oxford, 1912). My quotation is from p. 53.

[6]*Poetics*, IX, XV. See *Rhetoric*, III, vii, for ideas about suitability of language to the character and occasion.

[7]*Rhetoric* (Jebb-Sandys), I, ii [1356b].

[8]*Rhetoric*, I, ii [1356a]; II, i [1378a].

character (ἦθος), a subject which he found it necessary to discuss in his *Rhetoric* (I, ix). Good will is, rather, related to the affection, the passing emotion (πάθος), that part of human nature which must especially be touched—and touched well—by the effective speaker. So in Book II, sections iv to ix, of the *Rhetoric* he considered these affections in a theoretical way, and, in order to illustrate the affections as well as to provide the student of oratory with further insight into the nature of the different groups of men, he then added a set of descriptions, already referred to, of old men, young men, men in their prime, rich men, well-born men, men of power, and fortunate men.[9] The crux of the matter for our study of the Character lies in the notion that a speaker must know the natures of men in respect to moral virtue or character, in respect to affections, age, and fortune;[10] that he must also, for adequate persuasiveness, know the "moral character peculiar to each form of government";[11] and that a good way to master these subjects is to compose, as Aristotle did, descriptions of representative men. In the *Ethics* the examination of moral virtue and the affections is carried on mostly through abstract discussion but with a few particularized characterizations as well. In the *Rhetoric* the character-sketches may be no more numerous, but their significance is somewhat greater: they are not only to clarify the subject-matter for the student, but also they are pedagogical examples themselves, to be copied for their method by the student of oratory. It is impossible either to affirm or deny the suggestion of Otto Immisch[12] that Theophrastus' *Characters*, written about fifteen

---

[9]Rhetoric, II, xii-xvii.

[10]So listed, *Rhetoric*, II, xii [1388b].

[11]*Rhetoric*, I, viii [1366a].

[12]In his introductory essay in *Theophrasts Charaktere* (Der Philologischen Gesellschaft, Leipzig, 1897). The idea is attacked by Navarre, not very effectively, in *Caractères de Théophraste Commentaire*, p. xi.

years after Aristotle's Rhetoric, were composed for a classroom in rhetoric. But is is obvious that he omitted ethical and psychological commentary as Aristotle had not done even in the, for him, relatively objective descriptions of character in the *Rhetoric* and that, whatever his intent, his accomplishment was the creation of a compact literary form capable of affording a special aesthetic satisfaction to the general reader. With that advantage in addition to a putative connection with Aristotle's teaching of ethics and rhetoric, the Characters were eventually adopted by teachers of oratory and written composition. It was the medieval pedagogues in rhetoric to whom England was indebted for its first acquaintance with the Character.[13]

2. THE CHARACTER AND CLASSICAL RHETORIC

The *Characters* of Theophrastus, it has been said, came into England in the sweeping train of medieval rhetoric. Casaubon's important edition of 1592-1599 and the subsequent familiarity with the *Characters* among bookish folk of the Jacobean and Caroline periods were possible only because in the ninth century and several times later a recension of the *Characters* had been included as a minor, probably illustrative, part of a collection of writings on rhetoric and logic. The fundamental and regularly reappearing section of these manuscripts consisted of rhetorical works by Hermogenes and Aphthonius.[14] In order to understand the connections between Theophrastus and the rhetorics of the sixteenth and seventeenth centuries we must consider four topics: first, the question of the influence of Theophrastus' teachings relating to the subject of oratory; second, his possible influence on Menander, who, according to Diogenes Laertius (V, 36), was a pupil of his; third, evidence that the literary charm of the

---

[13]Gordon, p. 65.
[14]Immisch, pp. xxix-xxxvi, and Navarre, pp. xiii-xvi.

Characters was recognized in ancient times; and, finally, the theory of Character-writing as under various headings and in rather vague fashion it was passed on by early rhetoricians to later teachers.

If we may trust Diogenes Laertius (V, 47-48), Theophrastus composed several treatises on rhetoric and poetics. The references to Theophrastus' pronouncements which one finds in Cicero suggest that he dealt with large matters of tone and style; they offer no hints useful to us in our problem. A more interesting tack but one that requires aid from the dubious wind of inference can be started from the fact that Horace, who in his epistle on poetry addressed to the Pisos drew brief pictures of the typical boy, youth, mature man, and old man, was acquainted with Philodemus of Gadara. Philodemus, though an Epicurean, was interested in Theophrastus' *Characters*. And because Philodemus, like Horace an associate of the house of Piso, was among other things a rhetorician, one might allow that there is at least a chance that Philodemus carried on some of the teachings of Theophrastus as well as a taste for character-sketches and, further, that Horace's *Ars Poetica* may reflect the ideas of Theophrastus even if very much altered by transmission through two centuries of time and a shift from Peripatetic to Epicurean point of view[15] But such speculation is not very helpful. Quintilian, writing about one hundred years later, mentioned Theophrastus half a dozen times, deferring to him, as Cicero had done, as an authority on the more philosophic aspects of style. One reference (X, i, 27) is suggestive: the reading of poetry, says Theophrastus, will benefit the orator by teaching him to treat characters appropriately ("in personis decor"). From his pupil Demetrius and from other sources

---

[15]On Philodemus and the elusive matter of Theophrastus' rhetorical ideas see Tenney Frank, *Vergil, a Biography* (New York, 1922), Chapter V; George C. Fiske and Mary A. Grant, "Cicero's *Orator* and Horace's *Ars Poetica*," *Harvard Studies in Classical Philology*, XXXV (1924), 3-11.

we learn that appropriateness of style was one of Theophrastus' impressive ideas.[16] Hermogenes, the authority on rhetoric of the second century after Christ, appears to have advanced beyond the earlier teachers in analyzing and classifying the kinds of style, but so far as I am aware there are no specific allusions to Theophrastus in his treatises. And thus, with the final disappearance of the text of Theophrastus' works on rhetoric, we are left in murky darkness on the question of what they said about Character-writing.

The second route of transmission, through his effect upon his younger contemporary Menander, would seem to offer more basis for study, provided one enjoyed the hazards of pursuing resemblances and announcing literary debts. Actually, we do not know the contents of Theophrastus' lectures or if Menander heard any of them or if, hearing, he was impressed. Yet certainly there is a kinship in spirit and method in the creations of the two writers. The debts, in turn, of Terence and Plautus to Menander are patent, as is the fact that the comedies of the former pair served well the schoolmasters of England in the sixteenth century. Textbooks in rhetoric, like the theatres of London, plundered the Latin plays, and the Aristotelian doctrine of characterization by type came to be familiar to most people by observation and to some by literary experiment. There is the possibility, then, that the prose sketches of Theophrastus had an influence upon Menander's drawing of type characters, thence upon the similar work of Plautus and Terence, and finally upon the taste of Elizabethan audiences and readers. But proof that Theophrastus started this long tradition in comic drama is lacking.

That his *Characters* gained imitators through their own

---

[16]See the Introduction of W. Rhys Roberts' edition of *Demetrius on Style* (Cambridge, 1902); G. L. Hendrickson, "The Origin and Meaning of the Ancient Characters of Style," *American Journal of Philology*, XXVI (1905), 249-290.

attractiveness seems likely.[17] Possibly, too, it became customary with the Peripatetics to compose such sketches. About seventy-five years after Theophrastus' death, Ariston, a Peripatetic, illustrated a discourse on morality with Characters of several types of pride, written in a manner duplicating that of Theophrastus. Lycon, of the same school and period, also imitated him.[18] One example of his work survives in a translation made by Rutilius Lupus somewhere near the end of the second century before Christ, and six of Ariston's Characters were inserted some years later by Philodemus of Gadara in the same work (Περὶ κακιῶν) into which he copied Theophrastus' "Self-seeking Affability" (v). Evidence of acquaintance with the genre after this date exists in the rhetorical treatises, but the paucity of true Characters in extant Roman literature forces one to conclude that they were no longer very popular. In literature as in sculpture Roman taste seems to have found as much satisfaction in portraiture as in generalized figures. To be sure, at least one abridgement of the *Characters* was made a century or more after Philodemus, and the original pieces by Theophrastus somehow survived until the time of our first manuscript, the ninth century.

The Character at its best—in Theophrastus or the Overbury collection or John Earle—is a highly artificial form. It is lively, yet basically it is neither dialogue nor drama; it represents a class, yet it must seem to possess the reality of a flesh-and-blood individual; it pleases by graphic detail and illuminates by hints, yet it must not be endangered by the merely local and temporary.

---

[17]Gordon, p. 65, declares that the Characters seem to have become popular at once and to have retained their popularity throughout antiquity. Such research as I have been able to make has failed to disclose sufficient evidence to warrant either part of his sweeping statement.

[18]Satyrus Atheneus and Heracleides Ponticus have also been mentioned as early imitators of the *Characters*. See Navarre, pp. xiii-xvi; Edmonds, *Characters of Theophrastus*, p. 6; Pasquali, pp. 143-150.

of the psychological training of an orator and out of the *inventio* (that is, the investigation of material) of his speech into the department of style, there to be treated with the figures of speech. In order to follow it, one must be prepared to consider something besides a correct imitation of it, and one must not be put off by a shifting terminology.[20]

The basic idea in Theophrastus' Characters as we have them is the depiction of types of moral characters—three or four more or less professional types do not alter the main fact—fashioned by means of an accumulation of suggestive, characteristic actions and words, and representative of a group of similar individuals. Although I have found no definitions in the rhetorical treatises that present this concept exactly and completely, there are indications that it was recognized. For example, in the *Schemata Lexeos* of P. Rutilius Lupus, written near the end of the second century B.C., it was explained that just as a painter describes persons by appearances, so an orator may by a certain device depict the virtues and vices of people.[21] This device Rutilius labels χαρακτηρισμός, and he illustrates it with a passage translated from Lycon.

> What hope remains for him who spends all his life in a single, despicable habit? Satiated with too much food and drink from a former day, at noon he is with difficulty awakened drunk, first with eyes wet with wine, blinded with moisture, heavy, unable to look at the light steadily; exhausted because his veins are filled with wine rather than blood, he cannot raise himself; at last, leaning on two

---

[20]According to William G. Crane (*Wit and Rhetoric in the Renaissance*, New York, 1937, pp. 58-59, 157) the Character received attention under about twenty-five names in the early rhetorics. It would be more exact to say that matters and forms sometimes closely, sometimes remotely related to the Character were treated under these various headings. Mr. Crane's collection of such passages has been of great service to me.

[21]See C. Halm, *Rhetores Latini Minores* (Leipzig, 1863), pp. 16-17.

servants, languid, tired from lying in bed, clothed in a
tunic but without a mantle and wearing slippers, his head
bound in a little cloak to keep off the cold, his head bent,
eyelids lowered, face pale, he is raised from the couch in
his bed chamber and is dragged to another in the dining
room. There a few daily guests await him, summoned
by the same desire. Here indeed as a petty chief, with
what he has left of his mind and senses, he hastens to
proffer the cup; he challenges to drink, he incites just as if
he were in battle and surmounting or striking most of
the enemy, thinking the greatest share of the victory his
own. Meanwhile he proceeds to mock time in drinking;
his eyes, weeping wine, make mists about him; the drunk
scarcely recognize the drunk. One man without cause
provokes his neighbor to a quarrel; another, surrendering
to sleep, is kept awake by force; a third gets ready to
quarrel; the doorman restrains a fourth from corrupting
the company with a desire to go home; he beats him, forbids
him to leave, pointing out the master's injunction. Meanwhile a boy supports another fellow, abusively pushed out
of the door reeling, and leads him away, the man dragging
his mantle through the mire. At last left alone in the
dining room, our man cannot put the cup down before
sleep overcomes him as he drinks; the cup slips from his
shaky hands as he collapses.

The Latin version of this passage was made familiar by being
reprinted as *"Ebriosi hominis character"* in Casaubon's editions
of Theophrastus. It is more long-winded and less keen than
the sketches of the master; it gives us a scene rather than a mis-
cellany of representative actions of one type of man.

Cicero used the words χαραχτῆρα and *descriptio* for a representation of the nature and way of life ("natura et vita")
of the miser, the flatterer, and other types.[22] Seneca cites
Posidonius in connection with the description of the character-

---

[22] *Topica*, LXXXIII (22).

istic conduct of moral types, giving *ethologia* and *characterismos* as its proper labels.[23]   Seneca's interest in the form, however, was not rhetorical but moral, as was the case with Joseph Hall, who made good use of his suggestion that the Character might deal with both virtues and vices ("virtutis ac vitii et notas"). Both the *characterismos*, the method of which is to describe, and the precept, the method of which is to preach, serve, says Seneca, to lead men to better lives. It was apparently something similar— a description, with moral implications, of the rustic, the miser, the coward, and so on—which Quintilian alluded to under the titles *ethologia, mores,* ἤθη.[24]   These, he reveals, were among the written exercises assigned to boys in grammar school.

Earlier than Quintilian's *Institutio Oratoria* there was the rhetorical treatise *Ad Herennium,* a work of enduring popularity attributed to Cicero until the sixteenth century.   Among the rhetorical devices "of words" and "of thoughts" listed in Book Four are *effictio* and *notatio,* the former being a description of the physical appearance and the latter of the nature ("natura") of a man.[25]   Both definitions, as well as the appended illustration of *effictio,* imply that the picture is to be of an individual. But the illustration of *notatio* is not limited in that way.

> *Notatio* is the description of the nature of someone by definite signs, certain marks, as it were, bestowed upon that disposition.   Suppose you wished to describe someone who is not rich but is ostentatious with his money.   You might say, "That man, judges, who thinks it is wonderful

---

[23]*Epistulae Morales,* XCV, 65-66.

[24]*Institutio Oratoria,* I, ix, 3; VI, ii, 17.   In IX, iii, 99, Quintilian seems to object to the classification of Rutilius' χαρακτηρισμός as a figure of speech.

[25]In the seventh-century *Rhetorica* of Isidore of Seville *characterismus* seems to include details of voice and external appearance rather than of conduct and, hence, to be closer to the *effictio* of *Ad Herennium.*   See Halm, p. 521.

to be thought rich, just look at him as he gazes at us. Does he not seem to say: 'I should give something away if you weren't so offensive to me'? When indeed he has smoothed his beard with his left hand he thinks that his appearance far outshines that of anyone else because of the gleam of his gems and the lustre of his gold. When he looks upon this certain boy whom I know—I think you don't—he calls him by one name, then by another, then by another still. 'Ho, there, you,' he cries; 'Come, Sannio, don't let those boors disturb you.' Anyone who hears him who doesn't understand might think that he was calling one servant from a retinue of many. He says in the boy's ear that the couch at home should be provided with cushions, that an Ethiopian should be asked for from his uncle to be sent to the baths, that a place for the Austurian horse should be designated in front of the door, and that any other brittle grandeur should be prepared for false glory. Then he shouts so that all may hear: 'See that everything is well accounted for by nightfall, if you can.' The boy, who by now well knows the man's nature, says, 'You had better send several of us if you would have everything well reckoned today.' 'Well,' says the man, 'take Libanus and Sosia with you.' 'Surely,' replies the boy. Then it so happens that the foreigners whom this fellow had given an invitation to while he had been traveling so showily do appear. In truth he is genuinely disturbed by this, but he doesn't back away from the flaw in his nature. 'You do well in coming,' he says, 'but you would have done better had you come straight to my house.' 'We would have,' they reply, 'if we had known the house.' 'But it's easy enough to find from any direction. Just come with me.' They follow him. His conversation meanwhile consists wholly of boasting. He inquires about the quality of his crops. Because his villas are burned down, he says he can't approach them nor dares rebuild them just now, 'although in Tusculanum I really began to go crazy and rebuild on the same foundations!' While he is talking thus he comes to a certain house in which there is to be a party that day; as if the master of the house he walks in with the foreigners. 'Here's where I live,' he explains. He looks over the silverware spread out, tries the couch-cushion, and gives his approval. A servant enters and clearly tells the man that his master will soon come—in case he wishes to leave. 'Is that so,' says the man. 'Let's go, friends. My brother is coming from Falernus; I shall go meet him. Come back at ten o'clock.' The guests disperse, he hastily betaking himself to his own house. At the tenth hour as they were instructed they come. They ask for him, find out whose house it really is, then as laughing-stocks troop back to their inn. The next day they see this man, explain what happened, expostulate, and accuse. He argues that they, deceived by the similarity of the place, must have gone astray by the covered passage; he had waited for them late into the night at the expense of his health."[26]

And on the story goes, the man telling an elaborate lie to explain the modest household to which he has to take the visitors.

This picture of the pretender to wealth, mentioned by Erasmus in the *Copia* under the heading "Personæ Descriptio" and printed in Casaubon's *Theophrastus* as well as in the text of the widely-read treatise itself, must have been known to many students in the sixteenth and seventeenth centuries. Resemblances between certain details in it and in Theophrastus' "Pretentiousness" (XXIII) could no doubt be explained without resort to the idea of literary indebtedness. Furthermore, this sketch is much longer than the Greek Characters and, unlike all but two or three of the latter, consists of a continuous narrative. But the sketch of the Roman pretender to wealth has the objectivity, faint humor, and simple language of Theophrastus; it likewise de-

---

[26]The Latin text may be found in W. Friedrick's edition of Cicero's *Opera Rhetorica* (Leipzig, 1884), I, 109-111.

pends on action and speech for a revelation of character; and in depicting one case it suggests the short-comings of a whole class of men. *Notatio,* defined in the rhetoric *Ad Herennium* and, about twelve centuries later, described in almost the same words by Geoffroi de Vinsauf as the presentation of the nature of a man by "certain signs," need not be, we have seen, exactly like the Character. But the definition and its example, if interpreted in the light of classic notions of *decorum,* could easily lead the student toward the true Character.[27]

The theory of the latter genre, though not its form, received attention from rhetoricians also in connection with the two figures, *ethopoeia* and *prosopopoeia.* These, like *characterismos,* were *figurae sententiarum* and were studied in the grammar school. But they were not always conceived or defined in the same way. Quintilian explained *ethopoeia* merely as the orator's imitation of another person's character or habits ("imitatio morum alienorum").[28] *Prosopopoeia* is almost the same thing, but with a dramatization of the person as well as the giving of his words. In both figures the words must be suited to the subject matter and situation—for example, to Cicero speaking for Titus Ampius on a specific occasion. It is, said Quintilian, a most useful exercise for future poets, historians, and orators. The latter are required to impersonate "sons, parents, rich men, old men, gentle or harsh of temper, misers, superstitious persons, cowards and mockers, so that hardly even comic actors have to assume more

---

[27]That it did not always lead very far can be seen in the illustration of *notatio* offered by Evrard l'Allemand about 1213 in his *Laborintus,* 11. 551-552:

> Iste sub hypocrisi permulcet nectare linguae
> Indoctos, virus inde propinat eis

(Edmond Faral, *Les Arts Poétiques du XIIe et du XIIIe Siècle,* Paris, 1924, p. 357).

[28]IX, ii, 58.

numerous rôles in their performances on the stage."[29] *Prosopopoeia* aims not to be objective but to reveal the thoughts as well as character of the speaker (who may be a living man, a man summoned up from the shades, an historical or fictitious figure, an inanimate object, a state or nation), and it presents the speech of an individual. But because the ubiquitous classical doctrine of *decorum*, of suitability of style to speaker, audience, mood, and situation, had entered into the instructions so completely, the effect of teaching both *ethopoeia* and *prosopopoeia* was eventually to encourage the presenting of types.

As *ethopoeia* and *prosopopoeia* were carried on by the manuals of Hermogenes in the second century, Aphthonius in the third, and Priscian in the fifth,[30] the applicaton was ostensibly to the representation of particular men on particular occasions— Aristides in the speech against Plato in defence of the Four, or what Hercules might rightly be imagined to have said when Eurysthenes laid his commands on him. But the Aristotelian and Horation injunction about suitability persisted conspicuously with attention to Aristotle's distinction between the basic moral habits or character (ἤθη) and the passions (πάθη), between the permanent and temporary states of mind.[31] Hermogenes' in-

---

[29] III, viii, 51, as translated by H. E. Butler in *The Institutio Oratoria of Quintilian* (The Loeb Classical Library, 1920-1922). See also VI, i, 26-27; IX, ii, 30.

[30] Hermogenes' Προγυμνάσματα (*Elementary Exercises*) was adapted by Aphthonius, who gave his work the same name. Both have been edited (1913 and 1926) by Hugo Rabe and printed at Leipzig. I have made use, too, of a Latin translation of Hermogenes' longer works and the Προγυμνάσματα of Aphthonius, published without date at Basel under the title *Hermogenis Tarsensis Philosophi ac Rhetoris Acutissimi De Arte Rhetorica Praecepta*. Priscian's *Praeexercitamenta*, a slightly expanded version of Hermogenes, uses the word *adlocutio* ("imitatio sermonis, ad mores et suppositas personas accommodata") to translate ἠθοποιία

[31] See the translation of Hermogenes printed in Baldwin's *Medieval Rhetoric and Poetic*, pp. 34-35.

sistence upon truth to type in *ethopoeia* as explained in his *Progymnasmata* was repeated in a section (II, ii) of his longer treatise on the kinds of style (Περὶ ἰδεῶν). There again he observed that for a general or an orator, a greedy man or a coward, there is an individual, suitable kind of expression.

That Hermogenes or Aphthonius or Priscian meant to teach Character-writing under the heading of the separable *ethopoeia* or *prosopopoeia* is unlikely. Yet those two figures, like the Character, aim to present human nature, and they employ the same means—speech, conduct, and sometimes even appearance. To be sure, *ethopoeia* and *prosopopoeia* are both a kind of oration; in both description is subordinate to speech, and typicalness a handmaiden to individuality. No definition of either figure would of itself create the Character. But both could take Theophrastus' sketches under their wings with some sense of family feeling. Such, at least, seems to be the most plausible explanation of the fact that the *Characters* have survived solely and yet many times in manuscript collections built around Hermogenes and Aphthonius.[32] Certainly the *Characters*, vivid and pungent and quietly droll, must have come with such a welcome to the medieval teacher of rhetorical distinctions and divisions as would a beautiful, inspired writing to an ignorant priest laboring among the benighted. It was not, perhaps, exactly what he had been teaching, but he might accommodate one to the other.

The desire for appropriateness or *decorum*, always emphasized in classical and medieval treatments of *ethopoeia* and *prosopopoeia*, is, to borrow a figure from Mr. Fiske,[33] bifocal. The insistence upon suiting the speech, character, and conduct of rhetorical or

---

[32]Immisch, p. xxxv, suggests that the *Characters* were regarded as supplementary to the discussion of these two figures and also to Περὶ ἰδεῶν, II, ii-ix.

[33]Fiske and Grant, p. 17.

poetic creations to their type—that is, to their age, social and economic position, and particular circumstances—is just the nearer view, stemming from Aristotle's dictum that characterization in poetry, which is a more philosophic branch of writing than history, should be probable and universal. The doctrine sweeps over all art. Cicero passed it on in its larger phase in echoing the master's idea that what is becoming in one place may not be so elsewhere and that what is always good is the mean between excess and defect.[34] This broader question of *decorum* in style is something which apparently was treated in Theophrastus' rhetorical treatises; from them, indeed, Horace, Cicero, and Quintilian may have imbibed respect for the doctrine. The Roman delight in appropriateness in characterization and in the giving of type names to figures in comedy, as recommended by Aristotle,[35] will be mentioned again in a later section. Horace provided the *locus classicus* for the doctrine of *decorum* in his famous letter to the Pisos. Pathetic accents, he observed, suit a sad face, lascivious words the jester; a matron of noble family should not be made to talk like a sedulous nursemaid, nor a cosmopolitan merchant like a farmer. Achilles must be fierce, angry, inexorable; Ixion must be perfidious; and Orestes, sad. What is typical of a class should be observable in the individual. To illustrate this statement Horace offered brief pictures of the universal character and conduct of the boy, the youth, the man in his prime, and the old man. These sketches, well remembered by succeeding rhetoricians, merely condense what Aristotle had provided for the instruction of orators in his character-analyses of the same four ages. Horace's habit of seeing men in their general aspects appears also in one of his epistles (I, ii) in which he treats Homer's people as if they in-

---

[34] *Orator*, XXI-XXII.
[35] *Poetics*, IX.

terested him mostly as illustrations of moral types—Paris the impractical lover, Achilles the man of rage and love, and Ulysses the model of virtue and wisdom:

> Rursus, quid virtus et quid sapientia possit,
> Utile proposuit nobis exemplar Ulixen.

How Horace gave support to Character-writing will be seen as we proceed.

A kind of unimaginative exaggeration of the ubiquitous doctrine of *decorum* appears in the eventual fate (if not indeed in the origin) of the rhetorical scheme called *descriptio personae*, which differs from both *effictio* and *notatio* as defined in the *Rhetorica ad Herennium* and from χαρακτηρισμός or *descriptio morum* as used by Rutilius, Cicero, and Seneca. Properly, it includes an account of the person's appearance, temperament, and entire biography, and originally it was to apply to an individual, either an actual man or a fictitious character in a literary composition. The authority for this figure was Cicero's *De Inventione* in the discussion of *confirmatio*. All argument, Cicero says (I, xxiv), is from either persons or things, and in arguing from persons there are eleven points that one may consider: name, nature (*natura* including sex, nation, family relationship, age, physique), way of life (*victus* including education, associations, domestic habits), fortune (*fortuna* meaning whether rich or poor, free or enslaved), physical appearance (*habitus*), passions (*affectio*), interests (*studium*), reasons for doing things (*consilium*), one's deeds (*factum*), what happens to one (*casus*), and one's discourses (*orationes*). In Cicero such description subserves argument, and, one gathers, not all the eleven points must be included. But inevitably, sophistic rhetoric made *descriptio* one of the devices for amplifying any oration, a separable but decorous ornament of style. It also used a modified version of Cicero's list in its instructions for the encomium.[36]

Descriptio took an important place in later medieval theory. According to Matthew of Vendôme, an authority of the twelfth century, description in all its varieties constitutes the supreme art of poetry. M. Faral's valuable collection of twelfth- and thirteenth-century manuals provides plentiful information, by precept and example and in verse and prose (for the *poetria* of those centuries confused the forms as well as the theories of poetry and rhetoric), of what *descriptio* should be. Tedious completeness was required along with appropriateness to the person. Matthew explained the matter of *decorum* in the large, then composed extensive *descriptiones* of a prelate, a Caesar, a clever orator (Ulysses), a cynic, a virtuous woman, a beautiful woman (Helen), and an old woman; finally, lest any reader improbably escape in doubt, he discussed the epithets suitable for each type and ran over Cicero's whole list of points.[37] Geoffroi of Vinsauf, who carefully illustrated *effictio* and *notatio* as established by the *Rhetorica ad Herennium,* devoted only a few words to explaining *descriptio,* but he illustrated[38] it in respect to the presentation of physical appearance,[39] and he employed Horace's pictures of the four ages to strengthen his insistence upon *decorum* in such passages.[40] Although the original function of *descriptio* was to

---

[36]The list of eleven points, slightly rearranged, appears in the rhetoric of Fortunatianus, a Roman sophist. The meeting of the list and of the idea of *decorum* can be observed in Isidore's seventh-century rhetoric under the heading of *ethopoeia;* see Halm, pp. 514-515. In the ninth century, one Radbert composed a portrait according to Cicero's eleven points and called it in his Latin text by the Greek name χαραϰτηρισμός (Faral, p. 79). See pp. 75-81 in Faral for remarks on description in these manuals and pp. 30-32, 187n. in Baldwin's *Medieval Rhetoric and Poetic* for the encomium.

[37]*Ars Versificatoria,* I, 41-45, 62-92.

[38]*Poetria Nova,* 11. 1260-1265. Geoffroi, like Matthew, is included in Faral's *Les Arts Poétiques.*

[39]*Poetria Nova,* 11. 563-621.

[40]*Documentum de Modo et Arte Dictandi et Versificandi,* II, iii, 138-139.

present some particular person, the result of carrying out the theory literally would be a merely conventional drawing. As M. Faral says, "Les hommes du moyen âge, partant de ces indications, y ont tout ramené: ils ont perdu de vue les individus pour ne plus considérer que les catégories dans lesquelles ils entraient."[41] In spite of its elaboration the heavy rhetorical machine squeezed the portrait of an individual into the familiar outlines of some type. The process is not unlike the task, though less consciously and less imaginatively undertaken, of the Character-writer.

We see, then, that though no rhetorician appears to have written a complete, technical definition of the Character as Theophrastus composed it, several Roman writers came close to it (as χαρακτηρισμός, χαρακτῆρα, *notatio, ethologia, descriptio*), and they valued it for its ethical and educational uses. We notice, too, that after the classical period the "figures of thought" called *ethopoeia* and *prosopopoeia*, merely decorative in function, and the universal and authoritative principle of *decorum* kept the idea of the Character alive. Before tracing the history of these rhetorical doctrines in the sixteenth century it will be interesting for us to consider how a medieval poet responded to them.

The Middle Ages, it is well known, loved authorities and rules and categories, so that its characterization "was almost purely typical."[42] Chaucer's transcendent genius often carried him out of the limitations of thought and practice of his time, and he could poke fun at the rhetorician's blunder of putting Cicero on Parnassus and at Geoffroi's grotesquely amplified

---

[41]Page 79.

[42]G. L. Kittredge, *Chaucer and his Poetry* (Cambridge, Mass., 1939), p. 29. See also Frederick Tupper, *Types of Society in Medieval Literature* (New York, 1926), pp. 15-17.

lament on the day Friday.[43] But complete superiority to an essential (that is to say, rhetorical) part of medieval education as well as to medieval poetic would be unthinkable even in Chaucer. He knew the rules, laborious and unimaginative and inartistic as they may seem now, and he followed them often, though exactly how often and with what degree of success is a question as yet not completely explored.[44] *Prosopopoeia* he employed in *The Parlement of Foules* and elsewhere; *effictio* in brief form he introduced unexpectedly and irrelevantly late in *Troilus and Criseyde*.[45] Description of persons is abundant, of course, in all his poetry. What it was at the first of his career can be seen in the artificial, laboriously-complete picture of the Duchess Blanche, a description composed in accordance with both the implied theory and the practice of the subsequently ridiculed Geoffroi.[46] The description is long and detailed, but that it is not still longer may be due to the fact that even Geoffroi had not brought himself to follow out all of Cicero's eleven points. Later, Chaucer's characterization gained infinite deftness in realism and dramatic technique, so that within the better

---

[43]In the "Nonnes Preestes Tale," B. 4537-42. See Charles S. Baldwin, "Cicero on Parnassus," *Publications of the Modern Language Association*, XLII (1927), 106-112.

[44]A suggestive survey of the subject was made by J. M. Manly in "Chaucer and the Rhetoricians," *Proceedings of the British Academy*, London, 1926. Traugott Naunin's dissertation, *Der Einfluss der Mittelalterlichen Rhetorik auf Chaucers Dichtung* (Bonn, 1929), covers the ground with greater detail and suggests that French and Italian poetry as much as the treatises taught rhetoric to Chaucer. But neither Manly nor Naunin specifically analyzes the Prologue for rhetorical procedure.

[45]See Manly, p. 105; Naunin, pp. 39-40; L. A. Haselmayer, "The Portraits in *Troilus and Criseyde*," *Philological Quarterly*, XVII (1938), 220-223.

[46]*The Book of the Duchess*, 11. 817-1033. Manly, p. 103, calls the passage a free paraphrase of lines 563-597 of the *Nova Poetria*. That Machaut provided a model has also been suggested; see *The Complete Works of Geoffrey Chaucer*, edited by F. N. Robinson (Boston, 1933), p. 885, and also Naunin's comments.

of *The Canterbury Tales* there probably are few reminders of the *descriptio*.

A tantalizing aspect of the question of Chaucer's connection with the rhetoricians lies in the characterization of the pilgrims in the Prologue. One's first inclination is to deny that anything so vivid and charming as the initial pictures of the Knight, the Prioress, the Monk, the Clerk, and the Parson could have been done by rule. Yet one would be rash to deny that the rules had made their contribution, the rules, that is to say, of Matthew perhaps more than of Geoffroi and as suggested to Chaucer by examples of *descriptio* scattered through medieval writing as much as by recollection of the precise dicta. It would be a weary task to calculate mathematically how many of Cicero's eleven points are touched on in each of the descriptions in the Prologue. Obviously and happily, not many of the sketches seem to approach completeness, especially as to *victus, affectio, consilium, casus,* and *orationes,* these points being handled more naturally in the links and tales, and Chaucer apologized on occasion for inability to supply a man's name, the very first requirement on Cicero's list.[47]

The result of strict obedience to the rules of *decorum* and of method would be, as we have said, to produce a representative rather than individual portrait. Are Chaucer's pilgrims as set forth in the Prologue types of medieval society, or are they individuals created out of Chaucer's fertile imagination or perhaps drawn from actual people he knew? This question, returning to us in every new book on Chaucer, can probably never have a final answer, and indeed we shall need to return to it for further consideration ourselves. But this much can be

---

[47]Tupper, p. 17, suggests that the failure of Chaucer (and other medieval writers) to give names to individual characters was a result of the medieval preference for the typical and general.

said: whichever they were meant to be, the pilgrims seem more typical in the Prologue than in the links and tales, and they doubtless seem so in part because of a certain repeated attention to *nomen, natura, fortuna, studium,* and the rest, which to the knowing, then and now, sounds a faint echo of the rhetorical *descriptio.* Medieval characterization by types carries a tenuous thread from Greek rhetoric onward toward the seventeenth-century Character-writers.

3. THE CLASSICAL TRADITION AND THE CHARACTER IN SIXTEENTH-CENTURY ENGLAND

A broad and solid ground for the later popularity of the Character was laid in the academic tradition of sixteenth-century England. Throughout the century, the student's reading in classical literature did not ordinarily include Theophrastus, although a rare scholar like Erasmus or John Hoskins apparently knew him. But elsewhere there were pictures of representative individuals which bore some resemblance to those of Theophrastus and which an especially learned teacher might discourse upon in a way to display his esoteric knowledge of the ancient Character. The scholars who at the end of the century saw Casaubon's new edition of Theophrastus read there the sketches from Rutilius and the *Ad Herennium* which I have quoted in Section 2 as well as the "Garruli hominis character" in Horace's Satire (I, ix), which has only a limited resemblance to the genre. In an appended note in the 1612 edition readers were referred by Casaubon to other descriptions "close (*prope*) to those of Theophrastus" in Synesius (Letter CIV), Petronius, Lucian (the "Professor of Rhetoric"),[48] Dio, Martial (III, lxiii), and

---

[48] There are many thumbnail sketches of special types of frail mortality scattered through Lucian in addition to his full-length exposures of the rhetorician and of the illiterate bibliomaniac. Lucian was read by Jonson and Earle (see his Character of a Prison).

Chrysostom.[49] In his Prolegomena Casaubon had mentioned in the same connection the lost work of Varro and Satyrus and the brief contrast in the *Iliad* (XIII, 278-285) of the brave man and the timorous. Among these passages only the epigram of Martial has both the form and the method of the true Character. Yet Synesius' entertaining account of the exploits of Joannes the long-haired Phrygian, a real *miles gloriosus*, is, as Casaubon said, similar to Theophrastus' pictures, resembling his "Cowardice" both in matter and in the continuous narrative procedure. Dio's attempt in his fourth discourse on kingship to draw the type and form (χαρακτῆρα καὶ μορφὴν) of the avaricious man, the hopelessly sensual man, and the man given over to love of fame produced descriptions that are analytical and moralistic, the unshaped material of the short, objective sketch.

In addition to the classical representations of the character and conduct of moral types mentioned by Casaubon, the sixteenth-century reader might also know Plato's account of the philosopher-king in the *Republic* (VI), Epictetus' wise man (*Encheiridion*, xlviii), and Cicero's description of the truly great orator (*De Oratore*, III, xiv). But these are idealized and discursive pictures like those in Aristotle's *Ethics* and are perhaps of the sort that Seneca was thinking of (in his ninety-fifth epistle) as moralistic descriptions.[50] Plutarch's picture of the flatterer, though drawn at great length and interrupted by commentary and digressions, comes closer to the style of

---

[49]The homily ("XXXVIII in Acta Apostol.") to which Casaubon refers contains nothing very close to Theophrastus' sketches. The probable contribution of Martial to the English Character I have discussed in the next chapter.

[50]His descriptions of Stoic wise men in Epistles XLV and LXXXI are too subjective and hortatory to resemble the true Character. But Seneca may have called such things "characterismi."

Theophrastus in its many concrete details and dramatic touches,[51] and it probably was known to more Elizabethan readers than were the passages in Dio and Synesius. The letters of Sidonius Apollinaris contain vivid portraits of a dissipated, beastly parasite (III, xiii) and of a "young man of fifty" (IV, xiii) which, regardless of the possibility that they represented actual persons, figure forth two classes (the second small) very much as Theophrastus or Sir Thomas Overbury might do it. Classical literature unquestionably would afford other passages like these.[52] It is true that, in one respect or another—concentration, objectivity, graphic and dramatic method, typicalness—they all fail of being true Characters; yet they must have served, as the rhetorics did, to preserve some taste for the sort of sketch Theophrastus had drawn.

But much more effective than any of these passages in creating the habit of looking for the typical in the fictitious and historical persons of literature would be Menander and Plautus and Terence, but above all Terence, the familiar companion of the English schoolboy and university student. No one who has read Plautus or Terence needs to be told that the personages of their plays engage the reader's interest not by any rare and subtle qualities of their individual selves but through the situations in which they are placed and through the ability to suggest the immemorial habits of obvious classes of human folk. Menander, Plautus, and Terence used the same simply-outlined and easily-recognized

---

[51] See especially sections IV and VIII in Plutarch's "How to Tell a Flatterer from a Friend" (*Plutarch's Moralia* with an English translation by Frank Cole Babbit [The Loeb Classical Library], I [1927], 273-275, 285-287).

[52] Juvenal's Satires VIII and IX, mentioned by E. C. Baldwin (*PMLA*, XIX [1904], 77) as containing Characters, are not important parallels. But the drawing of the lover of law courts in *Wasps* (ll. 87-134) is properly recalled by Gwendolen Murphy (*A Cabinet of Characters*, London, 1925, p. ix n.). Both Baldwin and Murphy list other relevant passages.

types over and over again.[53] To be sure, a modern admirer may undertake to argue[54] that "perhaps six" of Terence's people rise above the expected level of characterization in comedy of manners, the expected low level, that is, of an "ethical description on two legs." Donatus, whose essay on Terence was customarily printed with sixteenth-century texts of the plays, remarked that Terence had been bold enough to create kind mothers-in-law and honorable courtesans. But in the Prologue to *Eunuchus* Terence in all candor avowed his intention of choosing characters from stock, of making courtesans evil, parasites hungry, old men gullible, and slaves tricky. Donatus of course approved, and so, in faithful apostolic succession, did the later pedagogues. Gnatho, the parasite, and Thraso, the braggart soldier, in the play to which Terence prefixed his creed were sufficiently vivid and entertaining to make their names and their types common in sixteenth-century writing. As Sidney remarked in his *Apologie for Poetrie* and as Shakespeare's Rosalind demonstrated in her allusion to "Caesar's thrasonical brag," the Terentian figures had merged into modern trades and types: one need not read very widely to come upon their names and significances. Captain Bobadil and Sir John Falstaff descend from Thraso by a more direct line than do the Overburian "Vain-

---

[53]See F. G. Allinson, *Menander* (The Loeb Classical Library, 1921), p. xvii, on the standardized characterization of Menander. Allinson believes that suggestions of the "influence of Theophrastus reappear now and again in Menander's character-drawing" (p. xiii), an idea considered "unsound" by an anonymous reviewer of C. E. Bennett's and W. A. Hammond's *Theophrastus* in the New York *Nation*, LXXVI (1903), 338. Gordon withholds specific comment on this possibility but seems to imply, p. 80, that Characters are always abstracts from comedy.

See Gilbert Norwood, *Plautus and Terence* (New York, 1932), pp. 12-13, on stock characters in the Latin comedies. Budgell in the preface to his 1714 translation of Theophrastus suggested that Terence's Thraso and Gnatho were "Copies" of Theophrastus' flatterer and coward. The question of Seneca's reliance on stock characters in his plays is discussed by C. W. Mendell in *Our Seneca* (New Haven, 1941), chap. X.

[54]Norwood, pp. 131-140.

glorious Coward in Command" and other Characters that likewise have Theophrastus' "Cowardice" in their complex family
trees. But the existence of a sketch by Theophrastus as the Adam
of the genealogy of a Character must not make us forgetful of the
collateral lines, particularly the important and often renewed line
of Plautus and Terence. It accentuated the association of humor
and social conduct with the "ethical description on two legs." It
also made certain obvious type-characters so very familiar that by
1614 the educated reader was happy to have the more conceitful,
more peculiarly British sketches of Overbury and the rest.
Furthermore, by the ancient and honorable tradition of baptizing
each creature with a name suggestive of his principal feature of
character—Gnatho, from "jaw," for the parasite; Thraso, from
"bold," for the cowardly blusterer; Chremes, from "to spit," for
the old man—classical comedy prepared for the eventual adop-
tion by eighteenth-century Character-writers of such names as
Lady Betty Modish and Sir Andrew Freeport.[55]

Not only in the student's reading of classical authors was he
unwittingly prepared for the Theophrastan revival in Jacobean
times. In his daily school tasks the boy was drilled in many of
those rhetorical figures with which we have been dealing in
earlier pages. In grammar school and in college, rhetoric, which
embraced both written and oral composition, took a forward place
in the curriculum. As in Chaucer's day, the average schoolmaster

---

[55]"Nomina personarum, in comœdiis duntaxat, habere debent rationem
& etymologiam" (Donatus' note on the first line of *Adelphi* [*P. Terentii
Comœdiæ sex*, Paris, 1541, p. 334]). See James C. Austin, *The Significant Name in Terence* (University of Illinois Studies, 1922).

The tantalizing question of costuming in Elizabethan life and in
school performances of the Latin plays I leave unattempted. There is
certainly the possibility that the distinguishing of various professions and
trades by their clothing, which seems to have been far more striking in
Shakespeare's day than now, was exaggerated in interesting ways in the
theatre. If such was the case, the Character-writers were probably
somehow responsive to the custom. See p. 112.

seems, furthermore, to have incorporated poetic in the study of rhetoric. The textbooks chosen were in part the ancient treatises—especially Hermogenes and Aphthonius for the younger students, and Cicero, the treatise *Ad Herennium*, and Quintilian for later study—and in part they were the more or less contemporary works of Erasmus (the *Copia*, used particularly in lower schools), Talaeus (Omer Talon, Ramus's follower), Charles Butler, Wilson, Sturmius, and others, all these latter being based to some degree upon the former and upon Aristotle's *Rhetoric*. Aristotle's treatise itself was not well known, though Ascham mentions it and Bacon's discussion "Of Youth and Age" suggests that he had seen its analyses of the natures of the different ages of men. At Rivington and Sandwich, at Durham, at Eton, at Winchester, and at many other schools, the schoolboy was required to take either Hermogenes or Aphthonius for his guide in composition and presumably was made to attempt *ethopoeia* and *prosopopoeia* with all their tedious requirements of appropriateness and their subdivisions into "morally habitual" (ἠθικαί), "emotional" (παθητικαί), and "combined" (μικταί). Both authors, having been printed first in the Aldine *Rhetores Graeci* of 1508, were reprinted, translated into Latin, commented upon, objected to (very boldly!), and often adopted *in toto* throughout the century. So if by good luck one escaped them in their original form—Ascham, Elyot, Brinsley, Hoole, John Milton, and several Italian critics urged one not to do so[56]—one probably got their approach and certainly some of their special teachings about the figures and about decorum from contemporary authorities.[57]

---

[56]*The Scholemaster*, II; Elyot, *The Boke Named the Governour*, I, xi; John Brinsley, *Ludus Literarius*, XIII; Milton, *Of Education*; Charles Hoole, *A New Discovery Of the old Art of Teaching Schoole* (1660), edited by T. Campagnac (Liverpool, 1913), p. 172.

[57]For information about the curricula of English schools in the six-

Of the sixteenth-century treatises dealing with rhetoric which were used in schools, the first in time and probably in importance was Erasmus' *De Duplici Copia Verborum ac Rerum*. Published in 1511, it was prescribed in Colet's school of St. Paul's in 1518 and in several other schools later in addition to being recommended for study by most of the rhetoricians of the following hundred years. With the major exception of Aristotle's *Rhetoric* Erasmus seems to have been acquainted with the body of ancient writing which I have discussed. Drawing on these sources, he assembled his remarks concerning the Character under the heading "Personæ Descriptio" in the second book of the *Copia*. Most striking is his statement that Theophrastus' *Characters* looked to him like the work of a grammarian, not a philosopher.[58] Knowing those Characters and the picture of "pseudoplutus" illustrating *notatio* in the *Rhetorica ad Herennium*, Erasmus had a perfectly good idea of the form and spirit of the Character, though he did not use that name for it. Instead, "descriptio" or "notæ" served him. But to "notatio," the word used in the *Rhetorica ad Herennium*, he gave a special meaning (I, xv). It was the description of the nature of someone through the use of a suggestive, unimportant detail: thus, "he scratches his head with one finger" signifies an effeminate, petty man, or "he blows his nose on his elbow" denotes a dealer in salt fish. Erasmus' con-

---

teenth century I have drawn especially on Foster Watson, *The English Grammar Schools to 1660* (Cambridge, 1908); Hastings Rashdall, *The Universities of Europe in the Middle Ages*, edited by F. M. Powicke and A. B. Emden (Oxford, 1936), III; Arthur F. Leach, *Educational Charters and Documents* (Cambridge, 1911); the introduction to F. H. Colson's edition of Quintilian's first Book (Cambridge, 1924); Marvin T. Herrick's discussion of the slow progress of Aristotle's *Rhetoric* in England, in *Philological Quarterly*, V (1926), 242-257; A. M. Stowe, *English Grammar Schools in the Reign of Queen Elizabeth* (New York, 1908); George Saintsbury, *A History of Criticism* (Edinburgh and London), II (1902); Crane, *Wit and Rhetoric in the Renaissance*; J. Howard Brown, *Elizabethan Schooldays* (Oxford, 1933).

[58] *Desiderii Erasmi Roterodami Opera Omnia* (Leyden, 1703), I, 80.

necting the Character with the type-personages of Plautus and Terence indicates his understanding of one aspect of the former which escaped some writers, that is, that the Character should represent some prevailing trait of personality but that the representativeness should not destroy the vitality of the imagined figure.

Richard Sherry's *Treatise of the Figures of Grammer and Rhetorike* (1555) echoed Erasmus' *Copia* in many respects, but its illustrations of *characterismus*, for which it gave "effictio" as a synonym, demonstrate that Sherry had no exact notion of what the term originally meant. To him it signified a vivid presentation of someone in a little dramatic scene.

Thomas Wilson, on the contrary, knew what the classical Character was and composed for his *Arte of Rhetorique* (1553) his own *descriptio* of the pinch-penny to illustrate it.

> There is no such pinch peney on live as this good fellowe is. He will not lose the paring of his nailes. His haire is never rounded for sparing of money, one paire of shone serveth him a twelve moneth, he is shod with nailes like a Horse. He hath bene knowne by his coate this thirtie Winter. He spent once a groate at good ale, being forced through companie, and taken short at his worde, whereupon he hath taken such conceipt since that time, that it hath almost cost him his life.[59]

Brevity, representativeness, graphic and suggestive detail are here, and also acid humor and a sting in the final sentence.[60] This piece, though buried in the profuse abundance of Wilson's book, must have come under the eyes of countless Englishmen, for the book lived on in edition after edition. Had Wilson used the proper label for it rather than the word "descriptio," which in

---

[59] G. H. Mair's edition (Oxford, 1909), p. 187.

[60] The second illustration, a reference to the description of Piso in Cicero's most vituperative oration against Piso, might cause one to doubt if Wilson knew what he was doing in his Character of the pinch-penny. Its justification here was perhaps that its harshness would excuse Wilson's.

43

many rhetorics had a much more general or even a different meaning, the Theophrastan genre might have been reëstablished sooner.

There may have been other definitions and illustrations of the strict classical Character in the treatises used in English schools between 1553 and 1592, but I have not come upon them. Both the term and the precise form appear to have fallen out of use, though approximations to the latter were, as we shall see, frequent. Casaubon's 1592 volume, containing twenty-three of Theophrastus' *Characters* in both Greek and Latin, was followed in 1599 by another containing five more Characters. Both editions presented an elaborate annotation and learned "Prolegomena" on the Characters and their literary connections. The text of Theophrastus and of the excerpts from Lycon and the *Ad Herennium* would clarify the nature of Character-writing for those who had eyes to see. But Casaubon did not push his observation of the nature of the genre beyond the notion that it gave a vivid picture of the character and conduct of a moral type;[61] objectivity and the telling of much by well-selected, concrete detail were not requirements in his definition. Students who followed his references to other examples of description "prope Theophrasteam" would in consequence either have a rather loose idea of the Character, or, being acute and analytical, they would appreciate that Casaubon's "prope" was very important.

The effect of Casaubon's publications did not immediately appear. But in a very few years Jonson for some reason was composing a set of near-Characters for the printed edition of *Every*

---

[61]"Erat namque hoc tanquam exemplar & speculu[m] quoddam morum, ubi virtutis & vitij cuiusque expressæ notæ cernebantur" (ΘΕΟΦΡΑΣΤΟΥ ἠθικοὶ χαρακτῆρες. *Theophrasti Notationes Morum. Isaacus Casaubonus recensuit,* Lyons, 1612, p. 89). Information about the 1592 and 1599 editions of Casaubon was supplied by Sylvia L. England from copies in the British Museum.

Man Out of his Humor, and in 1608 Joseph Hall led off the long procession of Character-books with his *Characters of Vertues and Vices.* Four years later, John Brinsley, Hall's brother-in-law, recommended in his *Ludus Literarius: or, The Grammar Schoole* that students of theme-writing should seek ideas and sentences in "the French Academie, the morall part of it: Charactery, Morall Philosophy, Golden grove, Wits Common wealth, Civill conversation."[62] Most of Brinsley's titles are of easily identified books, and "Charactery" doubtless refers to *Characters of Vertues and Vices,* the author of which wrote the commendatory preface for Brinsley's book. Hall said of his own Characters that they were done as nearly as possible in the manner of "that ancient Master of Moralitie," Theophrastus.[63]

Across the Channel, Nicholas Caussin, confessor to Louis XIII, published in 1619 an enormous tome, *Eloquentiæ Sacræ et Humanæ Parallela Libri XVI,* which had some circulation among the more energetic in England. Caussin put the Rutilius-Lycon sketch verbatim under the heading *Characterismus* in Book VII, Chapter xvii, and to illustrate *hypotyposis* filled Book XI with an ambitious collection of "epidictici characteres," beginning with embracive descriptions of "Homo," then of the parts of the body, then of classical statues, then of abstractions ("Calumnia" from Lucian, and so on), and, at last, in Chapter xxiv-xlviii, of moral and social types of people. "Avarus Dives" is, Caussin says, from Cyprianus; his "Avarus, et Tenax" is from Theophrastus, Plautus, and others; "Garrulus" is obviously and admittedly patched together from Horace and Theophrastus. These Characters, though composite and hand-me-down, are of the classical sort and could aid the learner. In 1665, when the original Theophrastan form and the Overburian successor had both nearly run their course,

---

[62] Page 183.
[63] "Procme," *Characters of Vertues and Vices* (1608).

Ralph Johnson included in his *Scholar's Guide from the Accidence to the University* a full and helpful set of "Rules for making a Character."[64] Although I have not attempted to discover exactly how long schoolmasters continued to require of pupils some practice in this kind of writing, my knowledge of the profession encourages me to guess that the tradition, once established, was not modified soon. Edward Everett Hale's diary has an interesting note on what he did on November 24, 1837, when he was a student at Harvard: "Wrote some on a theme this morning. It is 'Draw a Character of a Misanthrope.' Sketching character was never my forte. I don't like the subject much."[65]

But not all the instruction that led students in the direction of the Theophrastan Character came under that heading. "Prosopographia," a word chosen by Erasmus for descriptions of real persons as well as for personifications,[66] was adopted by the author of the *Arte of English Poesie* (1589) for the description of actual people as distinguished from *prosopopoeia*, the counterfeit representation or personification of abstractions like Avarice or Old Age. *Prosopographia* gives the "visage, speach and countenance of any person absent or dead . . . as *Homer* doth in his *Iliades*, diverse personages: namely *Achilles* and *Thersites*, according to the truth and not by fiction. And as our poet *Chaucer* doth in his Canterbury tales set forth the Sumner, Pardoner, Manciple, and the rest of the pilgrims, most naturally and pleasantly."[67] But to Henry Peacham "*prosographia*" is the exhaustive kind of description done by resorting to Cicero's eleven points plus others. His illustration, not so tedious, perhaps, as his precepts

---

[64] Page 15.

[65] *The Life and Letters of Edward E. Hale*, edited by E. E. Hale, Jr. (Boston, 1917), I, 33.

[66] *De Duplici Copia*, p. 81.

[67] *The Arte of English Poesie by George Puttenham*, edited by Gladys D. Willcock and Alice Walker (Cambridge, 1936), pp. 238-239.

might lead one to fear, is not a Character, but one could be constructed upon it: an old man may be drawn

> in this manner, with crooked limmes, and trembling iointes, his head white, his eies hollow, his sight dimme, his hearing thicke, his handes shaking, his legges bowing, his colour pale, his skin wrinkled, weake of memory, childish, yet covetous, suspicious, testy, greedy of newes, credulous, misliking of the present world, and praising the former times.[68]

Hamlet's tart account of what "satirical rogues" say about old men (II, ii) might have been abstracted from this example of *prosographia*.

Prosopographia leads us across the nearly obliterated borderline between rhetoric and poetic and into the matter of creating the personages of poetry and drama. At once the ubiquitous and international law of *decorum* rises up, as if all Renaissance rhetoricians and critics were poor Mr. Dick and *decorum* were King Charles' head. To set forth here all the passages in sixteenth- and seventeenth-century textbooks on this basilisk of theory would be unnecessary punishment, though to do so would clinch beyond any cavil the argument that sixteenth-century criticism guaranteed a well-disciplined audience for the Character as soon as it should be presented. From Erasmus to Sidney, from Sidney to Milton, from Milton to Dryden, from Dryden to Fielding, everywhere the idea of making characters normal and representative is echoed, but in most authors—Castelvetro, Hoskins, Dryden, and Fielding perhaps being exceptions—the echo is not of Aristotle so much as of the petrified doctrine made obligatory by Horace. The illustrations of *decorum* in the manuals also clarify one reason for the prevalence of the doctrine—the aristocratic point of view of the Renaissance, which caused Milton to think in terms of social strata and which produced the noticeable emphasis upon the acci-

---

[68] *The Garden of Eloquence* (1593), p. 135.

dents of economics and social life in sixteenth-century creations of character.[69] Erasmus' discussion of *decorum*, apropos of *Personæ Descriptio* and Theophrastus, lists a goodly number of moral types—"amantis, luxoriosi, avari, voracis," and so on—and also of national types that may be described according to Cicero's eleven points and with Horatian appropriateness. *Miles gloriosus,* the old man, and the rest must be true to type as they are in Terence and Plautus, even if—and here, as often, Erasmus was more penetrating and more artistic than most of his successors—there are individual traits that humanize the figures of old men or parasites in the Roman comedies.

Sixteenth-century instruction for *ethopoeia* and *prosopopoeia* inevitably handed on the rule of *decorum* from Hermogenes, from whom, indeed, Richard Rainolde and Charles Butler, Abraham Fraunce and the *Arte of English Poesie* derived, directly or at second hand, their remarks on these two figures.[70] Likewise, in the speech of praise or blame, Wilson and Coxe[71] both taught that a man's character and ancestry, his national tendencies, his education and habits, what he did and what he might have done, and several other points of biography and description might be considered and developed with strict observance of propriety for the class to which he belonged.

Perhaps speeches of praise and blame always tend toward the

---

[69]See J. E. Spingarn, *A History of Literary Criticism in the Renaissance* (New York, 1899), p. 87; Vernon Hall, "Decorum in Italian Renaissance Literary Criticism," *Modern Language Quarterly*, IV (1943), 177-183.

[70]Rainolde, *A booke called the Foundacion of Rhetorike* (1563), fols. xlix-liij; Butler, *Rhetoricæ Libri Duo* [1600], Book I; Fraunce, *The Arcadian Rhetorike* [1588], sig. G₂; *Arte of English Poesie*, III, xix. ἠθικάς. See his Prolegomena, p. 90.
Casaubon recognized the kinship between the Character and ἠθοποιίας

[71]*The Arte of Rhetorique*, edited by G. H. Mair (Oxford, 1909), pp. 12-13, 91, 177-179; Leonard Cox, *The Arte or Crafte of Rhethoryke* [*c.* 1530], edited by F. I. Carpenter (Chicago, 1899), pp. 75-77. See also Rainolde, fol. xliiij.

conventional, and Wilson was not far wrong. But the hallowed law of *decorum* had fatal possibilities for art—or so it seems today—when it became fixed in that department of poetic theory which concerns the projection of character in literary forms. It is not surprising, to be sure, that critics should have pointed out the typicalness of the dramatis personae in Plautus and Terence, nor was it odd that Sir Thomas Elyot in 1531 or Charles Hoole in 1660 should publish in books of pedagogical intent their belief that the old comedies were "full of morality," that they possessed "the true *decorum* of both things and words," and that they taught "how apt young men are to be enticed, old men to chide, servants to deceive," and many other lessons about the "behaviour and properties of sundry . . . sort of people."[72] Students of the age of which Elyot and Hoole were thinking may conceivably need to have the simple categories of human nature drilled into their understandings. At any rate, one gathers that the habit of seeing men as types must have been as firmly established in the English mind as pedagogical persistence could make it.

One could hardly deny the presence of *decorum* in the personages of the plays Elyot and Hoole were speaking of. But some of the Italian critics, whose books eventually influenced English theory, went farther and thought of character in all poetry as a "prescribed norm," believing in their theoretic madness that all angry men, for instance, were alike and should be projected in the same way. Englishmen, Scaliger would have his readers believe, must always be seen as "perfidi, inflati, feri, contemptores, stolidi, amentes, inertes, inhospitales, immanes."[73] Other nations and

---

[72]Hoole, *A New Discovery Of the old Art of Teaching Schoole*, edited by T. Campagnac (Liverpool, 1913), pp. 137-142; *The Boke Named the Governour*, edited by H. H. S. Croft (1883), I, 125.

[73]*Iulii Cæsaris Scaligeri . . . Poetices* (Heidelberg, 1607), p. 234; quoted by H. B. Charlton in *Castelvetro's Theory of Poetry* (Manchester, 1913), p. 104. Respecting the enormous question of *decorum* in Renaissance criticism I have used, besides Charlton, Spingarn, Donald L. Clark's

other states of mind have their proper characteristics (which, if as universal as Scaliger intimates, would hardly need so precise a catalogue). Character developed according to such fixed notions could, of course, not change during the progress of the play or poem, and readers have been heard to mutter dissatisfaction with the creations of Fielding, if not of Spenser and Jonson, on just this score. But whatever damage slavish obedience to *decorum* did to the creating of the imagined folk of literature, it prepared for and, perhaps one might be allowed to say, created the revival of the Character.

Not, indeed, that the espousing of suitability was always rigid and inartistic. Castelvetro, opposing unintelligent respect for mechanically decorous character-drawing, declared that the situation and action of the poem should govern the character, which by itself was nothing. Shakespeare rose above the tradition while honoring it: Jaques' little harangue on the seven ages of man has its value as rhetorical decoration (of the most ancient kind) but even more as an illustration of the whimsical sententiousness of that second-rate, second-hand philosopher. The critic who knew Aristotle might be more imaginative about appropriateness than were the merely Horatian theorists. John Hoskins, a cultivated gentleman of the circle of Jonson, Donne, Daniel, and Raleigh, put into his "Directions for Speech and Style," written about 1599 or 1600, some remarks about characterization on the universal Aristotelian pattern. "[H]e that will truly set down a man in a figured story must first learn truly to set down an humor, a

Rhetoric and Poetry in the Renaissance (New York, 1922), and Lane Cooper's *The Poetics of Aristotle Its Meaning and Influence* (New York, 1927).

The development of the Character of national types out of the decorous *descriptio* of Nations was discussed by Mr. Greenough in "Characters of Nations," *Proceedings of the Massachusetts Historical Society,* LXV (1940); reprinted in *Collected Studies by Chester Noyes Greenough,* edited by W. C. Abbott (Cambridge, Mass., 1940).

passion, a virtue, a vice, and therein keeping decent proportion add but names and knit together the accidents and encounters."[74] The "perfect expressing of all qualities," he said, could be learned from Aristotle's *Ethics* and *Rhetoric*. The characterization in Sidney's *Arcadia*, which Hoskins particularly admired and which was his subject in this passage, was learned there, but Sidney also "had much help out of *Theophrasti Imagines*." This, the first reference I have found to the possible connection between Theophrastus and the development of characterization in English fiction, is followed by a catalogue of Sidney's main personages and the moral qualities they individually represent; in each of them Hoskins observed "steadfast decency and uniform difference of manners."

Hoskins did not publish his "Directions," but Thomas Blount put practically the entire text into his *Academy of Eloquence* (1654).[75] A more famous admirer of the original conception of *decorum* was John Milton, who alluded to it in his tractate *Of Education* (1644) as the crowning reward of one's final studies of poetry in Aristotle, Horace, and Castelvetro. As we have it in these authors, the doctrine is much as it was in Aristotle, but the Greek's reason for composing character-sketches of representative people has been completely ignored. One cannot but wonder whether Joseph Hall, "chosen to the rhetoric lecture in the public schools" at Cambridge for two years together,[76] introduced that question in his discourses.

Finally it may be noted that the schism in rhetorical theory

---

[74] Hoskins, *Directions for Speech and Style*, edited by H. H. Hudson (Princeton, 1935), p. 41.

[75] Hudson in the Preface to his edition says that Jonson's *Timber* also quoted the "Directions" and that John Smith's *Mysterie of Rhetorique Unvail'd* (1657) pillaged Blount.

[76] See his autobiographical remarks, *The Works of the Right Reverend Joseph Hall* (Oxford, 1863), I, xxvi.

brought about late in the sixteenth century by the revolt of Peter Ramus did not affect the teachings with which we have been concerned. Ramus and his disciple Talaeus, in spite of their break with the Aristotelian tradition, did not materially alter the time-honored conception of *decorum* nor the contents of the ornamental figures of rhetoric. Hence, as we have seen, both the authorities loyal to Aristotle—Cicero, Quintilian, Hermogenes, Aphthonius, Erasmus, Wilson—and the other group devoted to the doctrines of Talaeus—Brinsley, Butler, Hoskins, Blount, Hoole[77]—trod the same ground and wore a clear path to guide all the educated.

To Aristotle's interest in teaching Athenian orators more about human nature, to χαρακτηρισμός and the amplification of the Roman sophist's harangue, to Renaissance docility in accepting Roman rhetorical theory as law and decorous Roman drama as perfect, to Horace and Terence and Erasmus and Wilson as well as to the little-known sketches of the "philosopher"[78] Theophrastus the early seventeenth century was obligated for the vogue of one of its favorite literary forms.

---

[77]See Perry Miller, *The New England Mind* (New York, 1939), p. 322.

[78]See Ascham, *The Scholemaster*, edited by J. E. B. Mayor (1884), p. 111; *Gabriel Harvey's Marginalia*, edited by G. C. Moore Smith (Stratford-upon-Avon, 1913), p. 115.

III

THE
NATIVE BACKGROUND
OF
CHARACTER-WRITING

> For the human mind the absolute continuity of motion is inconceivable. The laws of motion of any kind only become comprehensible to man when he examines units of this motion, arbitrarily selected. But at the same time it is from this arbitrary division of continuous motion into discontinuous units that a great number of human errors proceeds.[1]

The Greek text of twenty-three of Theophrastus' Characters, accompanied by Casaubon's Latin translation, his Prolegomena, and annotations, was published in 1592 in Lyons. Five more Characters were added in the edition of 1599. Not until nine years later did the first collection of avowed imitations, Hall's *Characters of Vertues and Vices*, appear,[2] and the real vogue of the genre came only after the Overbury collection in its simplest form was issued in 1614. As every student of the seventeenth century knows, the Character-literature of the next hundred years had great richness and vitality, varying widely from Theophrastus in matter, attitude, and style but somehow maintaining, in spite of free divergence, a conscious artistic succession. It seems beyond doubt that the sketches of Theophrastus and the edition of Casaubon provided the genre with certain fundamental

---

[1] *War and Peace*, XI, i, Constance Garnett's translation in The Modern Library edition.

[2] Wendell Clausen in an interesting article ("The Beginnings of English Character-Writing in the Early Seventeenth Century," *Philological Quarterly*, XXV [1946], 32-45) suggests that Casaubon's editions did not come into England very soon because of British suspicion of books issued at Lyons, a center of Catholic publication.

elements of its form as well as giving it its name. The Greek sketches, supported by the rhetorical tradition, also contributed life and artistic self-sufficiency. But there must be other explanations for the eventually enthusiastic development of Character-writing, especially in view of the fact that there had been editions (not ever complete, to be sure) of Theophrastus in 1527 (Nuremberg), 1531, 1541 (Basel), 1552 (Venice), 1557 (Paris), and several times later before the edition of Casaubon. Not just the authority of Casaubon, not mainly the rhetoricians, certainly not Joseph Hall alone could have established the type effectively. There were healthy native roots, intellectual and artistic, which were not ready to produce blooms until the end of the century. The Character, quite as truly as the epic or drama of Shakespeare's day, illustrates the nature of the English Renaissance: classical and medieval together, and only together, could have created the popularity of this literary form in the span of years from Hall to Addison.

A study of the history of the Character in England might quite as properly begin, then, with early English literature as with Theophrastus. Not that there were actual Characters in English before 1608. But some, though not all, of the literary intentions of the Character-writer can be seen operating in numerous authors of earlier date. The well-known preference of the Christian and educated Middle Ages for the universal rather than the individual and the visible delight of medieval writers in codifying and classifying might lead one to expect to discover many anticipations of the Character in the works of this period. With important reservations, such will prove to be the case. The kinds of writing which provide the earliest native background for Character-writing are, first, the homiletic works and, second, that body of literature, sometimes identical with the other, that treats the Estates of society. Both literary kinds continued vigorously into the first decade of the seventeenth century, and much of the breath of life of the English Character came from them.

The early religious writers of England tended to compose pictures of representatives of viciousness and virtue in two different ways. When the homilist spoke to the imagination and deeper thoughtfulness of his listeners, when his mind wandered into the realm of theory and causes, he clothed his abstract ideas in allegory. The resulting figures personify some one aspect of human nature or one element in the spiritual life, and though they may be constructed by means of descriptive detail drawn from real life, such figures were meant to remain outside the ranks of mankind and live only in the imagination. Such passages, as Howard R. Patch has suggested in a helpful study of the earliest anticipations of the Character in English literature,[3] probably owed something to the thirteenth chapter of I Corinthians ("Charity suffereth long and is kind; charity envieth not; charity vaunteth not itself, is not puffed up"), and they had precedents in the sermons of St. Ambrose and St. Augustine. The pictures of backbiters, flatterers, and the greedy glutton in the *Ancren Riwle* and those of the envious man in the *Ayenbite of Inwyt* and *Handlyng Synne* are mostly subjective and symbolic, though the descriptions contain sentences that dramatize a lifelike, representative man. The poet-preacher of the *Vision of Piers Plowman* is known as a frank and observing critic of fourteenth-century life. He was, nevertheless, a theorist, and the Seven Deadly Sins in his presentation are abstractions, personified with more than ordinary vividness. "Avaricia" in Passus V has an ugly face and wears old clothes; he has stolen from hedges and at fairs; among the drapers he has cheated buyers while his wife has woven very thin woollens and

---

[3] "Characters in Medieval Literature," *Modern Language Notes*, XL (1925), 1-14.

has adulterated her thin-brewed ale; he has pared pennies, been pitiless to the poor, lent money at exorbitant rates. He has, in fact, moved from youth to age and through all the ranks of society. He is not a picture of the Avaricious Man, an actual representative man, but a horizontal study of one tendency, avariciousness, in all men. The virtue of the Character is *vraisemblance;* the virtue of the figures in *Piers Plowman* and of those in *Everyman* is symbolism, for they are fictions or fancies pointing at the inner natures of all unregenerate men.

Not everyone can be reached by abstract symbols. So to some auditors the preacher had to speak directly, embodying his rules of life in concrete, realistic pictures of such folk as one should strive to imitate and of such others as one would shudder to be. The Bible again furnished a literary model, this time in the last chapter of Proverbs. The text as printed in a Geneva Bible of 1584 reads as follows:

> Who shall finde a vertuous woman, for her price is farre above the pearles.
>
> The heart of her husband trusteth in her, and he shall have no neede of spoyle.
>
> She will do him good, and not evil al the dayes of her life.
>
> She seeketh wooll and flaxe, and laboureth cheerefully with her hands.
>
> She is like the shippes of marchantes: she bringeth her foode from a farre.
>
> And she riseth, whiles it is yet night: and giveth the portion to her housholde, and the ordinarie to her maides.
>
> . . . . .
>
> She putteth her handes to the wherne, and her hands handle the spindle.
>
> She stretcheth out her hand to the poore, and putteth forth her hands to the needy.
>
> She feareth not the snow for her family: for all her family is clothed with skarlet.

56

She maketh her selfe carpets: fine linen and purple is her garment.

Her husbande is knowen in the gates, when he sitteth with the Elders of the land.

She maketh sheetes, and selleth them, and giveth girdles unto the marchant.

Strength and honour is her clothing, and in the latter day she shall reioyce.[4]

"Writers of pulpit manuals and treatises, from the thirteenth century onwards, were accustomed to illustrate each separate 'branch' of Vice or Virtue . . . with . . . vivid little sketches of contemporary men and women and their ways. Thus grew up a natural tendency to identify topic with illustration, and blend them into one."[5] Consequently, Mr. Owst has shown, as sermons became more realistic, the abstraction became a living person. "The Vices themselves now strutted upon the scene as well-known types and characters of the tavern or market-place. The Virtues appeared in the guise of noble women of the times." Instead of employing an imaginary figure of Sloth or Gluttony, one four-teenth-century preacher spoke directly to the knowing and acting faculties of his auditors' natures in a picture of priests who

neither know the law of God, nor teach others. By giving themselves up to sloth, they spend their time upon banquet-ings and carousals, they covet earthly things, they grow wise in earthly things, constantly in the streets, rarely in the church, slow to investigate the faults of their parishioners, *ready to track the footprints of hares*. . . More freely do they offer food to a dog than to a poor man; more wait upon them at table than at mass; they wish to have men

---

[4]The "proverb clusters" dealing with kings and fools (Proverbs 25-26) and the bad wife (Ecclesiasticus 25:16-26) similarly combine suggestive metaphor and description of conduct. Their tendency is especially toward the precept-Character.

[5]G. R. Owst, *Literature and Pulpit in Medieval England* (Cambridge: Cambridge University Press, 1933), p. 87.

servants and maid servants with them, but not clerics. These are they whose chamber is more ornate than their church, their table better prepared than their altar, their drinking cup more costly than their chalice . . . their shirt more delicate than their alb, (their horse dearer than their missal).[6]

Such a description, if put into the third person singular with the title "A Worldly Priest" and with the opening words somewhat altered (as thus, "A Wordly Priest is one who, neither knowing the law of God nor wishing to teach it, idly spends his time upon banquetings" and so forth), would constitute a genuine, if partially subjective and not very exciting, Character. Here rather than in the allegorical creations is the first stage in the development of a native feeling for the Theophrastan form. Yet the abstractions assisted, both as they popularized the idea of types and as they utilized costume and personal appearance to suggest qualities of character. One of the most obvious differences between Theophrastus and Overbury is in the greater dependence of the latter upon physical appearance, upon the data of *effictio* required by the rhetorics and made easier by the gawdy costuming of northerly England.

The literature of Estates classified men primarily on social rather than moral grounds, and lacking so complete and elaborate a doctrine as the Church had provided for the homiletic writer, it was perforce more empirical, at least in its satiric moments, however theoretic it might become in its less frequent descriptions of good conduct. Of the four characteristic features of Estates literature[7]—enumeration of the estates or ranks of men, lament over the shortcomings of each, belief in the divine ordination of the three chief estates, and the suggestion of remedies for the defections of the estates—the first two are

---

[6]Quoted by Owst, pp. 278-279. See also pp. 491-496, 521.
[7]Thus set forth by Ruth Mohl in *The Three Estates in Medieval and Renaissance Literature* (New York, 1933), pp. 6-7.

important for the history of the Character. The tendency of writers to enumerate more and more classes of people according to economic, academic, sectarian, professional, and other differences proceeded so far by the end of the sixteenth century that the innumerable categories of the Character-books were almost inevitable.[8]

Although the Prologue to *The Canterbury Tales* is not a perfect example of the literature of Estates, its connections with that kind of writing and frequent references to jt in historical comments on the Character make it the most interesting example to consider. But two warnings seem necessary. In the first place, it should be said that there is no evidence that Chaucer knew Theophrastus' *Characters*. In the Prologue to the Wife of Bath's Tale and in the Merchant's Tale there are signs that he was acquainted with the *Aureolus Liber de Nuptiis* of a "Theophrastus." But this book, known to us and doubtless to Chaucer only in a monkish excerpt included in Jerome's treatise against Jovinian, appears to be unrelated to the Characters or their author. Secondly, since our concern is with the Character and not with characterization in fictitious narrative, we must limit our discussion to the sketches in the Prologue; what the Cook and Wife and Pardoner developed into as, along the road to Canterbury, they talked about themselves and each other and spun out long stories rich in personal meanings—these developments are precious to the reader of Chaucer, but they are irrelevant in the present discussion.

Chaucer chose his pilgrims first on a basis of social and professional, not moral, classification,[9] though as usual in the literature of Estates he set forth the moral defections of each Estate, and he did that so persistently that we should weep if, fortunately, we were not made to laugh instead. We have the

[8]Cf. Mohl, p. 385.
[9]See Emile Legouis, *Geoffrey Chaucer* (London, 1913), p. 144.

Knight, the Monk, the Summoner, the Clerk, the Cook, the Prioress, the rich middle-class Wife, not the noble man, the hypocrite, the lecherous man (and woman), and so forth. To be sure, my titles are too simple: the pilgrims are the Brave and Selfless Knight; the Wordly, Pampered Monk; the Shameless, Beastly Summoner; the Downright Scholar; for Chaucer like Earle saw the groups within the groups. Yet he preserved the professional aspect throughout the sketches: it is the knight's battles, the friar's perversion of a friar's opportunities, the parson's faithfulness as a shepherd, the cloth-making wife's interest in coverchiefs and color and husbands and the tangible evidence of pilgrimages[10] that Chaucer tells us of in the Prologue. The "estat" or "degree," to use his own words, is preserved.

The result is a set of types, professional types, many with a further moral classification and, as W. C. Curry has argued,[11] in some cases—the Pardoner and the Wife, for example—an astrological or physiological classification besides. To the lay reader[12] it appears in some of the sketches that Chaucer must have meant the figure to be an individual: why else the Summoner's "Questio quid iuris," the Wife's deafness, the Prioress' brooch, and, worst of all, that shocking mormal on the Cook's shin? The answer, I believe, is that, like Theophrastus and his seventeenth-century imitators, Chaucer "vitalized the types,"

---

[10]H. S. V. Jones' suggestion (*Modern Philology*, XIII [1915-16], 45-48) that the Wife represents the estate of matrimony takes care of her case perhaps as well as does my suggestion that she represents the rich bourgeois weavers.

[11]*Chaucer and the Mediaeval Sciences* (New York, 1926).

[12]And to some scholars also. J. M. Manly, whose efforts to discover actual portraiture in the Prologue are well known, wrote a somewhat evasive discussion, "The Pilgrims—Types or Individuals?" for his edition of the *Tales* (New York, 1928, pp. 70-74). See also C. Looten, "Les Portraits dans Chaucer: Leurs Origines," *Revue de Littérature Comparée*, VII (1927), 436.

to borrow a phrase from G. L. Kittredge, by using concrete details that would call up the image of a special man as well as pictures of many others more or less like him.[13] And that mormal in revolting proximity to the Cook's pies and blanc-mange—if one were to describe the waitress in the corner drug-store and remarked that she interrupted the making of a sand-wich to scratch the top of her oily head, would this not be a similar killing of many familiar birds with one stone? Undoubtedly Chaucer's contemporaries saw more of the typical in his people than at this distance we can see.

Chaucer's sketches are not Characters in verse. There is still too much *effictio,* too much of face, figure, and "array" in the manner recommended by the thirteenth-century *poetria;* and some pieces of exactitude such as the Wife's deafness, though they do not destroy the type, do not assist with it. Furthermore, though a master of indirection and also of dramatic characterization, Chaucer often tells us exactly what a man thinks instead of merely describing behavior that would indicate his nature. Chaucer's method and his intention are not, on the whole, Theophrastan, but because of his psychological insight, his con-creteness, and his scheme of social-moral types, the effect of the portraits is in some cases very similar.

One of the unfailing sources of our delight in Chaucer, one which occurs all too rarely in his predecessors and even in his successors, is his genuinely artistic attitude. He takes pleasure in discovering what his pilgrims are, and in the "array," the "con-dicioun," and the motives of each he finds ample scope for humor and intelligence. The preacher in him and in us is allowed at moments to go a-blackberrying. This check on the moralistic

---

[13]A similar idea was expressed by Lowell in his *Literary Essays* (*The Writings of James Russell Lowell,* Boston, 1892, III, 358-359). See also Frederick Tupper, *Types of Society,* pp. 15-16; and above p. 35.

faculty by the descriptive—a restraint necessary to the Character —appears momentarily again in two popular works of the beginning of the sixteenth century. Both works—the Brant-Barclay *Ship of Fools* and Erasmus' *Praise of Folly*—were written by men who were acquainted with classical satire, to which they may have been indebted, as later writers were, for hints about composing a general satire in specific illustrations. Both are related to the literature of Estates and the treatises on virtues and vices.

The headings of Barclay's fifty-odd sections or "satyres" indicate that what he wished to do was not to reveal classes of humanity through fair examples but to assail countless abuses, ranging from such necessarily limited mistakes as "the folisshe begynnynge of great bildynges without sufficient provision" to the fundamental and common sins of gluttony, avarice, and so on. Although there is considerable variety in method and proportion among the satires, the usual components are outright exposition, sermonizing, enumeration of sub-classes and of details about the appearance and behavior of representative sinners, illustrative anecdotes, and classical instances. "Of ryches unprofytable" is entirely a moral essay, not a picture of a miser, and there are others like it that do not concern us. "Of glotons and dronkards" offers numerous facts about the characteristic conduct of such creatures, but the facts are distributed, hardly more than one apiece, among so many sub-classes—the maudlin, the bawdy, the profane, the singer—that no one sketch is complete. Not content as Rutilius was to preach his temperance sermon by dramatic representation, Barclay intersperses explanation, lamentation, and judgment between the brief pictures. On the other hand, among the sermon-like passages in "Of flaterers and glosers" one can find numerous lines that re-create, in spite of a wavering between *he* and *they*, the typical flatterer as Theophrastus drew him. He can

> pyke up the fethers properly
> Of his maysters clothys if they syt nat right
> He maketh them yet for to syt more awry
> To take occasion them clenlyer to dyght
>
> . . . . .
>
> They laughe out lowde if that theyr lorde do smyle
> What ever he sayth they to the same assent.[14]

In certain sections, such as those on people who make noises in church, on disobedient children, on people who despise poverty, and on the extortion practised by military men, the medieval traditions persist unaltered. Elsewhere, however, Barclay builds a picture of the vicious type, not just of the vice, and does so with suggestive data seemingly observed in actual men and women.[15] Probably the realistic and dramatic merits of the *Ship of Fools* derived something from the increasing vividness of the type-figures in contemporary sermons. Probably, too, sixteenth-century readers saw resemblances between Barclay's fools and the strongly but simply characterized figures in current miracle and morality plays.

In the same combined tradition but subtler and more intellectual is Erasmus' *Moriae Encomium*. Remembering that Erasmus in the article on "Personæ Descriptio" in his *Copia* had referred to the "facientes notæ" of Theophrastus, we might hope that he would here cast his observations on the particular follies of lawyers, scientists, old men, and other groups into true Character form. Actually, in the *Copia* Erasmus had held up typicalness and *decorum* as the important features and had not insisted upon objectivity or a dramatic revelation. Hence in the *Praise of Folly*, though his sketches are vivid and *decorous*, they employ

---

[14] *The Ship of Fools Translated by Alexander Barclay*, edited by T. H. Jamieson (Edinburgh, 1874), II, 212.
[15] The woodcuts accompanying the satires are frequently much less lifelike than the verses, often being only symbolic.

analysis often and make moral judgments. The preceptual sketches of Epictetus and Seneca come to mind. In fact, Erasmus' picture of a Stoic wise man[16] is a stinging reverse view of the idealized Stoic as drawn by those two ancients. A less subjective sketch presents "those who pursue fame by turning out books":

> Of the same brand also are those who pursue fame by turning out books. All of them are highly indebted to me, but especially those who blacken paper with sheer triviality. For the ones who write learnedly for the verdict of a few scholars, not ruling out even a Persius or a Laelius as judge, seem to me more pitiable than happy, since they continuously torture themselves: they add, they alter, they blot something out, they put it back in, they do their work over, they recast it, they show it to friends, they keep it for nine years; yet they never satisfy themselves. At such a price they buy an empty reward, namely, praise—and that the praise of a handful. They buy it with such an expense of long hours, so much loss of that sweetest of all things, sleep, so much sweat, so many vexations. Add also the loss of health, the wreck of their good looks, weakness of eyes or even blindness, poverty, malice, denial of pleasures, premature old age, and early death—and if there are other things like these, add them. The scholar considers himself compensated for such ills when he wins the approbation of one or two other weak-eyed scholars.[17]

Theophrastus would exclude some of this matter or express it through concrete actions. Overbury and Earle would have a more figurative style. And of course the plural should be changed to the singular. But the mood is right, and the piece as it stands would give pleasure to connoisseurs of the Character in any period.

---

[16]*The Praise of Folly by Desiderius Erasmus*, translated by Hoyt H. Hudson (Princeton: Princeton University Press, 1941), pp. 39-40. I am indebted to Mr. Hudson for calling my attention to the approaches to the Character in this work.
[17]*The Praise of Folly*, pp. 73-74.

In the prose and verse and drama of the Elizabethan decades there are many pictures of human nature, whether mere sketches in a single sentence or elaborate pictures a page or more in length, that remind one to some extent of those of Theophrastus and that foreshadow the pattern or the tone, the cadence, the favorite phrases, the especial subject matter, or in one way or another the idea of what the best English practitioners of the seventeenth century worked out as the Character. To speak of these as embryo Characters or even ancestors of the form would often be inaccurate. But the history of the genre cannot be understood without considering the many literary forces that moved in the direction in which Hall, Overbury, and Earle were to continue. Pamphleteers, dramatists, homilists, handbook-compilers, and the imitators of Martial all did much. In the following pages I shall endeavor to indicate the principal avenues down which the Character-impulse was proceeding between 1550 and 1608.

The medieval tradition of homiletic writing, still powerful in Shakespeare's day, continued to supply analyses and personifications of the Deadly Sins, the Cardinal Virtues, and their subdivisions. In Bishop Guevara's *Golden Epistles* as translated by Fenton (1575) there is a letter that is really an essay on envy—how it operates in different men, how and why it is wicked. But in telling what envious men are, Guevara also dramatized them momentarily in what they do:

> They say no ill of the poore, but speake at large of the riche: They minister no succours themselves, and restreine others from Charitie: They have mindes voyde of all compassion, but readie hands to receive all that comes: They never speake wythout murmure, nor use scilence wythout pretence of malice: They are suspicious of their enemies, and Traytors to their friendes: They seeke not to salve what is a misse, but are diligent supplantors of men of vertue.[18]

[18]Fol. 141.

But the didactic purpose obviously leads writers into analysis, digression, generalities. George Gascoigne's *Droomme of Doomes Day* (1576) contains much of the latter in its descriptions, with an occasional sentence that demonstrates the "properties" of moral types more graphically: "The proude arrogaunt man loveth the highest seates in the Synagoges . . . He sytteth highest, he goeth stately, he would have all men to ryse when he passeth by, and he will give a beck to every man."[19] Many other passages could be cited[20] to illustrate how moralistic writers, resorting, in a seemingly haphazard way, to description of physical appearance and analysis of motive and character, also tried to reveal character through depiction of a man's habitual conduct. The Characters of good types in Hall's collection of 1608 benefited from the wholly objective, concentrated examples of Theophrastus, but they also have visible ties with these nearly shapeless passages, written, as Hall's pieces were, to carry out the Christian preacher's function.

As for the genuine sermons delivered in the pulpit, one cannot

---

[19]*George Gascoigne The Glasse of Government . . . and Other Poems and Prose Works*, edited by J. W. Cunliffe (Cambridge), II (1910), 255. The marginal note here, "Of the properties of arrogant men," should be recalled in connection with the heading in the King James Bible of the account of the good woman in the last chapter of Proverbs, "The praise and properties of a good wife." Gascoigne has notable pictures of the covetous man (II, 243), of the ambitious (II, 249), and of the proud man (II, 251, 254), but I cannot agree with Charles R. Baskervill (*English Elements in Jonson's Early Comedy*, University of Texas Bulletin, 1911, p. 70) that there is much of the art or point of view of Theophrastus in them. The same three passages, all based on the work of Innocent III, appeared in a slightly different phrasing in Henry Kirton's *Mirror of Mans lyfe* (1576).

[20]William Bullein (1578) *A Dialogue against the Fever Pestilence* (Early English Text Society, 1888), pp. 94-95; "Pierce Pickthanke" in Ulpian Fulwell's *Arte of Flatterie* (1579), sigs. Fiiv-Fiii; the "paynting of a Curtizan" in Part II of John Grange's *Golden Aphroditis* (1577); "The description of an envious and naughtie neighbour" in Thomas Tusser's *Five hundred pointes of good Husbandrie* (1580), chap. 53; the ambitious man in Thomas Timme's *A Plaine Discoverie of ten English Lepers* (1592).

tell how much they contained of realistic type-portraiture. The kind of sermon that would be most likely to resort to such a direct and popular means of affecting an audience is not the kind that usually got into print. Rather, the formal, learned, and exegetical discussions survive, and in these even when a cleric undertook such tempting subjects as "Atheists, Temporizers, Newters, and Humorists"[21] he kept within the polite limits of abstract terms and traditional imagery.

It must have been habit of mind as much as a conscious belief in the social necessity of preserving the feudal hierarchy[22] that caused the literature of Estates to persist into the seventeenth century and that prompted Prince Hamlet in the churchyard to suggest that the skull was that of "my Lord Such-a-one, that prais'd my Lord Such-a-one's horse when he meant to get it" or that it belonged to some lawyer, dealing as usual in quiddits and quillets, secure behind his actions of battery. The Estates scheme contributed to our genre in the Elizabethan age chiefly in collaboration with some other literary pattern, especially the older vices-and-virtues scheme and the classical epigram. In James Sanford's translation of Cornelius Agrippa's *Vanitie and uncertaintie of Artes and Sciences* (1569) are descriptive accounts of Church magistrates ("blinde guides, false and deceitfull") and, at great length and very graphically, "Dukes & Erles," the "noble *Thrasoes*, which dote in pride, riote, and pompe." But Agrippa's plenitude of detail lacks the drama and economy of the Character. By combining the analysis of Estates with the compact form of the epigram and a modicum of its wit, Thomas Dekker in *The Double PP* (1606) came somewhat closer to the Character, though in verse. His ten poems on Catholic types (all bad) and ten more on judges, nobility, the ploughman, and so forth, do not

---

[21]See Thomas Playfere's "Path-way to Perfection," preached in 1573, in his *Whole Sermons* (1633), pp. 172-177.   [22]See Mohl, p. 253.

go very far towards completeness; they are crudely carved, like wooden figures made to ornament a patriotic pageant. Dekker, who is thought to have contributed to the Overbury collection, could do better.

The well-known coney-catching books of the Elizabethan years may be considered a special development of the literature of Estates. Their ostensible *raison d'être* was, as Lodge said at the beginning of his *Alarum against Usurers* (1584), "that the offender seeing his own counterfaite in this Mirrour, might amend it, and those who are like by overlavish profusenesse, to become meate for their mouths, might be warned by this caveat to shunne the Scorpion ere she devoureth." In the process of educating the public the writers of these books at first indulged freely and solemnly in classification and differentiation, then, less soberly, in narrative and characterization; a century later the borderline between the moralistic-informative guidebook and the picaresque romance had largely vanished. It is a far cry from the brief and scarcely literary descriptions of the tricks of "A Freshe Water Mariner or Whipiacke" (whose ships were drowned in Salisbury plain) in Harman's *Caveat or Warening, for Commen Corsetors* (1567) and of the habits and methods of the rogues in Awdeley's *Fraternity of Vacabondes* (1561) to the absorbing exposure of the artful practices of a gifted criminal who assumed the revealing name "Moll Flanders." Between the two come a host of Characters of horse-coursers, bawds, quacksalvers (for instance, that in the Overbury collection), and sharks (see that by Earle) to which the short, really lexicographical descriptions by Harman, Awdeley, and Copland are early poor relations and of which *Moll Flanders* is a brilliant connection by a rich collateral line. The coney-catching pamphlets were not concerned with character, as Theophrastus was, but rather with professional techniques. The exposure of crime became something different,

68

however, in Dekker's *Seven Deadly Sinnes of London* (1606), for here Dekker's sympathy with human nature was too intense and his artist's eye too keen to allow him to rest in either definition or abstraction. In the first section of the pamphlet the account of the career of "Politick Bankruptisme," a high-class rascal whose tricks remind one of the art of business as practised by Bunyan's Mr. Badman, reveals mind and feelings as well as professional conduct. Parts of the report seem like an unconstructed Character; here in the third person singular are the characteristic actions and, through them, the essential nature of a social type.[23]

Some of the most interesting anticipations of the consciously-formed and labeled Character are to be found in two pamphlets composed under the joint influences of Estates literature and the literature of vices and virtues. In these two works, Nashe's *Pierce Penilesse* (1592) and Lodge's *Wits Miserie* (1596), perhaps the best prose pamphlets either author produced, there is flagrant evidence of literary borrowing. Lodge's largest debt is to a work of a medieval sort. That there were other influences is not improbable; both men were bookish, and both may be assumed to have known the character-delineation of the Latin and English epigram.[24]

In *Pierce Penilesse* both the matter and the form that we associate with the Character began to emerge, and the more con-

---

[23] The way in which a realistic analysis of a professional and corrupt type can suggest the Character (as well as the literature of Estates) without being one is illustrated by the passages on the tailor and the broker in Greene's *Quip for an Upstart Courtier* (1592). Greene, never very far from the main currents of his day, was not far from them in these satiric sketches.

[24] They also may have known *A Looking Glasse for Englande*, published anonymously in 1590, in which the anatomizing of the "Enormities and foule abuses" of a Christian commonwealth is done on a dual basis of Estate and moral character and, in the case of the description of an ideal bishop, with something of the effect of a mild preceptual Character.

spicuously because of the prose style—a scoffing manner; sentences loaded with epithet, colloquialism, and slang; short, pronounced cadence; and an abundance of photographically vivid details from real life. It is this racy style that Overbury and his associates imitated and that Earle adopted, with greater restraint and refinement in feeling; indeed, it gave a salty taste to the genre even in the eighteenth century. The passages in *Pierce Penilesse* to which I refer depict a swaggering young social upstart[25] and "Mistress Minx," an affectedly proud merchant's wife

> that lookes as simperingly as if she were besmeard, and iets it as gingerly as if she were dancing the Canaries: she is so finicall in her speach, as though she spake nothing but what shee had first sewd over in her Samplers, and the puling accent of her voyce is like a faíned treble, or ones voyce that interprets to the puppets. What should I tel how squeamish she is in her dyet, what toyle she puts her poore servaunts unto, to make her looking glasses in the pavement? how she will not go into the fields, to cowre in the greene grasse, but she must have a Coatch for her convoy; and spends halfe a day in pranking her selfe if she be invited to any strange place? Is not this the excesse of pride, signior Sathan? Goe too, you are unwise, if you make her not a chiefe Saint in your Calender.[26]

One misses the usual first-sentence definition of the Theophrastan Character; the illustrative details in this case are perhaps too few and too much colored by the author's bias; the conclusion here (but not in the picture of the upstart) ties the piece too quickly to the old medieval framework. Yet one can see the resemblance

---

[25] *The Works of Thomas Nashe*, edited by R. B. McKerrow (London, 1904-1910), I, 168-169.

[26] I, 173. McKerrow notes (IV, 102) that the name "Mistresse Minkes" was given to Lechery in *Dr. Faustus* and to a shopkeeper in a pamphlet of 1615. In Lodge's *Alarum against Usurers* (1584) an old harlot is called "Mistres Minxe"; and in Guilpin's *Skialetheia*, Satire 5, the name again seems to belong to a harlot.

to the old Greek sketches which in a Latin translation were being issued in Lyons in the year in which Nashe's book appeared.[27] On the other hand, because there are pictures of other types— Greediness, Dame Nigardize, a counterfeit politician, a "prodigall yoong Master"—which, as Mr. Aldington says, are merely "burlesque developments of the old fashion of allegory,"[28] one cannot be sure that the two passages came close to the genuine Character for any reason other than accident (that is to say, through the inevitable maturing of earlier tendencies in type satire). Furthermore, the surrounding framework of almost medieval moralizing and of vigorous yarn-spinning dwarfs the pieces and puts one off from the idea of the Character, which in its natural state grows in a recognizable cluster.

In the case of Lodge's *Wits Miserie,* in which the character-sketches are both more numerous and more elaborate, the temptation to discover a formative compulsion from classic Greece as well as from the two medieval traditions is at first glance strong. For though the subtitle, the manner, and three specific allusions to Nashe declare that the chief model was *Pierce Penilesse,* the name of Theophrastus also appears three times.[29] And two of these references come in connection with the character-sketches, the second being embedded in "Adulation" which suggests Theophrastus' "Flattery." Lodge's method—we may as well summarize now the case for a Theophrastan influence—does resemble Theophrastus' in revealing a man's nature through characteristic actions, and Lodge like the Greek chooses fundamental character

---

[27]E. C. Baldwin says (*PMLA*, XIX [1904], 79 n.) that Nashe had read Theophrastus in the original. But the Theophrastus whom he alluded to in his *Anatomy of Absurdity* is the presumably medieval author whom Chaucer mentioned. E. A. Baker (*The History of the English Novel*, London, 1924-1939, II, 223 n.) repeats Baldwin's error.

[28]*A Book of Characters* (London and New York, n.d.), p. 10.

[29]*Wits Miserie, and the Worlds Madnesse: Discovering the Devils Incarnat of this Age* (1596), pp. 8, 20, 100.

for the heart of his constructions. His "Adulation," as I have said, reminds one of Theophrastus, though mostly because of a common subject, and his "disordinate babler,"[30] developed by a quoting of the man's too ready flow of talk, shows a likeness in both subject and method to Theophrastus' "Garrulity."

But the argument against any direct indebtedness to the Greek Characters is at least as persuasive. The three quotations attributed to Theophrastus are not from the Characters; rather, they are moral sentences, the first originating in Diogenes Laertius' life of Theophrastus, the second coming, along with much of its surroundings, from the sketch of "Adulation" in Jean Benedicti's Somme des Pechez,[31] and the third beyond a doubt deriving from some of the many compendious manuals of wise sayings upon which Lodge was astonishingly dependent.[32] The types of humanity chosen for description in Wits Miserie (and set forth as ministers and vice-ministers of the devil) could probably all be found in earlier English sermons, satires, coney-catching pamphlets, and phrase-books: "Vainglory," the boastful traveler and man of the world;[33] "Curiositie," the addict to astrology and magic who is never "without a book of characters in his bosome";[34] "Adulation," quoted below; "Fornication," the

---

[30]Wits Miserie, pp. 85-87.

[31]Paris, 1595, IV, x, 1.

[32]See Alice Walker, "The Reading of an Elizabethan: Some Sources of the Prose Pamphlets of Thomas Lodge," Review of English Studies, VIII (1932), 264-281. The name of Theophrastus was attached to various sentences in some editions of Erasmus' Adages and in Palfreyman's version of William Baldwin's Treatise of Morall Philosophie (I, lvi, VII, vii). But these "quotations" are not from the Characters; it is possible that they may be apocryphal (see D. T. Starnes, Sir Thomas Elyot and the "Sayings of the Philosophers," University of Texas Studies in English, 1933, no. 13, p. 15 n.).

[33]Wits Miserie, p. 4.

[34]Pages 11-12. The title and first line are from Benedicti, III, vi, 10. The "book of characters" was presumably made up of magic symbols

lecherous gallant smelling of perfume and Bandello;[35] "Brawling contention," a brutal Captain Pistol;[36] "Sedition," the professional trouble-maker;[37] "Immoderate and Disordinate Ioy," the gay parasite;[38] and the "disordinate babler." There are also a number of sketches done in the older, more or less allegorical style—for example, "Usury," "Lying," and "Ire"[39]—which tie Lodge's work closer to Nashe's and which accentuate the medieval atmosphere. "Cousenage,"[40] furthermore, sets forth a bawd in the manner of the coney-catching work. According to classic standards, even the most Theophrastan of the drawings degenerate at the end; instead of concluding abruptly they usually spread out into a tiresome plumage, a shapeless and disproportionate brush of anecdote, patristic or classic quotation, piecemeal sermonizing, scraps of verse, and proper names. Narrative elements and horizontal division in satire sustain the medieval line.

But in the best parts of the best sketches, the quality and method are excellent and foretell Overbury. "Adulation" goes

> generally ietting in Noblemens cast apparrell, he hath all the Sonnets and wanton rimes the world of our wit can affoord him, he can dance, leape, sing, drink upse-Frise, attend his friend to a baudie house, court a Harlot for him, take him up commodities, féed him in humors; to bée short, second and serve him in any villanie: If he méet with a wealthy yong heire worth the clawing, Oh rare cries he, doe hée never so filthily, he puls feathers from his cloake if hée

used in his calculations. I am not aware that the word "character" was used in English for the Theophrastan picture until Hall adopted it in 1608. Lodge's "Curiositie" was freely pillaged by Rowlands in his *Letting of Humours Blood* (see below p. ???).

[35]Pages 46-47.
[36]Pages 62-63.
[37]Page 67.
[38]Page 84. From Benedicti's "Ioye desordonnee," III, xiii, 3.
[39]Pages 27, 35-36, 74-77.
[40]Pages 37-38.

walke in the stréet, kisseth his hand with a courtesie at
every nod of the yonker, bringing him into a fooles Paradise
by applauding him; If he be a martiall man or imploied in
some Courtly tilt or Tourney, Marke my Lord (quoth he)
with how good a grace hée sat his horse, how bravelie hée
brake his launce: If hée bée a little bookish, let him write
but the commendation of a flea, straight begs he the coppie,
kissing, hugging, grinning, & smiling, till hée make the
yong Princocks as proud as a Pecocke. This *Damocles*
amongst the retinue caries alwaies the Tabacco Pipe, and
his best living is carrying tidings from one Gentlemans
house to another: some thinke him to be a bastard intel-
ligencer but that they suspect his wit is too shallow. This
is as courtlie an *Aristippus* as ever begd a Pension of *Dion-
isius*, and to speake the only best of him, he hath an apt and
pleasing discourse, were it not too often sauced with
Hiperboles and lies: and in his apparell he is courtly, for
what foole would not be brave that may flourish with beg-
ging? The sword of a persecutor woundeth not so déepely
as he doth with his tongue. Neither dooth the voice of a
Syrene draw so soone to shipwrack as his words: yet (as
Aristotle and *Cicero* thinke) he is but a servile fellow, and
according to *Theophrastus*, he is an ant to the graine of
good nature: Of al things he cannot abide a scholer.[41]

Let us stop here, chopping off a huge coda on flattery. The
detail of the feather, which reminds one of the straw plucked by
Theophrastus' Flatterer from the beard of his victim but which
also could have been derived from the feathers of Barclay's flatterer,[42] will do very well to suggest the involved and uncertain
genealogy of the Jacobean Character. Lodge may have known
Theophrastus; he certainly knew the fleering, colorful writing
of Nashe and the hardly less vivid medieval school of moralistic

---

[41]*Wits Miserie*, p. 20. As has been suggested, much of the abstract
and moralizing comment here comes from Benedicti.
[42]See the passage quoted p. 63.

type-portraiture, and almost as surely we may say that he had read many epigrams. In *Wits Miserie* the English character-sketch went as far as perhaps it could go toward becoming a genuine Character without direct appeal to the classic model.

But several other kinds of writing that favored the appearance ultimately of something like the Character must be considered. Before we contemplate the epigram, prose fiction, or the drama we should notice how certain humbler types of writing contributed to the idea of compact portraiture of moral and social types.

One variety is the more or less scientific discussion of the various physical and psychological natures of men. The theory behind such writing, as ancient as Galen, is well known for its extensive development in Shakespeare's day of the idea of the four humors, but the theory also contained more elaborate possibilities of classification according to age, sex, physical state, and nationality, with emotional and intellectual concomitants for the physical differences. Lyly, Spenser, Marlowe, and Jonson appear to have read *Batman uppon Bartholome* (1582),[43] a book based on a thirteenth-century encyclopedia of natural history that had chapters on the constitution and conduct of children, maidens, mothers, nurses, servants, and so on. A more up-to-date treatment of the doctrine of physiological types could be found in Thomas Wright's *Passions of the Minde* (second edition, 1604). Its tenth chapter explains the physical and mental make-up of youths, old men, women, and alludes more hastily to the different passions of rustics, citizens, Flemings, Frenchmen, Spaniards, Italians, short men, tall men, and others. John Barclay's *Icon Animorum* (c.1614), translated by Thomas May as *The Mirror of Minds* (1633), surveyed the "chiefe kinds of dispositions and

---

[43]*Medieval Lore . . . from the Encyclopedia of Bartholomew*, edited by Robert Steele (1893), p. 3.

affections, of which men use to be composed, and by them wholly swayed, and notably distinguished from other men." Barclay carried the classifying tendency far, giving a good deal of space to the interesting matter of national groups;[44] in the analysis of psychological types—for example, the timorous nature discussed in chapter eleven—he showed surprising penetration. And the book repeatedly just misses producing a Character. Since men could be classified according to their "differences of wit," it was natural that there should have been some such work as Huarte's *Examen de Ingenios. The Examination of mens Wits . . . Englished . . . by R. C.* (1594), which tried to facilitate proper vocational placement on the ground that "to every difference of wit there answereth in preheminence, but one only science." In these works, in Roger Ascham's contrast of "quicke wittes" and "hard wittes" in *The Scholemaster* (1570),[45] and, one may hazard, in thousands of diagnoses of cases by Elizabethan physicians the idea that certain kinds of conduct are symptomatic of certain kinds of temperaments prepared readers for the principle and even the art of the Character.

Somewhere between the scientific description and the manners book enticing one into an admired pattern of conduct lies a special type of composition giving the "marks to know a man." William Vaughan in *The Golden-grove* listed the tokens for knowing a flatterer thus:

> First, a flatterer is accustomed to prayse a man before his face, and yeeldeth his consent with him in all matters, as well bad as good: Secondly, a flatterer is wont to commend the deformitie of his friend, when hee is present, and to admire his stammering voyce. Thirdly, a Flatterer, when a man hath need of him, turneth his backe. Fourthly,

---

[44]Mr. Greenough's article on the use of national types in the Character is mentioned p. 50 n.
[45]Mayor's edition, pp. 79-84.

a flatterer will take upon him at first to contradict a man, and by little and little hee will yeeld as vanquished, and will shake handes with him: these bee the properties of a Flatterer, of whom lette every honest man beware.[46]

Such a flat-footed passage is of service to counterbalance the frequent subjectivity and vagueness of the homiletic tradition in characterization.

That the manners or courtesy book should have facilitated the development of our genre is to be expected. Books written to form a splendid prince or to guide the ambitious tradesman, books on table manners or the military art or the proper acquiescence in one's rank in life, pamphlets for the traveler to Spain, books on the pathway to heaven, and manuals for the maiden of high degree—here *in extenso* is at least the material of the Character-writer. But the Renaissance was too much fascinated with the glass of fashion and mold of form to relish brevity, which in some degree, certainly, is a requirement of the Character. Furthermore, the pedagogue, regardless of his epoch and even if he be so delicate a gentleman as Castiglione, is theoretical, discursive, and thorough. So although in reading manners books one repeatedly has the experience of supposing that in the next sentence a real Character will begin to unroll itself, one is almost always disappointed.

But not always. At least, in James Cleland's treatise entitled ΗΡΩ-ΠΑΙΔΕΙΑ, *or The Institution of a Young Noble Man* (1607) the discussion is occasionally pointed by the listing in parallel columns of the characteristic impulses and actions of a pair of virtuous and vicious types, with the result of producing pieces that have the concentrated attention and representativeness and even the repeated sentence-form of the Character. With

---

[46]I quote from the 1608 edition, book I, chap. 74. See also Thomas Breme's *Mirrour of Friendship: both how to knowe a Perfect friend, and how to choose him* (1584).

greater concreteness the following passage (which is only part of an extended contrast) would merit that label.

Your frend that loveth you with a true and faithful affection beareth that same mind towards you in your adversitie, that he did in your prosperitie. Hee is the same man in your sicknes, which he was in your good health and alwaies remaineth constant.

The flatterer wil honour, & respect you so longe as he seeth your fortune in credit, but when as he perceaveth but the least turning of her wheele, he staieth no longer, then the swollow doth winter, where she had her neast in sommer . . .

A freinde followeth you not for anie respect of lucre or gaine . . .

The flatterer is altogether for his own private commoditie and profite . . .

Your freind when hee is private or in company alone with you or with others is ever without ceremonies, & goeth roundly and squarlie to worke, not regarding whether hee have the first or the second roome. He careth not so much how to please you, as how to profite you.

Wher the flatterer shall alwais give you the first place and shal praise you, studying onlie how to please your humor without al respect of your profite. *Non imitatur amicitiam sed præterit.* In companie he wilbe iealous if you entertaine any other then himselfe, and ever you shall have him tatling, something or other in your eare.[47]

The conduct book says, in effect, that if one wishes to be regarded as such-and-such, one must act in the way to be specified in the following pages. The Character proceeds almost identically: a man who is such-and-such habitually acts as follows. But there are differences in intention and style, and, because the majority of Characters, from Theophrastus' down to Kenneth

---

[47]Pages 194-195.

Fearing's portrait of the "successful" metropolitan business man,[48] are ironic or sarcastic, there are also differences in tone. But the Grobian piece, picturing with ironic admiration the brilliantly bad manners of the glutton-fool, is the satiric *verso* of the Catonian courtesy book.[49] The best known Elizabethan example, Dekker's delightful *Guls Horne-booke* (1609), started out as a modernization of Dedekind's *Grobianus* (1549) but, after the third chapter, undertook to represent in Dekker's racy prose the conduct not of the beastly fool but of the spurious man of fashion. It is a parody conduct book, but its main difference from an Overburian sketch of the same social type is that Dekker uses a chapter for what a Character would put in a sentence.[50] The *Guls Horne-booke* reveals more clearly than do the serious manuals like George Herbert's *Priest to the Temple* (written not later than 1632) the relationship between the two kinds of literature. When at last the classic Character was consciously attempted in England, what the conduct books had said "Of decencie in Apparell" or "Of behaviour at Church" or of folk who "eate and Drinke all the while they sit at the table, glutton-like" came happily to hand to fill out the new form. The manual of instruction and exhortation continued after 1608 to do its daily task in its more or less practical fashion. But the Character, somewhat the stronger and, indeed, the gayer for the existence of the other, utilitarian

---

[48]*Dead Reckoning* (New York, 1938), pp. 34-35.

[49]Of course, the courtesy book, by occasionally describing what one should *not* do, assembled everything that the Grobian writer or the Character writer needed except art. Fleming's *Schoole of good Manners* (registered 1595, printed 1609) explains that at the table people should not dip bread into the common sauce if they have bitten it off the loaf and that they should not stuff food into the mouth until "their cheeks swel like bagpipes" (D_3v).

[50]In the first scene of *Every Man Out of His Humor* (1600) Carlo Buffone's explanation of what one should do to become a gentleman is a kind of condensation of Dekker's not yet published pamphlet and looks consequently, even more like a Character.

genre, rose above it in prestige for a time, ultimately to become almost obsolete.

The gradual emergence of something like the Character was doubtless assisted in a small way by a still more utilitarian kind of Renaissance production: the phrase book, the collection of "flowers" of poetry and wisdom. These books varied a good deal, some being in Latin and some in English, some collecting prose sentences from ancient sages, some assembling quotations of verse, and others mere phrases. Commonly the scattered subject matter was ordered under alphabetical headings. As one casts an eye down the index—Abstinentia, Adolescentia, Adversitas, Adulatio, Adulterium, Aetatis, Affectus, Afflictio, Aliena, Ambitio (I quote from Mirandula's *Illustrium Poetarum Flores*, Lyons, 1570)—not every topic is suggestive. But the *sententiae*, phrases, verses, and classical allusions under such headings as "De Adulatione," "De Hypocrisi," "Of Youth," "Of Bravery" often half create a type for the reader to complete in his own mind. The phrases offered in *Synonymorum Sylva* (in the 1639 London edition of this already ancient book) under the heading "an expert and valiant souldier" would be of use primarily, one guesses, to an author plagued with the necessity of observing *decorum* in characterization; but that use would hardly operate against the development of the Character. And several of the prose flowers in Nicholas Ling's *Politeuphuia: Wits Common wealth* are mildly dramatic: "The iealious man, lyving dyes, and dying, prolongs out his lyfe in passions worse then death; none looketh on his love, but suspition sayes this is he that covets to be corival in my favours, none knocketh at the doore, but starting up, hee thinketh them to be messengers of fancie, none talkes, but they whisper of affection; if shee frowne, shee hates him,"[51] and so on.

---

[51] I quote from the 1598 edition.

In the phrase books the philosophy and literature of Greece and Rome were pillaged in little fragments which, with small flints and blocks of Christian origin, were sorted and collected in bins from which the not very energetic and not very scholarly writer could choose ornaments and props for his own constructions. The labels for the bins often remind one of medieval thinking, but the doctrine of *decorum* and the main ideas of classical ethics could be found among them. The phrase books, furthermore, like the collections of epigrams, should have taught Thomas Lodge, who used the former, that human types as types are interesting without being in a heavy frame.

Equally mixed of elements classical and Christian was the English essay, and like the phrase book, but far more artistically, it was a collection of "dispersed meditations"—anecdotes, quotations, sentences. The essay emerged into self-consciousness almost exactly at the moment the Character first became recognized as a literary type. Plutarch and Seneca provided Montaigne and Bacon with ideas about the prose form that they especially were to develop and dignify. But the interest of Plutarch and Seneca in moral disposition, the precept-description discussed by Seneca, and the concise, pointed sentences in which Seneca expressed himself became contributory influences on the Character also.

Although from medieval times through the seventeenth century many an English writer seems not to have conceived of the essay and the Character as literary forms distinct from each other, the two did develop differently because they satisfied quite different needs. The essay is chatty and, as Bacon explained, both meditative and dispersed. The Theophrastan genre pleases, on the contrary, because it says what it wishes to say objectively, succinctly, and in a pattern. Casaubon found the Character to be something new, a form separate from poetry and from philosophy and from history, neither wholly abstract nor a portrait of a particular person. Joseph Hall repeated this observation in the "Premonition" set before his *Characters of Vertues and Vices*. But Hall knew definitely what he was doing, whereas many an essayist appears only to have had the notion of clinching a discussion of abstract or general matters by some concrete details of conduct and moral disposition. That such a method should occasionally have been resorted to by the essayist was natural and inevitable, and there was no need of a Theophrastus to cause a writer on the subject of envy to mention the common habits of an envious man. In Henry Crosse's *Vertues Common-wealth* (1603) there are curious sproutings of the Character manner. A passage opening with the remark that "Prudence, is a certaine brightnesse shining in the minde"[52] continues through two paragraphs with the abstract subject. But the first words of the third paragraph seem to promise a Character: a "prudent man, is so cautious and vigillant, as wel in the consideration of fore-passed daungers, as in pre-indicating perilles to come, that he meeteth with everie mischiefe, and is not overtaken with *non putavi*, had I wist, for having set his rest on a firme ground, doth not doubt but expect, not repent in the end, but reioice in the whole action: so that she regardeth things past, present, and to come, and bendeth her force to that part that is needful"—and thus we are back to prudence again. Crosse's juggling with "him" (the prudent man) and "her" (prudence in general) could be matched in other writers.

The pattern and the dramatic method of the Theophrastan sketch, features which Casaubon ignored, are hard to find in the essay-writers. Sir William Cornwallis often discussed types of people, but except for a few clauses scattered here and there he depended upon subjective analysis for clarifying the picture. Bacon's familiar "Of Youth and Age" illustrates the method of

---

[52]Fol. B$_2$v.

developing an essay by contrasting a pair of figures, somewhat in the manner of the presentation of a good and a bad woman in the twenty-sixth chapter of Ecclesiasticus. Bacon's habit was to be concrete, but it was also to be judicial and analytical and to use the more scientific plural, with the result that any resemblance is not to Theophrastus but to the venerable sketches of old men and young men in Aristotle's *Rhetoric* and Horace's *Art of Poetry*. In Elizabethan essays[53] there are descriptions of friendship, love, jealousy, and other abstractions, set forth with a feeling for pattern and concreteness, rather like the description of charity in I Corinthians or of wisdom in the Apocrypha.[54] They seem almost to be models for Breton's more self-conscious *Characters Upon Essaies* (1615). In none of them, however, is there more than a superficial resemblance to the Theophrastan genre. Indeed, in spite of the uncertain line between the developing essay and the Character in the years before 1608 (and often afterwards) the two forms have fundamental differences and give most satisfaction when kept distinct.

Although the new essay was too brief to contain anything longer than sentence-portraits of the famous men it often mentioned, the longer treatises, histories, and conduct books sometimes attempted more elaborate studies like those which had been admired in Tacitus, Plutarch, and other ancient historians. Actually, the connection between classical portraiture and the Character is slight. For though in Sallust's picture of Sempronia,[55] for ex-

---

[53]See Walter Dorke's *A Tipe or Figure of Friendship* (1589), fol. B₂; the passage on pride in Thomas Timme's *Plaine Discoverie of ten English Lepers* (1592).

[54]The Wisdom of Solomon, Chapter 7. See W. L. MacDonald, *The Beginnings of the English Essay* (Toronto, 1914), pp. 94-114, for a more extensive discussion of the inter-relations of Character and essay. Chapter X of Crane's *Wit and Rhetoric in the Renaissance* collects valuable material on this question; his use of the word "Character" seems to me too loose, however.

[55]*Bellum Catilinae*, xxv.

ample, or Nepos's interesting discussion of Alcibiades[56] the accumulation of detail about the moral quality, the intellectual capacities, and actual conduct of the man or woman is of the sort the Theophrastan could use, the subject is ordinarily interesting for his individuality. Plutarch, pairing off his heroes for comparison and contrast, did his job of biography so thoroughly that even the comparison sometimes fails to establish any simple outline. The function of the classical historian, which was to report the fact, however eccentric and puzzling, governed his form. But the Character "represents the antithesis of the biographical impulse"[57] in that its function is to reduce the disparate to a unit, to generalize, and also to give the satisfaction of a special literary design.

The moralistic habit of the Renaissance, abetted by a passion for *decorum*, sometimes prevented Elizabethan history from achieving the exact and lifelike effects of Roman historical writing. In translating an interesting characterization in the *Roman Historie* (1609) of Ammianus Marcellinus (Book 16, Chapter 2) Philemon Holland, forcing the issue of "suitability," provided the heading "*The vertues of* Iulianus, *beseeming a magnanimous prince.*" Archbishop Cranmer's secretary in writing of the life and character of his master produced a description[58] which resembles numerous other representations in Elizabethan literature of the ideal Stoic-Christian, the constant, calm, upright, brave, and humble man as Guevara and Hall and Daniel pictured him. There is, also, Jonson's famous description of Francis Bacon, actually based on Seneca.[59] Both Cranmer and Bacon seem to

---

[56]See *Vitae*, VII, i: "nihil illo fuisse excellentius vel in vitiis vel in virtutibus."

[57]Donald A. Stauffer, *English Biography before 1700* (Cambridge, Mass., 1930), p. 270.

[58]*Narratives of the Days of the Reformation*, edited by J. G. Nichols (Camden Society, 1859), pp. 244-246.

[59]*Critical Essays of the Seventeenth Century*, edited by J. E. Spingarn (Oxford, 1908), I, 223.

be portrayed for themselves, yet each represents a type, and the question arises as to whether the authors meant to be particular or general. In Renaissance portraiture many individual men have sat for the idealized type-figure, and, conversely, a man may be fitted, for reasons of flattery or reproach, into an established silhouette. That the same process occurred in Latin literature has been suggested in Chapter II apropos of the letters of Synesius and Apollinaris. The genuine portraitist, to be sure, hunts for the secrets of the individual sitter. But when out of discretion, which is the better part of valor, Bacon submerged the identity of his cousin Cecil in an abstract treatment of deformity,[60] or when Guazzo chose some one person as the original for a drawing of the modest fine lady,[61] or when Ulpian Fulwell assembled the qualities of Edmund Harman to create a picture of that rarity "A faythfull freend,"[62] the biographer leads us close to the boundary of the Character. Late in the seventeenth century, when the historian had learned to ornament his work with set analyses of character and when some novelists used the word "character" for a description of the person and nature and manner of a fictitious being, the boundary between two literary kinds was still not destroyed. Halifax's "Character of King Charles," absorbing and vivid and valuable as it is, affords a pleasure different from that we find in Theophrastus' "Distrustfulness" or Earle's "Downright Scholar" or Butler's "Virtuoso" or, in spite of its modification of the verbal pattern, the first sketch of Sir Roger de Coverley.

---

[60]Such at least was said to have been the case. See Edwin A. Abbott, *Francis Bacon* (1885), p. 437.

[61]*The Civile Conversation*, edited by Sir Edward Sullivan (London, 1925), I, 240-242.

[62]The picture is in verse. See *The First Parte, Of The Eyghth liberall Science* (1579), sig. Gii. Another idealized picture of an individual is Thomas Moffet's "Nobilis: sive vitæ mortis que Sydniadis Synopsis in Laudem magni illius Equitis Philippi Sydnij" (1593), edited by V. B. Heltzel and H. H. Hudson (San Marino, California, 1940).

We may say, none the less, that although the pen portrait could not create the Character, it would presumably further an interest in it.

What is the case with the actual portraiture of sixteenth-century painters and miniaturists? Again the tendency of the human mind to repeat one pattern, to discover similarity in spite of dissimilarity, to organize the world into a recognizable simplification—that psychological impulse which is at the root of Aristotelian logic and the Theophrastan Character—shows itself. Not merely in comparison with the masterly work of Holbein do the painted portraits of Elizabeth's day strike one as being almost uniformly poor, at least in respect to the central problem of revealing personality through the face.[63] To be sure, all the incredible details of ruff, jewels, embroidery, and lace, the color and shape of the beard and hair, in a word the removable differentiae of people are painted with excessive care and faithfulness in the miniatures as well as in the large canvases. But the faces, even Elizabeth's face, which one cannot believe was uninteresting, too frequently are expressionless, characterless masks. If there are divergences among the portraits, whether because of technical limitations or because of the powerful rule of *decorum* or because of some pre-Chesterfieldian respect for the "facade," they go only far enough to indicate the type. Isaac Oliver's charming miniature of Sir Philip Sidney presents a languorous, poetic, fanciful young man. But one cannot say whether this is merely a type or actually the rare Sir Philip, who after his death was apotheosized into a figure of the Renaissance gentleman. In many portraits the nature of the type appears principally in the costume.

---

[63] These remarks, for which in part I am indebted to Professor Lawrence Opdycke, are of course in general and do not deny the revealing quality of such a rare piece as Nathaniel Bacon's self-portrait.

The great majority of Elizabethan portraits, indeed, are little more than standardized fashion-plates ... [the] figure draped in clothing appropriate to the sitter's real or imagined importance—a sober gown for statesman, scholar and merchant, armour for the soldier, court-dress for the gallant and his lady. The rich ornaments and elaborate jewellery which give most of these portraits their sole interest, were probably nothing but stage-properties put in by the painter, who thus enabled his clients to indulge in an economic rivalry with Elizabeth herself.[64]

If contemporary portrait-painting had any effect at all on the development of the Character, it must have been favorable.

When Casaubon declared that the way of the historian and of the poet differed from that of the Character-writer (as well as from each other) he presumably included the writer of prose fiction among the poets. It hardly needs to be pointed out that the creation of individual human beings that are to move about in a story is not the same as creating a nameless type that acts not of its own accord but only when the author pushes it through its prescribed, representative motions. There are, to be sure, similarly restricted constructions in modern fiction, but a Sir Willoughby Patterne or Soames Forsyte in order to survive must have not only a name and particular address but also other special features of his own and the power of self-propulsion as well. Yet among the living, individualized people (I count Sir Willoughby as among the living in spite of some bad moments caused by the relentless determination of Meredith not to give in on his side) a novelist may sometimes need to place, if not an embodiment, a unit-description of the typical actions of a group of men. Lyly writes in *Euphues* of "the beasts which live by ye trenchers of younge gentlemen, & consume the treasures of their reve-

[64]G. H. Collins Baker and W. G. Constable, *English Painting of the Sixteenth and Seventeenth Centuries* (New York, 1930), p. 27.

newes, these be they that soothe younge youthes in their owne sayinges, that upholde them in al theyr dooinges with a yea, or nay."[65] Nicholas Breton, a future Character-writer, approached the method in Mavillia's description[66] of a miserly and lecherous old man; details already associated in English satire with the traditional old man, lecher, and miser are effectively assembled for the portrait. In Deloney's tales and in *The Unfortunate Traveler* (1594) there is nothing like the Character. But Lodge's Rosalynde describes some "Ovidians," who "holding *amo* in their tongues, when their thoughts come at haphazard, write that they be rapt in an endless labyrinth of sorrow, when walking in the large lease of liberty, they only have their humors in their inkpot. If they find women so fond, that they will with such painted lures come to their lust, then they triumph till they be full-gorged with pleasures; and then fly they away, like ramage kites."[67] Although there is something here of the objective presentation and stylized expression of the Character, Lodge went farther towards the Overburian product two years later, not in a pretty romance but in the homiletic-satiric *Wits Miserie*, where he compressed the Ovidians into a single figure and created other specific types each with its own separate milieu. The flowing, forward movement that gracefully caught up the Ovidians into Rosalynde's story has gone, along with the pastoral enchantment, and we are again in the harsh world of static, varnished, separately-framed, but firmly collected art. Nashe and Lodge, who wrote the best "near-Characters" before 1600, put them into didactic-satiric pamphlets rather than into their tales, thus demonstrating that the Character is a literary form that did not naturally develop in the art of story-telling.

---

[65]*The Complete Works of John Lyly*, edited by R. W. Bond (Oxford, 1902), I, 282.

[66]Quoted from *The Miseries of Mavillia* (1596) by Baker, II, 148.

[67]*Rosalynde*, edited by W. W. Greg (London, 1931), p. 80.

It may be with some surprise, then, that one comes upon the statement of John Hoskins, writing about 1599, that Sidney not only used Aristotle's *Rhetoric* in drawing the characters in his *Arcadia* but also "had much help out of *Theophrasti Imagines*."[68] What Hoskins meant, apparently, was not that Sidney attempted to compose sketches in imitation of those of Theophrastus but rather that he loyally and persistently followed the rule of *decorum* as it was then interpreted. He that will "truly set down a man in a figured story must first learn truly to set down an humor, a passion, a virtue, a vice, and therein keeping decent proportion add but names and knit together the accidents and encounters."[69] Hoskins goes on to explain "what personage and affections are set forth in *Arcadia*": "pleasant idle retiredness in King Basilius," unfortunate valor in Plangus, proud valor in Anaxius, the "mirror of true courage and friendship" in Pyrocles and Musidorus, a "mischievous seditious stomach" in Cecropia, "miserableness and ingratitude" in Chremes, and so forth. Certainly Hoskins is right. The adventures and occasionally the names—Chremes the old man, Clinias the wanderer from the right course, Zelmane the envious—suit the "humor" or "virtue" or "vice" Sidney has assigned to each, and every character is a recognizable type of person, with, as Hoskins says, "a steadfast decency and uniform difference of manners." Clinias's actions[70] are different, and differently revealed, from those in Theophrastus' "Cowardice," but Clinias quite as well exemplifies that quality. Cecropia indulges in unrelenting and unadulterated

---

[68]Hudson edition of Hoskins, *Directions for Speech and Style*, p. 41.

[69]*Ibid.* Hoskins was echoing Sidney's own assertion in his *Apologie for Poetrie* that by a concrete representation a poet may make a virtue or a passion real and affecting.

[70]II, xxvii; III, vii. The head-note for the former chapter is *"A verball craftie coward purtrayed in Clinias."*

fiendishness from her first appearance to her last. The "stead-fast decency" in her depiction, however, is at the expense of psychological probability and is spurious, for how could such a monster rear so brave and honorable a son as hers? Like Theophrastus' folk, Sidney's are built about one propensity of character, and everything they do is consonant with that propensity. The mistake in the Horation identification of rhetoric and poetic appears only too clearly in its result in the *Arcadia*. When a figure constructed with rigid *decorum* is set forth with other such creations to move about as if in life, the consequence will either be allegory or, in an Arcadian landscape of wooded hills and verdant meadows, a decorative design. Sidney's characters, with few exceptions, are hollow.

If we are to discover anything more literally indebted to "Theophrasti Imagines," and I believe we shall not, we may consider the picture of Chremes, to whom Pyrocles is brought by the old man's daughter. As Chremes "was of all that region the man of greatest possessions, and riches, so was he either by nature, or an evill received opinion, given to sparing, in so unmeasurable a sorte, that he had not onely barre him selfe from the delightfull, but almost from the necessarie use thereof." When Pyrocles and the daughter reach the old man's castle, where plentiful signs of his wretched nature appear, he receives his daughter, who has long been absent, without pleasure. Pyrocles relates that he saw Chremes, "a driveling old fellow, leane, shaking both of head and hands, alredie halfe earth, and yet then most greedie of Earth: who scarcely would give me thankes for that I had done, for feare I suppose, that thankefulnesse might have an introduction of reward. But with a hollow voice, giving me a false welcome . . . he brought me, into so bare a house, that it was the picture of miserable happinesse, and rich beggerie . . . In summe, such a man, as any enemy could not wish him worse, then to be himselfe."[71] The "such-a-one-as" formula suggests the Character. But really there is nothing here, not even the "steadfast decency," that could not have been learned from wholly English books. One may safely conclude, however, that the type figures and the personifications of moral and social tendencies set forth in the *Arcadia*, as in *The Faerie Queene*, bore a debt to classical theory as well as to the tradition of the *Ancren Riwle* and *Piers Plowman* and Ulpian Fulwell and Gascoigne.[72]

The satiric spirit rife in England in the last decade of the sixteenth century has been variously explained. We may postpone until Chapter VI any discussion of its cause and proceed to examine the verse satire and epigrams based on classical models that were being written at that time.

The satires of Juvenal and Horace differ from the poems of Martial in certain visible ways. The satirists exercise a right to discussion and broad judgment, they treat as many subjects— and objects—in one poem as they wish, and there is no immediate limit to the length of their poems. The Roman epigram (the Greek variety we may ignore, since the Elizabethans ordinarily did not copy it), on the contrary, is very short, often objective, and ends in a witty or ingenious turn of thought for which the rest of the poem has been a preparation.[73] In both kinds of poems it is sometimes difficult to say whether the people ridiculed are meant for individuals or types. The impertinent, shameless fellow

---

[71] *The Countesse of Pembrokes Arcadia*, edited by Albert Feuillerat (Cambridge, 1922), pp. 273-274.

[72] John L. Lievsay in his "Braggadochio: Spenser's Legacy to the Character-Writers" (*Modern Language Quarterly*, II [1941], 475-485) discusses the persistence in later satire and Characters of the type Spenser labeled Braggadochio. That Spenser's own characterization was done "in Theophrastian fashion" is true only in a loose sense. For partial, unintentional refutation of the idea of a Theophrastan debt, see the Variorum *Spenser*, II, 205-211.

[73] T. K. Whipple, *Martial and the English Epigram* (University of California Publications in Modern Philology, X [1925], No. 4), p. 282.

who attaches himself to Horace on his walk (the famous ninth satire of Book One) seems an individual, and equally well particularized are many of the innumerable people whom, usually for one fatal oddity, Martial stabs and mounts in his brilliant collection. Hundreds of Martial's specimens are preserved not because they are representative and classical but, instead, because they are eccentric, surprising, egregious. Such pieces suggest the Character only in their concentration and astringency. But there are also specimens of types. Part of Juvenal's powerful sixth satire consists of exaggerated pictures of women who, though seen only in a moment's glance, appear to have their many sisters—the mannish woman interested only in war and public affairs, the woman who will do anything for music or a musician, the learned woman, the woman whose life is in her dressing. Similarly Martial exposes types—the false wit (I, 41), the busybody (II, 7), the "Ned Softly" sort of poet (III, 44), and enough parasites to form a society. In the poem on Menogenes (XII, 82) Martial goes farther, adopting a dramatic method of exposition; Menogenes, Martial says, will pick up your muddy ball for you, praise your linen, comb your hair, or wipe away your sweat for you if you will then ask him to dinner. In the epigram on Cotilus, which the English especially liked, one has, except for the lack of prose, of an abrupt ending, and of the is-such-a-one-as-would formula at the beginning, a perfect classical Character.

> Cotilus, you are a beau; so say many, Cotilus, I hear; but tell me, what is a beau? "A beau is one who arranges his curled locks gracefully, who ever smells of balm, and cinnamon; who hums the songs of the Nile, and Cadiz; who throws his sleek arms into various attitudes; who idles away the whole day among the chairs of the ladies, and is ever whispering into someone's ear; who reads little billets-doux from this quarter and that, and writes them in return; who avoids ruffling his dress by contact with his neighbor's

sleeve; who knows with whom everybody is in love; who flutters from feast to feast; who can recount exactly the pedigree of Hirpinus." What do you tell me? is this a beau, Cotilus? Then a beau, Cotilus, is a very trifling thing.[74]

Although the Elizabethans did not always make a clear distinction between satire and epigram, the former was likely to be longer, more discursive, and its characterizations more complex. Such are Donne's witty satire (IV) on the confident, gossipy courtier who damns the court while meaning to praise it, Hall's pictures[75] of the famished but richly dressed gallant and of "old driveling Lollio" who worked hard and sacrificed all so that his son might pretend to gentility, and William Rankin's *miles gloriosus* and the foolish gallant.[76] Though they have neither the simplicity nor the economy of the Character, such satires catch a type and its own absurd motions, to record them with proper relish.

As for the imitators of Martial, if they had his habit of representing eccentric individuals they also appealed to the sort of literary taste which was to be more lavishly catered to by Overbury and Earle. Both Sir John Davies and Everard Guilpin reworked the Cotilus lines, Guilpin twice.[77] In the second and seventh poems of *The Letting of Humours Blood* (1600) Samuel Rowlands used a monologue in the first person to expose the actions of a type (the swaggering bully and the dissipated brute), with an effect akin to that of the Character. In *Pasquils Mistresse* (1600) Nicholas Breton outlined the revealing actions

---

[74]*Res pertricosa.* Translation from *The Epigrams of Martial* (Bohn's Classical Library, 1897), pp. 160-161.   [75]Satires, III, 7; IV, 3.
[76]*Seaven Satyres Applyed to the weeke* (1598). See Lodge, *A Fig for Momus* (1595), Satire IV.
[77]Davies, *Epigrammes* (Middleburg, 1590?), No. 2, "Of a Gull"; Guilpin's *Skialetheia* (1598), No. 20, "To Candidus," and No. 38, "To Licus." Jonson's twenty-eighth epigram, "To Don Surly," published in 1616 but perhaps written earlier, also resembles "Cotilus."

of a number of feminine types—the constant-patient, the clean within and without, the pious, and others—which are not always clear and never complete; but occasionally, as in the following example, the epigram approaches the Character.

> She that can have her breakefast in her bed,
> And sit at dinner like a maiden Bride,
> And all the morning learne to dresse her head,
> And after dinner, how her eye to guide,
> To shewe her selfe to be the childe of pride,
>   God, in his mercy, may do much to save her:
>   But what a case were he in that should have her![78]

Still a different English variety of the epigram might be labeled the precept-Character in verse. Seneca in his ninety-fifth epistle had pointed out the distinction between the description or "characterismos" and the didactic statement or precept. In his forty-fifth and eighty-first epistles he wrote what technically are descriptions but what in aim and spirit are really hortatory pieces, *praecepta*. This latter sort of composition had an interesting development with a special subject, the *beatus vir* conceived on Stoic-Christian principles. A versified description of the happy life and, by implication, of the behavior of the happy man (less Stoic than Epicurean, to be sure) was given several times by Martial and Horace.[79] Seneca and Epictetus[80] provided glowing accounts in prose of the Stoic wise man, self-judging, steady, just, his reason ever controlling his passions. A fusion of the material of the verse and prose passages can be seen in an epigram often printed in sixteenth-century editions of Virgil which earnestly sets forth the Stoic ideal ("vir bonus et sapiens").[81]

---

[78]*Pasquils Mistresse*, sig. D₈v.
[79]See especially Martial V, 20; X, 47, and Horace's Epistles, I, xvi.
[80]*Encheiridion*, xlviii.
[81]These lines, translated by Chapman in his *Petrarchs Seven Penitentiall Psalms* (1612) as "Virgils Epigram of a good man," and two

On the other hand, Christian homilists, assisted by the account of the *beatus vir* of the first Psalm, had also painted portrait after portrait of their ideal man—what he was and how he acted. Christian Stoicism being a popular faith among Shakespeare's contemporaries, there are many passages in prose and verse written near the turn of the century which combine Christian and pagan ideals of conduct and which are interesting for their resemblances to seventeenth-century Characters of laudable moral types.[82] In both the pagan and Christian precedents, it should be said, the method had been as much subjective as objective; since the true Stoic or Christian can be known ultimately only by his state of heart or spirit, even an effort to reveal him in what he does will perforce tell what his mind and heart do. Only thus can the hypocrite be distinguished from the genuine article. Theophrastus' method, which is that of an external observer, could hardly get at the crux of the matter. So the pictures of the essential good man—Samuel Daniel's splendid Horatian epistle "To the Lady Margaret Countesse of Cumberland,"[83] Thomas Thynne's epigram on "A godly mann,"[84] and Sir Henry Wotton's well-known "Character of a Happy Life"[85]—inevitably

similar, "original" epigrams entitled "A great Man" and "A sleight man," which were indebted to Wolfius' *Epictetus* (see *The Poems of George Chapman*, edited by Phyllis B. Bartlett, New York, 1941, pp. 447-448), present a general and analytical discussion of the theoretical types. A fourth piece, called "A good woman," is much more concrete. It sounds, in fact, like a versified condensation of some female manners book. I am indebted to Hoyt H. Hudson for calling my attention to these epigrams and to those, mentioned below, in the Ashmore collection.

[82]W. L. Ustick called Mr. Greenough's attention to a Character-like description (subjective in method) of a wise man in Charron's *De la Sagesse* (1601), II, vii. The description is based on Seneca, *Epist.*, LXXXV, and *Nat. Quaest.*, III, praef.

[83]There are Senecan suggestions in the poem. It was published in 1601.

[84]*Emblemes and Epigrames* (1600), epigram 69.

[85]Written in 1612; published in the fourth impression of the Overburian Characters, 1614. The title, it has been suggested (*The Life and Letters of Sir Henry Wotton*, edited by Logan Pearsall Smith, Oxford,

require a different manner. And a little group of poems printed at the end of Ashmore's *Certain Selected Odes of Horace, Englished* (1621) with the separate heading "Of a Blessed Life" show that in spite of the printed example of the Theophrastan *Characters* and Hall's and Overbury's imitations, the depiction of the ideal Christian stubbornly required the method of subjective analysis. Ashmore printed three epigrams on the Christian *vita beata* (and *beatus vir*) to oppose the ideas in Martial's two epigrams, which were here translated, and closed with an epigrammatized version of the mostly negative and figurative statement in the first Psalm.

When one turns back to the Virtues in Hall's *Characters*, especially the accounts of the "Wise Man," the "Faithful Man," and the "Happy Man"; when one examines the *"description of a good and faithfull Courtier"* and *"of a Christian"* in Hall's Epistles;[86] and even when one looks at Overbury's "Wise Man" and "Noble Spirit," one sees how continuously the tradition was maintained. The subject matter in both Characters and poems is that of the Senecan and Christian moralists combined; the tone, serious, exalted, hortatory, is likewise theirs; and the necessity of describing the inner man in subjective terms persists as well as the tendency to be general rather than vividly particular.

1907, I, 130), was not Wotton's. Certainly Wotton's procedure, analyzing the moral and mental condition of his man rather than reporting specific actions, distinguishes the piece from the majority of pieces with which it was published.

[86] Of the former, which appeared in *Epistles, The Second Volume* (1608), Hall said to the dedicatees of the sketch ("the Gentlemen of his Highnesses Court") that it was "The Character of *What you are*, of *What you should be*." It is more abstract than the description of a "rightfull Courtier in his kinde" which Spenser inserted in *Prosopopoia, Or Mother Hubberd's Tale* (1591), 11. 717-793. Spenser is sometimes thought to have been drawing a portrait here, but the effect is, as he said, of a "kinde." Both writers discuss the inner state of their courtier, who is a true Christian. The second of Hall's "descriptions" appeared in *Epistles, The Third . . . Volume* (1611).

Hall explained that in the *Characters* he was trying as well as he could to follow Theophrastus, and there are sentences and phrases in the Characters of good types to support his assertion. But as there was no model in Theophrastus for the description of a nature that one admired, for the representation of an ideal that was inward and remote, so it is not so much to Theophrastus that one should turn for the original of Hall's idealized Characters as to the Stoic moralists and Christian homilists, particularly as they spoke simultaneously in many English epigrams. The title of Hall's collection suggests a debt to Seneca's idea of composing "virtutis ac vitii . . . notas."[87]

What classical satire and epigram could contribute to the Character, once it was formally reëstablished and labeled, is clear. A stock of moral and social types of men had been ticketed and succinctly described; the description could be concrete and dramatic. From some, though certainly not all, of the epigrams the Character-writers could learn to use a light vein of mockery and a terse, witty ending which was foreign to Theophrastus but soon almost obligatory for the English imitators. From the later epigram as well as from the homiletic tradition came a tendency to tell what a person is rather than what he does. There was, in fact, a certain amount of cross-breeding between the epigram and the English moralistic prose genres, the results of which we must examine before we may consider our study of this aspect of our subject complete.

Both the epigrammatized homily and the epigrammatized literature of Estates can be illustrated in the work of Samuel Rowlands. In his *Letting of Humours Blood* (1600) he included a group of "Satyres," of which the first, third, and fifth are descriptions respectively of a lying, garrulous braggart, of a brutal, superstitious fellow, and of a contemptuous malcontent.

[87] *Epist.*, XCV, 65-66.

When one discovers that the first is constructed from "Lying" and "Vainglory" in *Wits Miserie*, the second from Lodge's "Brawling Contention," "Dicer," and "Curiositie," and the last from only his "Hate-Vertue" one understands why the former two seem to be complex individuals and the latter more nearly a type. The significant thing about these pieces is that Rowlands in his depredations took chiefly the graphic, dramatic material from which to build. Furthermore, his fifth satire actually raises the question of whether he did not know Theophrastus' "Backbiting." In *Looke to it: for, Ile Stabbe ye* (1604) Rowlands reverted to the old dance-of-death framework for its exposition of the evil conduct of kings, magistrates, divines, adulterers, quack doctors, disobedient children, and some twenty-five other "estates" and classes. The indiscriminate assemblage of moral and social groups combined with occasional preachment reminds one of Barclay's *Ship of Fools*. With the help of Lodge and Martial (who, as well as the preachers, habitually addressed his victims directly) Rowlands could produce the following picture of a "Counterfayte *Captaine*."

> You Captine mouse-trap, growne a desperat stabber
> You that will put your Poniard in men's guts:
> You that last Voyage, were no more but Swabber,
> Yet you cracke Blades as men cracke Hazel-nuts,
> You that try all your manhood with a Puncke,
> And fight most bravely when you are most drunke.
>
> You that protest the Feather in your Hat,
> Came from a Countesse Fanne by way of favour:
> Your Rapier, why the great Turke gave you that
> For mightie monst'rous *Marshal-like* behaviour:
> You that weare Scarfs and Gart'rings for your hose,
> Made all of Ancients, taken from your foes.
> Ile Stab Yee.

But we have still not arrived at the pleasure of the genuine

Character, whether of the seemingly unvenomed and easy Theophrastan sort or of the witty, lavish kind begun by Hall's *Characters of Vices* and perfected by Overbury and Earle. We lack the repetition of the formula "He is . . . He is one who . . . He goes . . . He says," a formula which when properly varied gives order and style to the Character. We also lack, unless in Nashe's and Lodge's pamphlets, the balance of interest in the peculiar conduct of a type and in his basic tendency of thought and motive. We notice, too, that the author still expresses his disapproval and releases his energy in harsh feeling and brutal language rather than in keen analysis and witty conceits. Can we find a closer approximation in the character-sketches prefacing the printed text of Jonson's *Every Man Out of his Humor* (1600) and in the others embedded in the dialogue of *Cynthia's Revels* (1601)? Some critics have in fact labeled these Characters.[88] In so doing they have tended to ignore their resemblance to the epigram.

The idea of writing comic drama in which each of the dramatis personae was either to be possessed by "some one peculiar qualitie," drawing "All his affects, his spirits, and his powers . . . all to runne one way" or was to pretend that he was so possessed, Jonson had already utilized before he wrote *Every Man Out of his Humor*. By the time he came to publish that play he himself was a possessed man. With a talkative passion for his scheme

---

[88]See G. S. Gordon, *English Literature and the Classics* (Oxford, 1912), p. 80 ("Jonson was the first man in England to produce the set Character on scientific principles"); A. C. Judson's edition of *Cynthia's Revels* (New York, 1912), pp. lxvi-viii; Aldington, p. 12; E. N. S. Thompson, *Literary Bypaths of the Renaissance* (New Haven, 1924), p. 7. In his Harvard dissertation of 1904 Mr. Greenough called the sketches before *Every Man Out* "real 'characters.'" Although I find no clear statement among his later notes to indicate his final judgment, his reading various comments on Jonson published later than 1904 would seem to indicate that he did not consider the question so simple as he once had done.

of "humors" that reminds one of the later theoretical Mr. Bayes, he not only prefaced the text of his play (which, to quote Cordatus, should itself "have made the Humors perspicuous enough") with a description of "the severall Character of every Person" in it; he also explained his theory absolutely and historically in the Induction and, for good measure, appended another picture of Carlo Buffone and a reiteration of the key-word "envy" for Macilente. Plautus in the prologue or early scenes of a play sometimes described one or more of his people, usually just to make the type he represented more conspicuous. Seeing Jonson's descriptions in their original surroundings, one realizes that their function was primarily practical, not aesthetic, and that the word used was "character" in the ordinary sense, not "Character."

As one reads through the list of descriptions before *Every Man Out of his Humor* one has no thought at first of the Theophrastan genre. Asper and Macilente are delineated simply and briefly. Puntarvolo and Carlo Buffone, however, are represented as more elaborate and picturesque beings. Puntarvolo as here described—and of course our concern is only with this description, not with what he does in the play—seems addicted to vainglory, travel, and fine language, and Carlo is parasite, liar, braggart, and slanderer. Both the contents and style of the description of Puntarvolo suggest what we have read in earlier English satire, epigram, and even the pamphlets on the Seven Deadly Sins.[89] Carlo suggests different figures in Plautus, Martial, and Lodge. But though it is often remarked that Jonsonian "humor" characters are simple and unified com-

---

[89]Compare especially Nashe's "greasie son of a Cloathier" in *Pierce Penilesse* (*Works*, I, 168-169) in which a determined "humorousness" unifies many vagaries. Baskervill in *Jonson's Early Comedy* upholds the theory that Jonson was deeply influenced by English traditions of writing. In his chapter on *Every Man Out* there is plentiful illustration to support the argument that Jonson's characters were already well-established English types.

pared with Hamlet and Prince Hal, it should also be said that
Puntarvolo, Carlo, and Fastidious Brisk in these prefatory
descriptions seem complex and Protean when set beside the
work of Theophrastus.[90] One can recognize Brisk, Shift, and
Deliro as the worthless courtier, the shark, and the uxorious
husband, and they are outlined with something of the dramatic,
objective method of Theophrastus as well as by direct explanation of their natures. Yet Puntarvolo and Carlo lack precise
definition. They are not universal human types but special
social phenomena, and what they are said to do is almost too
variegated to indicate to the uninitiated what they are. Although
their descriptions are not so truly conundrums as, for example,
the Overbury "Tailor" and "Apparator" are, the two figures
very nearly require a label, something not needed by the Theophrastan Character. The rest are too brief to be impressive.
If the longer sketches advance beyond those of Nashe and Lodge,
it is only in that they are not embedded in the continuous prose
of a pamphlet, the moralism of which might color them by
reflection or accretion. What Jonson was trying to do in these
paragraphs was to make it easier for the reader to "get" his
play. If there was any specific reason other than his own taste
to cause him to adopt a vivid, compact expression for his descriptions, it must have been Juvenal and Martial and the English
tradition of satiric portraiture rather than Theophrastus.[91]

---

[90]The more recent criticism of Jonson's drama has discounted the
idea that the characters are dominated by a single humor. See T. S.
Eliot, *Selected Essays* (New York, 1932), pp. 136-138; E. E. Stoll,
Shakespeare and Other Masters (Cambridge, Mass., 1940), pp. 98-100.

[91]The assertion of E. C. Baldwin ("Ben Jonson's Indebtedness to the
Greek Character-Sketch," *Modern Language Notes*, XVI [1901], 386)
that the sketches prefaced to *Every Man Out* are "except for their brevity,
exactly like those of Theophrastus" seems rash. The notion that Theophrastus was Jonson's model, accepted as probable by W. J. Paylor (*The
Overburian Characters*, Oxford, 1936, p. v) and M. G. Walten (*Thomas
Fuller's The Holy State*, New York, 1938, I, 26 n.), is modified by the

Yet the "quicker apprehension" and "learned eares" of certain of his readers may have enabled them to imagine a Theophrastan model, and in *Cynthia's Revels* one is at first less sure that there was not one. But the familiar Jonsonian interests in constructing characters out of real and imagined "humors," the allegorical intention of this play, and probably a desire to incorporate in drama the special methods and flavor of the recently prohibited formal verse satire[92] would sufficiently account for the seven pretentious, static descriptions of people spoken by Mercury in Act Two. The oddity of Madam Philautia, the artful phrasing of her portrait, and the stinging last sentence persuade one that Martial helped Mercury to fix her.

> Shee admires not her selfe for any one particularity, but for all: shee is faire, and shee knowes it: she has a pretty light wit too, and shee knowes it: shee can dance, and shee knowes that too: play at shittle-cock, and that too: no quality shee has, but shee shall take a very particular knowledge of, and most lady-like commend it to you. You shall have her at any time reade you the historie of her selfe, and very subtilly runne over another ladies sufficiencies, to come to her owne. Shee has a good

editors of the Herford-Simpson edition of Jonson (*Ben Jonson*, edited by C. H. Herford and Percy Simpson, Oxford: Clarendon Press, I [1925], 374) to include the influence of Martial. Clausen rejects the idea altogether. Baskervill and E. A. Tenny (*Thomas Lodge*, Ithaca, 1935, p. 152) have emphasized Jonson's debts in this play to *Wits Miserie*, with the consequence, it seems to me, of obliging us to abandon any idea of a single model or of a merely classical model.

[92]The thesis presented by Oscar J. Campbell in chapters III and IV of *Comicall Satyre and Shakespeare's Troilus and Cressida* (San Marino, California, 1938) that *Every Man Out* and *Cynthia's Revels* were written in "close adherence to the conventions of formal satire" such as Hall, Marston, and Donne wrote supports in a general way my contention that Jonson's sketches in the two plays are not primarily Theophrastan in aim or style. Mr. Campbell notices that the sketches in *Cynthia's Revels* are closer to the Greek ones than are those in *Every Man Out*; yet even here "Jonson's procedure is but an amplification of the method by which the figures were presented in formal satire" (p. 90).

superficiall iudgement in painting; and would seeme to have so in *poetry*. A most compleat lady in the opinion of some three, beside her-selfe.[93]

In the case of Crites, who is Jonson's variation of the Aristotelian high-minded man[94] and the Stoic-Christian wise man, he is analyzed both subjectively and objectively, as one might expect.

It is the descriptions of Hedon, "a gallant wholy consecrated to his pleasure" (II, i), Anaides, an "ordinarie gallant" (II, ii), Amorphus, a "travailer" (II, iii), and possibly Argurion (II, iii) that, because of the frequently dramatic and concrete style of their portraits, remind one of the classic Character and in wit and local color foretell Overbury. The personal manners of these folk, as Charles R. Baskervill pointed out, had already been made familiar by Skelton, Nashe, Lodge, Guilpin, and others, but Jonson imparted a somewhat less intense emotional atmosphere in his depiction, thus coming closer to the Character-writer. Yet even here the author's scorn for his subject strikes one. Theophrastus had never departed so far from the role of observer towards that of the reformer. What further separates Jonson's Hedon, Anaides, and Amorphus from Theophrastan creations is that no matter how many specific and lifelike facts Jonson accumulates for each, we shall never reach a moral core in them. Here is Mercury's account of Hedon:

> These are his graces. Hee doth . . . keepe a barber, and a monkie: Hee has a rich wrought wast-coat to entertaine his visitants in, with a cap sutable. His curtaines,

---

[93]*Cynthia's Revels*, II, iv (Herford-Simpson *Jonson*, Oxford: Clarendon Press, IV [1932], 77-78. This passage and that below describing Hedon are quoted with the kind permission of the publishers). The repeated "shee knows it" might be imagined to be an imitation of the repeated "et tamen pallet" in Martial's seventy-seventh epigram in Book I. See also XI, xlvii; lx.

[94]Baskervill, pp. 261-262.

and bedding are thought to bee his owne: his bathing-tub is not suspected. Hee loves to have a fencer, a pedant, and a musician seene in his lodging a mornings . . . himselfe is a rimer, and that's a thought better then a poet. He is not lightly within to his mercer, no, though he come when he takes physicke, which is commonly after his play. He beates a tailour very well, but a stocking-seller admirably: and so consequently any one hee owes monie too, that dares not resist him. He never makes generall invitement, but against the publishing of a new sute, marie then, you shall have more drawne to his lodging, then come to the lanching of some three ships; especially if he be furnish'd with supplies for the retyring of his old ward-robe from pawne: if not, he do's hire a stocke of apparell, and some fortie, or fiftie pound in gold, for that fore-noone to shew. He's thought a verie necessarie perfume for the presence, and for that onely cause welcome thither: sixe millaners shops affoord you not the like sent. He courts ladies with how many great horse he hath rid that morning, or how oft he hath done the whole, or the halfe *pommado* in a seven-night before: and sometime venters so farre upon the vertue of his pomander, that he dares tell 'hem, how many shirts he has sweat at *tennis* that weeke, but wisely conceals so many dozen of bals hee is on the score.[95]

Such a fellow is not fundamentally sensuality nor laziness nor foppishness nor boastfulness nor fraud, but a little of all. He is fashion plus sham, but he has no character. In all four cases, Jonson can only tell us about the creature's manners or style, a limitation which is sometimes imputed to Overbury, but not, I think, with equal justice in all his work. A comparison of Jonson's Amorphus and Overbury's "Affected Traveler" demonstrates that in learning from Jonson Overbury could improve upon his master in the direction of clarity of outline.

[95]Herford-Simpson *Jonson*, IV, 64-65.

The passionate need of the Traveler's dishonest soul asserts itself everywhere, but Amorphus' soul is wrenched from pride of travel to talkativeness to uncleanliness to cowardice (in a phrase that distracts us from the traveler in Amorphus to the braggart, reminiscent of Plautus' Pyrgopolinices) to excessive daintiness about his silk stockings. He is amorphous indeed, but he is also labeled a traveler, and a mixed impression is the clearest we can form of him. In the description of the "nymph" Argurian, Jonson almost equaled Theophrastus in objectivity, but what it is that drives a woman to be a nymph he failed to reveal.

Are these sketches, then, the first genuine English Characters? If we speak loosely, ignoring not only Theophrastus' mildness of tone and strict objectivity of method but also the classical requirement of a well defined moral or psychological propensity governing a number of tabulated actions, the answer must be yes, that they are. And in view of the many Characters written by Overbury and later authors of social and professional types that likewise have no moral or psychological core and that are presented sarcastically and subjectively, such a judgment seems proper. Yet the curious fact remains that Jonson's famous theory of a scientific construction of characters according to their "humors" appears in these descriptions to have permitted a merely picturesque and mechanical collecting of externals; it did not oblige him to find a ruling passion and unify the man's actions. In the plays themselves, particularly the great ones, Jonson surmounted this weakness.

These "first" English "Characters," the sketches in *Cynthia's Revels*, were composed, it seems probable, not only in accordance with the theory of "humors" and the rhetorical doctrine of *decorum* but also in imitation of the brief, devastating portraiture of formal verse satire and epigram, with recollections of the graphic and richly-contemporary sketches in English homiletic-satiric works in prose. The fact that Jonson used the word "character" in the title-page of *Every Man Out of his Humor* and in the dialogue of *Cynthia's Revels* to refer to these descriptive passages contributes only doubt to the argument, for in these cases as well as in the phrase *"Character principis— Alexander magnus"* at the head of an analytical and didactic discussion in his *Discoveries,* the common meaning of the word would serve perfectly well. Even in 1631, when Earle's as well as Hall's and Overbury's collections had made clear a technical, literary application of the label "Character," Jonson seems not to have adopted that special meaning. Before the text of *The New Inn* (1631) he put a list of "Persons of the Play" with a "short Characterisme of the chiefe Actors," but the "Characterismes" serve mostly to identify the situation of each person in the play. Still more interesting, in Act One of *The Magnetic Lady* (acted in 1632, printed in 1640) a number of the people in the play are presented in a description of their position, habits, privileges, manners, and sometimes morals, and twice (I, ii) the word "character" is used in reference to these more or less "set" passages. One is further called an "epi-gramme." At this point, certainly, a "character" was to Jonson almost any sort of description to explain the social background or situation or psychological nature or habits or several of these aspects of some individual. Even if it would be an insult to Jonson's classical learning to ask if he read Theophrastus,[96] only two short passages have been presented as evidence of specific borrowing, and the case for both is extremely weak.[97] Further-

---

[96]Aldington, p. 12.

[97]E. C. Baldwin (*Modern Language Notes,* XVI [1901], 385-386) offered as evidence two comparisons. In *Volpone,* IV, i, Sir Politick says: "A rat had gnawn my spur-leathers, notwithstanding I put on new and did go forth; but first I threw three beans over the threshold." Baldwin compares Theophrastus ("Superstitiousness") : "And if a cat

more there is lacking the sort of proud acknowledgment which Jonson might well have somewhere made of his acquaintance with an ancient author as yet not very familiar even to the widely read. It seems probable that the existence of the sketches in all four plays[98] was due to Jonson's particular dramatic intention and that their different forms were developed by his talents from a variety of literary impulses and precedents among which the *Characters* of Theophrastus, if they were present at all, were certainly not chief.

From the Theophrastan method of Hall, Overbury learned to unify his Characters. But to the encouragement of Jonson as well as of Hall and the pamphleteers, he owed his caustic, witty style and, to some extent probably, his free selection of social types,

---

cross his path he will not proceed on his way till someone else be gone by, or he have cast three stones across the street." Secondly, Mosca says (III, i) of flatterers that they "Echo my lord, and lick away a moth," which Baldwin says was taken from Theophrastus' flatterer, who "picks a speck from your coat; or if so be a morsel of chaff be blown into your beard, plucks it out."

The resemblance in the former passages, previously noted by Gifford, is not persuasive. John D. Rea in his edition of *Volpone* (New Haven, 1919, p. 212) thinks Del Rio's *Disquisitions*, III, lxxxiv, is a more probable source. References to similar superstitious acts must be plentiful in classical literature. But Percy Simpson and G. S. Gordon find the parallel cogent, Gordon adding that "borrowings from Theophrastus in Jonson are rare." Presumably he accepts the second parallel too; otherwise why "rare" instead of "unique"?

In the second case, one should compare as possible alternate sources the remarks (quoted above p. 74) of Barclay and Lodge on the conduct of flatterers as well as the antics of Mathew Merygreeke in *Roister Doister*, I, iv. Mathew picks an imaginary "fooles feather" or hair from his victim's coat, brushes the "foot of a gnat" from his gown, and picks a "lousy haire from your masterships beard" from his doublet. The idea, like the phenomenon, seems not to be rare. And even if one were sure of debts to Theophrastus in *Volpone*, that play appeared six years after *Every Man Out*.

[98]If one were attempting to collect every near-Character in Jonson one should certainly add Clerimont's picture of La Foole in *Epicoene*, I, iii.

especially the courtly sort. Mr. Aldington[99] entertains himself with the pleasant notion that King James, an admirer of Casaubon's theological opinions, was the one who led his courtiers Hall and Overbury into an English imitation of the ancient Characters. One might pardonably develop the picture further with the fancy that Overbury had been among the gentlemen who lent a learned ear to *Cynthia's Revels* in 1600 or 1601, that he had then been struck by Mercury's tangy portraits of Hedon, Amorphus, and the rest, and that now by copying Jonson's Mercury he proposed to dazzle the Royal Solomon with something which would be like the discoveries of the sober Swiss scholar but bolder, wittier, and truly James's own.

Besides the epigrammatized "estate" of Rowlands and the epigrammatized "humor" of Jonson there was the "Epigrammicall sonnet" as presented in *Choice, Chance, and Change* (1606). Fifteen examples were inserted in a cluster near the end of this half-narrative, half-expository volume as "idle notes" which the gentleman Tidero had formerly assembled "out of [his] observation of certaine Creatures." Many of the subjects painted—a "finicall Asse," a usurer, a pander, a "swaggering ruffe," a "Gull, that . . . was made a Gentleman," a true soldier—had already been made familiar by moralists, writers of epigrams, and comic dramatists. But it is a pleasure to read these pieces. Here is "a shamfast clown in gaie clothes."

> He that makes curtsie at a Ladies doore,
> And blusheth at a clappe upon the Cheeke,
> And saies good morrowe Mistresse and no more,
> And weares his silken clothes but once a weeke.

---

[99]Pages 9-10. Clausen argues that Aldington's suggestion is untenable for Hall. Instead he attributes to Jonson the first English interest in Theophrastus, using as the basis of his argument the very doubtful evidence of indebtedness to Theophrastus in *Volpone*.

Stoupes and goes backward, when he makes a legge
And saies forsooth at every word is spoken:
And onely keeps his Maidenhead for Megge
And in his hat will weare her true loves token:

Cannot endure to tast a Cup of wine,
And loves the Browne loafe better then the white:
Will at the spending of a penny whine,
And alwaies goes to bed at Candle light.

What will be written on his worshippes Tombe?
Wo to the Bride that meets with such a Groome.

In its consistent objectivity, its reliance upon behavior to reveal character, in its exactitude of observation, and in its
freedom from harsh language and crude judgments this passage
comes as close to Theophrastus as anything we have thus far
mentioned. The "Epigrammicall" thing about it, other than
the compact form and set ending, is the individuality of the
man's vulgarity. On the other hand, the picture of "a true
souldier," drawn with only slightly more subjectivity, is typical
throughout.

Next we should examine an interesting prose work of 1606
which will reveal the persistence of the "English" tradition
in type-satire in the face of the popularization of the epigram.
This book, Barnabe Rich's *Faultes Faults,* had its roots in
the literature of virtues and vices and of Estates, and it reminds one, perhaps, of the salty style of Lodge and the effect he created in *Wits Miserie* of a vibrant crowd of highly-
colored figures. Rich declares at the outset that he will treat
faults, not "humors," the latter having been made to play their
parts by Jonson. But faults as Rich portrays them in the
"Iestmonger," who like Carlo Buffone, "will rather choose to
loose a friend, then . . . a iest," and in the fashion-monger
and news-mongers and boastful travelers and malcontent, are

merely "humors" by another name. Behold the "Counterfeit Souldiour":

> I do knowe him by his Plume and his Scarffe; he looks like a *Monercho,* of a very cholericke complexion, and as teasty as a Goose that hath yong Goslings, yet very easie to please, but with a handfull of Oates. He lookes like *Haniball* . . . and good reason too; for hee that should but heare his Table-Talke, and how he will discourse among ignorant company, would think that the *Nine Worthies* were but fooles in comparison of his worth: He will talke of more proportions of Battels than ever *Langius, Vigetias* or *Machiavell* did know of. He will atchieve greater victories, but sitting at a dinner or a supper, than ever did *Alexander.* . . And what Towne so strong or Citydale so well fortified that hee will not surprize, but with discharging some two or three vollies of oaths: for there is not a greater Testimonie of a Captaines courage, than to sweare as if hee would make his audience to tremble. . . At a word, he will attribute the actions of a whole army to his own vertue, and worthinesse, and will beare fooles in hand, that neyther strong *Sampson* amongest his *Philistins.* Nor valiant Hercules against his ugly Monsters, were halfe so fierce and terrible.[100]

Jonsonian fluency is here; but the allusiveness, a coda of commentary and *sententiae* (including one wise paradox ascribed to "Theophrastus"[101]), and the unrelieved hodgepodge of preachments in later pages locate *Faultes Faults* in the line of *Wits Miserie* and its antecedents. An uncertain alternation from singular to plural also bespeaks an English parentage. These sketches illustrate how far, and only how far, the type-drawing could go with an impetus from many kinds of writing, ancient and modern, but without benefit of Theophrastus. The fact that in his revision of this work, published ten years later, Rich

---

[100]Fols. 12-12v.　　[101]Fol. 13v. See above p. 72 n.32.

easily incorporated in his sketches details drawn from the Overbury *Characters*[102] indicates not only Rich's original closeness to
the Character form but also Overbury's kinship to an ancient
English tradition. Yet what Theophrastus at his best taught—the
habit of keeping one's eye continuously on the subject, of generalizing not by abstract remarks nor the use of the plural but by piling
up many representative concrete details that reveal in many
ways the same essential nature; the happy variation of a repeated
sentence pattern; a more or less standardized size of canvas
more ample than that of the epigram but small enough to be seen
as a whole—cannot be found in *Faultes Faults* nor, so far as I
have discovered, in any other English book before 1608 with
the debatable exception of *Wits Miserie* and *Cynthia's Revels*.[103]

Of those two exceptions, the latter belongs to a department
of literature which merits more than a cursory glance as part of
the background of the Character. Precisely how important English drama was in encouraging the development of our genre
one could say only if one knew much more than we are likely to
know about the costuming and acting of sixteenth-century play-
ers. As one reads through the surviving dramas of the Eliza-

---

[102]See *My Ladies Looking Glasse . . . By Barnabe Rich* (1616), p. 53:
the malcontent's gait "as he passeth along the streete, cries *Looke upon
me:* and although to some mens thinking hee is but a man, yet in his
own opinion the wisest of men." The first part of the sentence is indebted to Overbury's "Affected Traveler," the second to Overbury's
"Courtier."

[103]Mention should be made here of Nicholas Breton's *Fantasticks*,
the only known issue of which was dated 1626. The work had been
entered in the Stationers' Register (Arber's edition, III, 272) as early
as 1604. Perhaps, then, there was an issue of the work about 1604. But
even so, it probably would give no impetus to Character-writing, its
relationship to the latter being of the sort that would clarify neither the
form nor the idea. The contention of F. H. McCloskey in his unpublished Harvard dissertation on Breton (pp. 9-10) that *Fantasticks* should
be called the first English Character-book remains debatable. I have
described the work in Chapter VIII.

bethan period one meets again and again representatives of the types—the gulls, the amorists, the scholars, and affected travelers—popular in the almost contemporary Character-books and reported by many a writer to be common in real life. How far did actors go in clarifying the estate or trade or station of each character by utilizing and exaggerating the costume and manner traditionally associated with it? The chances are that though the Admiral's Men and the Lord Chamberlain's Servants would not be pleased with the crude, conventionalized costuming of the miracle-play God or Satan, actors would make some use of the familiar visible distinctions of social groups and thus help to establish for each a body of detail about traits and dress which Overbury and Earle and their readers were to depend upon.[104]

That the habit of presenting current social types on the stage began early has been pointed out in connection with a similar tendency in the sermon: Cain and the Bad Husbandman, Noah's wife and the Shrew were paraded on the stage wagon many years before Courtly Abusion and pliable Iuventus and Hycke-Scorner appeared in the moralities. The personified abstractions of the earlier plays yielded later to figures that were only half symbolic; Strife in *Tom Tyler and his Wife* is a railing, drunken, gossiping shrew even if in an occasional line she also signifies strife in general. The interludes carry the tendency to lifelike characterization of types still further, as one can see in Ulpian Fulwell's *Like Will to Like* (1568) where Philip Fleming and Hance are mere, but genuine, drunkards but where Tom Tosspot must do double duty as a man and

---

[104]Some evidence for the idea that social and professional groups were distinguished by costume appears in George F. Reynolds' *The Staging of Elizabethan Plays at The Red Bull Theater* (New York, 1940), pp. 172-176. See also Candido's harangue on caps in *The Honest Whore*, Part II, scene 3.

as the seducing power of alcohol. Both Tom and Nichol New-
fangle explain themselves and the vice each personifies in extended monologues resembling those in Passus Five of *Piers
Plowman.*

The subjective and flagrantly homiletic procedure in these
plays met discouragement in the fortunate new interest in
Terence and Plautus, whose characters occasionally describe
themselves or others—witness Palaestrio's description of Pyrgopolinices in Plautus' *Miles Gloriosus* (prologue to Act Two),
imitated in Mathew Merygreeke's opening account of Ralph
Roister Doister—but enliven subjective analysis with concrete
examples of actual, characteristic behavior. From the Latin
comedies as well as from the rhetorics, Englishmen could learn
the lesson of *decorum*.[105] From Latin comedy, too, came broad
hints about the humorous possibilities in type characters and an
absolute authority for the device of the significant name for
dramatis personae.[106]

The ramifications of the drawing of types in Elizabethan
drama cannot be dealt with here, but the connections between
this matter and the Character are easily seen. Shakespeare affords nothing closer to the latter genre than Jaques' account of
the seven ages of man and Berowne's scornful portrait of "the
ape of form, Monsieur the Nice,"[107] but Portia's rapid listing
of her "horsey" Neapolitan suitor, the frowning County Palatine,
the mercurial Frenchman, the drunken German, and the oddly-
suited English wooer, and Maria's insistence that Malvolio is
not a Puritan but a "time-pleaser; an affected ass, that cons

---

[105]Nathaniel Woodes in the prologue to his morality play, *The Conflict of Conscience* (1581), echoes classical theory in saying that he has
omitted the actual name of his hero
> because, a Comedie, will hardly him permit,
> The vices of one private man, to touch particulerly.

[106]See pp. 38-40.
[107]*Love's Labor's Lost*, V, ii.

state without book and utters it by great swarths"[108] demonstrate how naturally the Elizabethans fell into anatomizing society and how in some cases the classification was indicated by a piece of representative behavior. The kernel of the Character is just such a thing as Maria's sentence. Jaques' epitome of the true soldier—

> Full of strange oaths and bearded like the pard,
> Jealous in honor, sudden and quick in quarrel,
> Seeking the bubble reputation
> Even in the cannon's mouth—

was worked out at length and dramatically in the splendid, humorous, and pathetic figure of Hotspur, in which Shakespeare utilized typical traits as the groundwork of the charming individual. A less winsome variety of the same genus and less vividly portrayed is Sir Cuthbert Rudesby in Chapman's *Sir Gyles Goosecappe* (1606). He is introduced in the first scene of the play in a speech that looks rather like a portion of some Character: he is

> blunt at a sharpe wit, and sharpe at a blunt wit: a good bustling gallant talkes well at Rovers; he is two parts soldier; as slovenlie as a Switzer, and somewhat like one in face too; for he weares a bush beard wil dead a Cannon shott better then a wool-packe; hee will come into the presence like yor Frenchman in foule bootes: and dares eate garlik as a preprative to his Courtship.

For Shakespeare the play was the thing, and though Hamlet, contemplative in a churchyard, might pause to consider the merely typical lives of a merely typical courtier and lawyer and buyer of land, Shakespeare's dramatis personae are not just studies of the time's abuses. Osric and the delicate fellow who maddened Hotspur on the field of battle are alive and have

---

[108] *Twelfth Night*, II, iii.

individualities that prevent their being lost in anyone's Character
of the courtier or fop, just as pressure and even violence are
needed to force Jaques into the mold of malcontent traveler
and Falstaff into that of Thraso-Gnatho.

But outside Shakespeare's plays and especially where the
comedy of "humors" is under way or when a thoughtful mood
seizes the dramatist or perhaps merely because of the stress of
an epigrammatic impulse, there are passages similar to the
Character in late Elizabethan drama. It is the contemplative
tendency which accounts for the thirty lines in Chapman's
Gentleman Usher (*c.* 1602) describing the virtuous woman.[109]
What we have is a subjective precept-description very similar to
a separate poem of Chapman's on the same subject.[110]   On
the other hand, the account of an exquisite fop (Dariotto) in
Chapman's *All Fools* (*c.* 1599)[111] sounds like an epigram of
Martial's even though the play was based upon Terence. Marston,
who was very much under the influence of formal satire and the
method of his sometime-enemy Jonson, put a Juvenalian list
of female types into the dialogue of a scene in *Parasitaster*
(1606),[112] had the actors in *Antonio and Mellida* (1602) in
an Induction epigrammatically describe the dramatis personae,
sometimes inserted a *descriptio* of a man's physical appearance,[113] and in *What You Will* (1607) exposed the manners of an "ordinary gallant"[114] and an "absolute Courtier" in

---

[109]IV, iii.   [110]See above, p. 94 n.81.

[111]V, ii, 5-22. See also the conceitful description of D'Olive, "the
true map of a gull" and impudent upstart, in Chapman's *Monsieur
D'Olive* (1606), I, i; but there is little here of what the gull *does*.

[112]III, i.   [113]See *Antonio and Mellida*, I.

[114]"He eats well and right slovenly; and when the dice favor him goes
in good cloathes, and scowers his pinke collour silk stockings; when he
hath any money he beares his crownes, when he hath none I carry his
purse. He cheates well, sweares better, but swaggers in a wantons chamber admirably; hee loves his boy and the rump of a cram'd capon; and
this summer hath a passing thrifty humor to bottle ale: as contemptuous

paragraphs that suggest those in *Cynthia's Revels*. Several of these passages, like the graphic description of a pair of flatterers spoken by Silius in the first act of Jonson's *Sejanus*, apply to specific individuals. The author means to damn a man by reference to a class, whereas the aim of the Character-writer is to reveal a class through an individual. The difference is of enough importance to explain why the sketches in these plays and even those in *Cynthia's Revels* fail to produce the feeling of finality, of sufficiency, which the true Character creates. Clever and typical though they may be, these spoken descriptions are still tied to one man whose career they are meant to illuminate.

Yet when drama existed not for storytelling but for criticism of society and when the audience consisted, if not of the philosophers desired by George Bernard Shaw, at least of the well-prepared members of one's university, the Elizabethan dramatist might conveniently use genuine types. Such was the case in the second of the anonymous plays called *The Return from Parnassus* (*c.* 1601). For in spite of the possibility that the characters in this play represent Nashe or Daniel or someone else, the author's real concern seems to be with tendencies and classes, not single souls. And having taken a hint from Jonson's method, as the Prologue half reveals, the author not only employs type characters but also inserts in the dialogue a unified portrait of a "meere Scholler" (II, vi) and the following comments on the fop Amoretto:

> he is one, that wil draw out his pocket glasse thrise in a walke, one that dreames in a night of nothing, but muske and civet, and talke[s] of nothing all day long but

as *Lucifer*, as arrogant as ignorance can make him," and so on (III, iii); see *The Works of John Marston*, edited by J. O. Halliwell (1856), I, 267-268. See also the description of an informer in Beaumont and Fletcher's *Woman Hater* (1607), I, iii.

his hauke, his hound, and his mistres, one that more admires the good wrinckle of a boote, [or] the curious crinkling of a silke stocking, then all the witt in the world: one that loves no scholler but him whose tyred eares can endure halfe a day togither, his fliblowne sonnettes of his mistres, and her loving pretty creatures, her munckey and her puppet.[115]

The method of this sentence is that of the Character. One wishes there were more freshness or more profundity in the reporting.

But dramatists properly refrained from expending their greatest powers of mind in static descriptions of people; *Cynthia's Revels* plainly cannot compare with *Volpone* as a play or as a picture of that somehow spoiled thing, human nature. Hence the sketches of types that we have noticed in Elizabethan drama want the insight that sometimes comes to the man concentrating his observation of life in a set of Characters. Nor are there as many "near-Characters" in the plays as one might thoughtlessly expect; Dekker and Webster, both believed to have been contributors to the Overbury collection, apparently put no Characters into plays written in the years before 1608.[116] The method of Theophrastus, it has been said often enough, is to reveal a man's nature through actual, typical deeds and words. But it is also to reduce much to little. Hence the dramatist will not ordinarily use up his material in Characters. Jonson and his imitators did so in the most extreme of the "humors" plays, but after leading that dance Jonson found a better way to his end. In the meanwhile, influenced probably by medieval al-

[115]III, v. Quoted from Macray's edition (Oxford, 1886), p. 125.
[116]Yet Hipolito's long account of what it is to be a whore and Friscobaldo's "true picture of a happy man" in the first and second parts of *The Honest Whore* (1604) show Dekker approaching the Character in two ways without reaching it. See Pearson's reprint (New York, 1873), II, 36-38, 103-104.

legorical habits and certainly by Roman comedy of types and by Roman verse satire and epigram, he produced a few passages that in most respects are Characters and that clinched for the genre a witty, pungent, allusive style of expression that had previously been flaunted before the public gaze in connection with type-satire by Nashe and Lodge. The more intangible encouragement given to Character-writing by the satiric and comic strains in Elizabethan drama, the encouragement, that is, that came from seeing portrayed on the stage again and again but in slightly different situations the same popular types of contemporary society, will be taken for granted, I trust, until someone with a taste for tabulation will examine the dramatis personae of every English play before Hall and Overbury and by statistics prove the extent of such repetition. The English theatre prepared for Hall and his followers by set descriptions in its dialogue, probably by costuming, and most of all by its willingness much of the time to accept characters that were so familiar as to have become types.[117]

The Aristotelian notion that any form of art exists by virtue of its capacity to satisfy certain instincts for pleasure[118] will

---

[117]It seems to me altogether contrary to the evidence of chronology for Paul V. Kreider (*Elizabethan Comic Character Conventions as Revealed in the Comedies of George Chapman*, Ann Arbor, 1935, p. 144 n.) to say that "the interest in books of 'Characters'" was one cause of the comedy of humors and for E. M. Waith ("Characterization in John Fletcher's Tragicomedies," *Review of English Studies*, XIX [1943], 145) to assert that characterization in Elizabethan comedy and tragedy "was based on certain types, derived from various literary traditions—notably, in the case of comedy, from Theophrastus and his imitators." *Decorum*, Latin literature, the medieval traditions in prose and verse rather than Theophrastus must account for similarities to the English Characters in dramas written before 1608 (and to some extent also, no doubt, after Hall's publication).

[118]See H. E. Mantz, "The Reality of Types," *Journal of Philosophy*, XX (1923), 393-405.

assist us in summarizing the preceding survey of type-portraiture in English literature before 1608. The man who composes a Character, whether he be Theophrastus or John Earle, regards men as belonging to more or less fixed groups, mental and moral and physical and social, and his delight is to describe one man who represents the whole group. Moral and spiritual classifications of the most profound import to men were provided by the early Church on an elaborate and orderly basis. In the vivid, simpler form of Deadly Sins and Cardinal Virtues they became the daily theme of preacher and teacher. The morality play almost always dramatized some conflict between the two familiar groups. Social orders developed with feudalism and thrust themselves into the lives of all. And Galenic science gave the authority of learning to what is probably a universal tendency in any well populated society, of supposing, whether with learning or in mere laziness of mind, that there are generic human types and situations into which the particular case can properly be fitted. With so many classifications surrounding them, countless English writers before 1608 were inevitably bound, the mimetic impulse being what it is, to anticipate one of the pleasures of the Character. The literature of Estates and of virtues and vices provided the clearest and strongest satisfactions of this sort, but the manners books—informative, polite, and even sometimes by burlesque—emphasized a more conscious sort of faithfulness to type that was a social parallel to the ancient doctrine of *decorum* in oratory and poetry. In the manners books and in the sophisticated character-descriptions of Ben Jonson the violence of feeling of the serious homilists was lightened, so that in Jonson's sketches as in Chaucer's there is the pleasure, native to the Character, of intellectual control and hence of some genuine humor. Furthermore, just as his sometime-friend Inigo Jones chastened the flamboyant, tasteless, half-Flemish Elizabethan architecture into Palladian symmetry, so Jonson reduced the shapeless, centrifugal, and florid sketch of *Wits Miserie* to something more compact and consistent. Gordon's neat theory that the Character always develops from comedy[119] gains some weight when we observe the superiority of Jonson to Lodge and the other moralistic writers in respect to intellectual aloofness and concentrated expression. But it is the epigram rather than drama as such which in this case the connoisseur of our genre should thank. Other special delights such as well sustained objectivity; the use of physical, outward behavior that reveals the inner nature of the man; the selection of details that are graphic, universal, and true and that really evoke a representative individual; the artistic variation of a sentence-formula beginning with *he;* the compact, uninterrupted-pattern—these idiosyncrasies of the Theophrastan Character were all visible separately but not together unless perhaps in *Wits Miserie* and *Cynthia's Revels* and *Faultes Faults.* But a final pleasure of this genre—the repetition of the whole pattern in a series of sketches that are interesting enough to stand by themselves and free enough to have their own effect and flavor—this was not provided by anyone before Hall. Subject matter, form, and style were developed by English writers who, though they profited from forms like the epigram and Plautine drama, appear not to have read Theophrastus or, if they knew his pieces, not to have penetrated to their artistic essence. Authors approached the Character from every side, yet they never quite reached it. The thin but none the less real barrier between Hall and the entire body of earlier work suggests how necessary the rediscovery of the twenty-eight or thirty little Greek sketches was. To the variously begotten tendencies towards type-portraiture Theophrastus gave the important bene-

---

[119]*English Literature and the Classics*, p. 80.

fit of a classical patron and the boon of a classical norm from which the uninspired could derive exact copies and from which Overbury and Earle and their followers could interestingly, yet not wholly, depart.

IV

JOSEPH HALL'S
CHARACTERS
OF
VERTUES AND VICES

When in 1608 Joseph Hall presented to the world his *Characters of Vertues and Vices* he put forward in such pieces as "The Superstitious," "The Vain-glorious," and "The Distrustful" what readers of my third chapter may be willing to acknowledge to be the first genuinely Theophrastan Characters in English. Although when he published his *Virgidemiarum* eleven years earlier he had boasted that his were the first English satires, he made no such boast concerning his Characters. Yet he openly declared an intention of following Theophrastus, a writer whose name had then rarely appeared in English books. Actually the 1608 volume was not only the first to offer Theophrastan Characters in English but also the first to consist of Characters that were not bound together by a framework of some kind. In addition, Hall inaugurated the use of the English word *character* for what Casaubon had at first called "Characteres Ethici" and later "Notationes Morum."[1] These pieces were not, it is true, the first trials Hall had made in the Character form. In his anonymous Latin *Mundus Alter et Idem* (1605) he had inserted descriptions that once or twice

---

[1] The title page of the 1592 edition reads: *Theophrasti Characteres Ethici, sive Descriptiones morum Græcè. Isaacus Casaubonus recensuit, in Latinum Sermonem vertit, et Libro Commentario illustravit . . . Lugduni.* The title page of the 1599 edition read: ΘΕΟΦΡΑΣΤΟΥ ἠθικοὶ χαρακτῆρες *Theophrasti Notationes Morum. Isaacus Casaubonus recensuit, in Latinum Sermonem vertit, & Libro Commentario Illustravit. Editio altera recognita, & aliquot capitibus aucta ex MSS. . . . Lugduni.* Before Casaubon the 1582 edition (Basel) had translated the Greek title *Theophrasti Morum Characteres;* the 1589 (Lyons) edition had used the simpler *Theophrasti Characteres.*

were almost Characters;[2] in the *Meditations and Vowes* (enlarged edition, 1606) he had briefly set forth in a general, subjective way the nature and habits of the worldling (I, 68); and in *Heaven upon Earth* (1606) he had done the same thing, though still more briefly, for the covetous man, the glutton, and the needy scholar.[3] But these exercises do not diminish the historical luster of his accomplishment in the *Characters*.

In the preface and in the first proem Hall made clear that, like Casaubon, he regarded Theophrastus' Characters primarily as "speaking pictures, or living images, whereby the ruder multitude might . . . learne to know vertue, and discerne what to detest." His own work had a similar purpose. "If thou do but read or like these, I have spent good houres ill; but if thou shalt hence abiure those vices, which before thou thoughtest not ill-favoured, or fall in love with any of these goodly faces of vertue; or shalt hence finde where thou hast anie little touch of these evils, to cleere thy selfe, or where any defect in these graces supply it, neither of us shall need to repent of our labor." As the title of his book would suggest, Hall was accommodating his classical model to the native literary tradition, which habitually—in morality play, in sermon, in prose and verse allegory—confronted the forces of evil with the forces of the Christian virtues.

The book contains nine Characters of virtuous types ("The Penitent" and "Hee is an Happy man" were added in 1614 when all were reprinted in Hall's *Recollection*[4]), followed by

[2]See especially the description of a flatterer in III, vi. See Huntington Brown's edition of the English translation, *The Discovery of A New World* (Cambridge, Mass., 1937), p. 107.

[3]XXII. I am indebted to Rudolf Kirk for calling my attention to this passage.

[4]In *A Recollection of such Treatises as have bene heretofore severally published, and are nowe revised, corrected, augmented. By Jos: Hall Dr of Divinity* the separate treatises have individual title pages bearing the date 1614, though the title page of the whole volume is dated 1615.

fifteen of vicious types, the total number not equaling by four
the number in Casaubon's 1599 *Theophrastus*. Just as Theophrastus' types were, with three exceptions in Casaubon's editions, fundamentally moral or psychological rather than social
or professional, so, with the exception of "The Good Magistrate," are Hall's. In Hall's table of contents the first eight
sketches are called by abstract nouns, duplicating the procedure
in the first sentence of each of Theophrastus' Characters;[5]
thereafter, as in modern editions, a descriptive adjective is used.
The proems before the two books seem to be in imitation of the
apocryphal proem printed in Casaubon's editions.

Of the virtuous types, not one took its theme from Theophrastus, for he painted only reprehensible classes. Instead
one should look to English homiletic literature such as I have
reviewed in Chapter III for numerous earlier descriptions of
the wise man, honest man, faithful man, valiant man (though
a hint in this case might have been taken from Theophrastus'
"Cowardice"), the humble man, the patient, and the truly
noble. The true friend had been expounded repeatedly by the
literature of virtues and vices and the manners book, and in
addition one notices in Hall an idea or two suggesting Seneca's
letter on this subject. The "Good Magistrate" is a contribution from the literature of Estates, by way, perhaps, of some
more recent adaptation in an epigram or homily. This character is of considerable significance, for it is the bridge between
innumerable analytic and satiric pictures of Estates composed
before Hall and the numerous Characters of social and professional classes (rarely now called Estates) written after 1608.
What one notices as one studies the descriptions of Hall's virtuous types is that they are all developments of one basic type,

---

[5]See p. 5 n. above. Within the volume itself the headings vary: "The
Characterisme of an *Honest man*," "The Characterism of the *Faithfull
Man*," "*Of the Humble Man*," and so on.

the Stoic-Christian wise man, calm and steadfast in a devout trust and with an absolute morality deduced from it.

Among the reprehensible types, at least seven[6] are indebted to Theophrastus for the main idea and many of them for particular details. Some six or seven others—the Characters of the hypocrite, the profane (drawn in connection with "The Superstitious," which was based upon Theophrastus), the "Unconstant," the slothful, the ambitious, the envious, the "Unthrift"—indicate by their themes that they, on the other hand, belong to the homiletic tradition, where each had frequently been anticipated.[7] One Character—"The Presumptuous," the

---

[6] "The Busy-body," "The Superstitious," "The Malcontent," "The Flatterer," "The Covetous," "The Vain-glorious," who reminds one of the pretender to wealth in the *Rhetorica ad Herennium*, and "The Distrustful." Baldwin discussed, rather carelessly, Hall's debt to Theophrastus in *PMLA*, XVIII (1903), 412-423.

[7] The hypocrite, for example, had been painted by Ulpian Fulwell in his *Arte of Flatterie* (1579) with the name Pierce Pickthanke, whose condition is

> to cloake his hollow harte, with a holy pretence, and his dissimulation is chéefely in matters of Religion, although in very déede there is in him no more sincerity than in an Ape. Hée will come sumetimes unto a Bishop, and sometimes to others that hee thinketh to bée zelous in Religion and hath under his arme a new Testament, or a Psalter, as though his speciall care, and onely study were in the Scriptures, under which pretexte hée beguileth both the wise and the learned. Hée will in their presence temper his talke with such a shew of godlinesse, as though he were rapt up into the thirde Heaven. Hée is a Saint outwardly and a Divell inwardly. And hée will seeme to bee greatly gréeved in conscience, that papistrie should beare such sway in mens harts, and that such papistes (naming this man or that) are not straitly seene unto and sharply punished . . .
>
> Then hée hath an olde Portas . . . and therwith hee commeth unto them that hee knoweth to bée of the olde stampe, and frameth his tale to this effecte.
>
> A good sir (sayth hee) the great anguish that I beare in my conscience, enforceth mee to seeke for the setlinge and satisfaction of the same at your handes or some such godly learned man,

and so on (sigs. Fiiv—Fiii).

Aristotelian extreme of Hall's "Distrustful" (based upon Theophrastus' "Distrustfulness")—seems new. The interesting aspect of Hall's material in these pieces is that even when he selected the subject and perhaps part of the development from Theophrastus he more often than not cast a religious coloring over the whole by the addition of especially Christian ideas and by the assumption, much of the time, of the preacher's gravity.

His method as well as his material reveals the usual Renaissance eagerness to imitate the classical without casting off the medieval Christian. And no literary form could better document Tolstoi's principle that human affairs are not discontinuous. In following Theophrastus "as [he] could," Hall learned of course how to suggest the inner nature of a type by describing some piece of external, visible conduct. Thus the "Vainglorious," "Under pretence of seeking for a scroll of newes . . . drawes out an handful of letters endorsed with his own stile, to the height; and halfe reading every title, passes over the latter part, with a murmur; not without signifying, what Lord sent this, what great Ladie the other; and for what sutes; the last paper (as it happens) is his newes from his honourable friend in the French Court." But it will be recalled that Barclay and Lodge could do that sort of trick intermittently, and except in "The Busy-body," "The Superstitious," "The Vain-glorious," and "The Distrustful," this objective, dramatic method is only intermittent in Hall. In his Characters of Virtues it does not appear at all. Often the most noticeably objective passages are built around details copied from Theophrastus, and these occur in the central and later sections of the Character. In fact it can be said that the more extensively Theophrastan Hall's material, the more concrete and dramatic (i.e., Theophrastan) his method.

The frequent generality of Hall's procedure is conspicuous.

In addition to whatever concrete data he may use, Hall builds out his Characters with metaphors and subjective analysis or descriptions of desires, thoughts, and traits of character, with his own judgments upon them. What the effect of a moral quality is he tends to express embracively, not in particular: the valiant man "forecasts the worst of all events, & incounters them before they come"; the humble man "loves rather to give, than take honour"; no anguish can master the patient man, "whether by violence or by lingring." This feature of Hall's method may remind one of Aristotle's in his *Ethics* and *Rhetoric*, but it has a closer parallel in English moralistic portraiture of the previous three centuries. Gascoigne's description of "the properties of a covetous man" who is "prompt to crave, slow to geve, and bould to denie"[8] and the less dramatic, rather long-winded discussion of beneficence in Barnabe Barnes' *Four Bookes of Offices* (1606)[9] show a similar generality in listing traits of mind and conduct, combined in Gascoigne's case, as in Hall's, with what Polonius would have called "art" in the phrasing. Joseph Hall, recently appointed chaplain to Prince Henry, was more concerned with questions of the spiritual life than with the picturesqueness of the court, and, naturally, he opened and closed his Characters of Vices with outright preachment. His Characters of Virtues, almost continuously subjective and abstract are not truly Theophrastan; but they could be prized as a manual of devotion.

One need not suppose, however, that Hall worked blindly. On the contrary he showed a strongly literary sense in his various productions, and in his experiments with the Character one can see that he was working out methods suitable to his purposes. As he said in his *Meditations and Vowes*, he de-

---

[8]*The Droomme of Doomes Day*, 1576 (George Gascoigne *The Glasse of Government*, II, 243). [9]Pages 93-94.

plored the clerics who neglect even for a moment their real function. In the *Meditations* he had gone over the ground to be covered later in his Characters of Virtues; earnestly and courageously he there explained the kind of thought and behavior necessary for a true Christian. Mostly the volume consists of soul-searchings, briefly and simply composed. There are, however, some efforts to be, if not witty, at least boldly figurative. We read that the "idle man is the divels cushion" and that the "covetous man is like a Spider, as in this that he doth nothing but lay his nets to catch every flie, gaping onely for a bootie of gaines; so yet more, in that whiles hee makes nets for these flies, he consumeth his owne bowels: so that which is his life is his death." In *Salomons Divine Arts*, published a year after the *Characters*, Hall invented something new—a Character put together from phrases and verses out of Proverbs and Ecclesiastes. Hortatory, general, rich in Hebrew metaphor, varying in length from one or two sentences to half the size of one of Hall's regular Characters, these sketches[10] are much less satisfying than the latter; they are diffuse and merge into the essay. But they suggest how many hints for his Theophrastan work Hall may have taken from the remarks in Proverbs on the proud man, the poor man, the slothful man, and others. The sketch called "He is an Happy Man," which was added to the *Characters* when they were reprinted in Hall's *Recollection* in 1614, was in a still different manner, being reminiscent of Seneca and Horace in its opening sentences. Its topic, the perfect Stoic Christian, required it to be more general and inclusive than any other of Hall's Characters. Possibly its addition to the set was prompted by the appearance

---

[10]The sketches are scattered throughout the whole work. The best are perhaps the description of the slothful ("Salomons Ethicks," III, xviii) and that of the good house-wife ("Salomons Oeconomicks," iii), constructed from the brilliant passage in Proverbs 31.

at the end of the Overbury collection, also printed in 1614, of Wotton's little poem on the subject and there labeled "The Character of a Happy Life."[11]

The Characters of Virtues remind us not only that Hall was a preacher but also that he "Two years together . . . was chosen Rhetoric Professor in the University of Cambridge, and performed the office with extraordinary applause."[12] Hall's method in his Characters implies what the textbooks on rhetoric had been saying since Augustan times about character-sketches (whether under *ethopoeia, prosopopoeia, descriptio,* or *decorum*), namely, that the picture should represent a man's nature and that he should be kept true to type. Hall's method ignores, furthermore, what all the instructions ignored—that the Theophrastan sketch is concrete and external and dramatic. Hall's pictures, unlike Overbury's and Earle's, contain so few specifically contemporary details that one could not tell from the mere substance of most of them that they were written in Shakespeare's England. There are, to be sure, references to churches, ordinaries, the Guiana voyage, and to leaping from Rome to Munster, but these are few, and Hall omits the journalistic spicings that Nashe and Lodge and other satiric moralists had character-

---

[11]See p. 95. To complete the roster of Hall's Characters I should mention the *"description of a good and faithfull Courtier"* which Hall "reserved" from his collection to put in the second volume (1608) of his *Epistles.* Less epigrammatic than the other Characters of that year, it also is less Theophrastan, for it was obviously arranged to serve as a manual of conduct for the Christian courtier. In the fifth "Decad" of the *Epistles* (1611) there is an extended *"description of a Christian"* which is somewhat similar in style to his Characters of Virtues but which is still more discursive and is broken by moralistic generalizations. In the sixth "Decad" Hall amplified his strictures on *"mis-education of our Gentry"* by describing representative groups of the mis-educated, but he did not try a unified type-picture. The best Characters Hall wrote were in *Characters of Vertues and Vices.*

[12]From J. Whitefoot's funeral sermon on Hall, printed in *The Works of Joseph Hall* (Oxford, 1837), I, lx.

istically employed. He keeps the type general even in its background, with a perhaps too colorless effect frequently but also with an occasional flavor of classical antiquity. He has more dignity and less dash than many of his clerical predecessors, and there is no doubting the sincerity of his moral purpose. If he is less visual, he is more Horatian and universal. His formal verse satires, published some ten years before, had represented their victims as Juvenal and Martial had variously done, by attention to dress and individual features, by scornful suggestion of the depraved social ideas and circumstances of the time, by sharply defined glimpses rather than by completeness. But now in the Characters Hall was consciously writing something different. In "The Slothful," to be sure, he provided an exact picture of the physical appearance of his man, but for that passage the medieval *descriptio* appears to have given the model, even if indirectly.

The tone as well as the method of the Characters of Virtues can be illuminated by a passage from Seneca's ninety-fifth Epistle quoted in Casaubon's Prolegomena. In the edifying of readers by descriptions of virtues and vices ("signa cuiusque virtutis ac vitii et notas") one may distinguish, Seneca says, between the precept, which says "If you would be temperate, act thus," and the description, which says "The temperate man is one who does this and abstains from that." Hall's accounts of virtuous classes are descriptions, technically, not precepts. Yet so habitual was the preacher's manner that he could not wholly escape it, and the reader feels the precept. As a matter of fact, when Hall explained in his *Epistles, The Second Volume* (1608) that the included "description of a good and faithfull Courtier" had been reserved from his other collection for dedication here "To the Gentlemen of his Highnesses Court," he revealingly said it was the Character not only of "What you are" but also of "What you should be." Because neither Seneca nor Cicero nor Rutilius nor Casaubon had said that *descriptio* or *ethologia* or *characterismos*[13] should be constructed without subjective analysis, Hall felt no necessity of avoiding it. And as a shepherd of souls he of course inclined in that direction. Yet he admired the art of Theophrastus too. The mixed method which he evolved from his several masters was to be adopted by practically all seventeenth-century Character-writers.

Hall's command of rhetoric shows in the verbal pattern of his Characters. Most of his sketches open with a generalization about the moral quality under consideration; in the Characters of Vices it is couched in metaphor or paradox. Thus "The inconstant man treads upon a moving earth, and keeps no pace," and, of the "Vain-glorious," "All his humor rises up into the froth of ostentation; which if it once settle, falles downe into a narrow roome." The development then follows, after a figure or two, with an occasional personification, plentiful examination of motive, and, in varying amounts, the concrete data of characteristic behavior in particular circumstances. All the Characters are longer than those of Theophrastus but are about equal among themselves (excepting the unusually long "Penitent" and "He is an Happy Man"). There is almost always a conspicuous rhetorical conclusion, frequently introduced by "in brief" or "finally" and consisting of a set of sharply cadenced and balanced descriptive phrases or a rather showy group of metaphors. The conclusion of "The Envious" has some of both: "Finally, he is an enemie to Gods favors, if they fall beside himselfe; The best nurse of ill Fame; A man of the worst diet; for he consumes himselfe, and delights in pining; A thorne-hedge, covered with nettles; A peevish in-

---

[13]It is possible that the word "characterisme" used in the secondary title pages and in some of the running titles was Hall's anglicizing of Seneca's "characterismon" (*Epist. Morales*, XCV, 65).

terpreter of good things, and no other then a leane and pale carcase quickened with a feend." Theophrastus, it should be recalled, did not formally conclude his pieces; he merely stopped them.[14] Lodge, on the other hand, indulged in finales more flamboyant than Hall's. The Malcontent, after the usual flourish of metaphors, is cast to the rewards of his merits: "Every eare was long agoe wearie of him, and he is now almost wearie of himselfe. Give him but a little respite, and he will die alone; of no other death, than others welfare." This sort of fillip Earle exploited delightfully.

Hall's sentences deserve further notice. For only too plainly they were works of art. Because of his admiration for the Senecan prose currently in vogue and also, no doubt, because of his consciousness of the emotional value of cadence, Hall indulged perpetually in antithesis and balanced short rhythm. His Valient Man "undertakes without rashnesse, and performes without feare." The purposes of his Wise Man are "neither so variable as may argue inconstancy; nor obstinately unchangeable, but framed according to his after-wits, or the strength of new occasions." Mannered, cadenced, polished, Hall's sentences are not like those of Theophrastus, but they were to be imitated by the Overburians, exaggerated into "quadrumania" by Breton, and gracefully varied by Earle. Antithesis and cadence, at first of the strongly Senecan "seesaw" variety,[15] hover over the Character from Hall to Addison.

Though the central portions of his Characters tend to be bare

---

[14]It should be remembered that general, moralistic sentences had been added to several of Theophrastus' Characters and that Hall would have supposed that Theophrastus intended those sketches to have formal endings. Casaubon, indeed, translated these apocryphal sentences as if part of the text. Hall's disposition would make him especially conscious of their value, both artistic and didactic.

[15]See George Williamson, "Senecan Style in the Seventeenth Century," *Philological Quarterly*, XV (1936), 321-351.

of imagery, the conclusions do not, particularly in the Characters of Vices. Many of the images strike one as neither remarkably vivid nor original, though once or twice a religious topic will produce something with a Biblical flavor—the Humble Man is "a lowly valley, sweetly planted, and well watered." One relishes Hall's saying that the Unconstant Man is a guest in his own house and, of the Distrustful, "There is nothing that he takes not with the left hand." If Hall's figures appeal, it is usually because of the wit or the picture. But when Hall writes that the Wise Man "stands like a Center unmoved, while the circumference of his estate is drawn above, beneath, about him," he may suggest Donne. His figures generally are not so thought-provoking, so "metaphysical," as this. Hall's real discussion is finished before he comes to his battery of figures; he uses them, rather, to heighten the emotional response and, it must be said, to afford glitter.

As the first true English Character-writer, Hall inevitably laid his own impress upon the genre. In the manner of the moralists and satirists immediately preceding, he painted his portraits with occasional witty flourishes, and of course he was bound to exaggerate the goodness or badness of human nature in such work. His chief interest was the religious condition of men's minds, the spiritual state of their souls; in ordinary, mundane details, consequently, he was less penetrating and less visual than he might have been. As a moralist he emphasized the chastening and humbling power of Christian belief, the restrictive virtues set forth by Zeno and Socrates and Seneca, whom in his sermons he was fond of quoting.[16] Although he indicated that the life of Mr. Spectator is the easier sort to maintain pure, he glowingly upheld the necessity of virtue in any sort of life and kept his eye,

---

[16]W. F. Mitchell, *English Pulpit Oratory from Andrewes to Tillotson* (London, 1932), p. 227.

both as a writer and as a divine, on his object. Our English
Seneca, to use Fuller's phrase for him, sketched no easy course.
He was an idealistic, an immoderate Christian. Even though in
the second book of *Salomon's Divine Arts* he allowed himself to
say that "Vertue consists in the meane; vice in extreames," there
is little evidence that he judged his types according to the Aristotelian code. The only good case would be the "Presumptuous," constructed to some extent as the opposite of the "Distrustful," for which Theophrastus furnished the original. Their mean,
the Man Who Knows his Merits and Limitations, is lacking. The
"Superstitious," who has too many gods, and the "Profane," who
"hath none at all," are otherwise not properly a contrast. The
"Humble Man" may be the logical opposite of the "Vain-
glorious" but not its Aristotelian extreme. For Hall the virtuous
types, the honest, the humble, the faithful, were not means but
extremes, absolutes. And in picturing the vicious, where Theophrastus was merely honest, Hall is relentless; there is much
less fun in his sketches than in the Greek gallery of frail mortals.
The homeliness of Theophrastus Hall also deemed beneath him.
Though there may not be enough vividness or moderation in his
Virtues to raise the weak nor enough subtlety to engage the
clever, Hall's wisdom is sound and good. He installed in the
Theophrastan department of letters a memorable model for the
depiction of good types to stand beside his figurative, "lesse grave,
more Satyricall," half-Theophrastan Characters of bad folk. The
modern reader, if he is a deep soul, may prefer Earle, or if he has
some of the devil in him, Overbury; but the Jacobean readers,
though they had the literature of Estates, journalistic homilies,
conceitful poetry, "humors" comedy, and formal satire, had nothing precisely like Hall's Characters and appear to have read them
attentively.

The immediate effect of their publication seems, however,

not to have been tremendous. But Hall judged them worthy of inclusion in 1614 in *A Recollection* of his earlier "Treatises," and they reappeared in 1617, 1621, 1625, 1628, 1633, 1634, 1639-1647, and 1662 in the various editions of his works. In 1610 they were translated into French—the first English work, possibly, to achieve that honor[17]—and it is conceivable that some one of the five French editions of Hall fell into La Bruyère's hands before he saw Theophrastus. There were three different German translations of Hall's *Characters* in the seventeenth century.[18] When irrelevant circumstances in the shape of murder gave Overbury's name greater notoriety than Joseph Hall's, the *Characters of Vertues and Vices*, as we shall see, still had readers and imitators.

---

[17]Sidney Lee, "The Beginning of French Translation from the English," *Proceedings of the Bibliographical Society*, VIII (1907), 274.

[18]Dated 1628, 1652, 1685; Gilbert Waterhouse, *The Literary Relations of England and Germany in the Seventeenth Century* (Cambridge, 1914), pp. 102-104. Professor J. A. Walz in a note to Mr. Greenough recorded another translation: *Characteres der Menschen oder Die Entlarvete Welt* (Amsterdam, 1701).

V

THE
OVERBURIAN CHARACTERS

If Casaubon's edition of Theophrastus was the spark that created the English Character out of ready materials and if Hall's
volume constituted the first conspicuous product, the Overbury
collection is the most famous of the seventeenth-century Character-books and the flashiest. It marks the point at which the
Character, profoundly indebted to the Greek model in two or
three particulars, could now neglect its model and branch out in
several ways, both old and new, for a fine flourishing. Most of
the later history of the Character can here in some fashion be
found in the bud. The bibliography of the collection as it grew
from a set of twenty-two Characters appended to the second impression in 1614 of Sir Thomas Overbury's poem *A Wife* to a
total of eighty-two Characters in 1615 and eighty-three in 1622
has been set forth carefully by W. J. Paylor in his excellent edition of *The Overburian Characters*.[1] In that volume, too, can
be found a summary of the evidence assembled by previous scholars indicating that thirty-two of the Characters added in the
sixth impression (1615) were by John Webster[2] and Mr. Paylor's own argument establishing the authorship of Thomas Dekker for the six prison Characters added in the ninth impression
(1616). In the ensuing pages I propose to discuss especially the
methods of construction and the literary qualities of the Overburian sketches.

One method commonly employed in the volume is the building up of a sketch by a listing of the opinions, the mental habits,
the moral values, the manners, and social habits of the type, all

---

[1]Oxford: Basil Blackwell, 1936. Quotations from the Overbury
collection are from this edition.

[2]See the articles by H. D. Sykes and A. F. Bourgeois in *Notes and
Queries*, 11th Series, VIII (1913), X (1914), XI (1915), XII (1915).

more or less in general, rather than by a dramatizing of a particular, revealing situation. A Good Woman is "much within, and frames outward things to her minde, not her minde to them. Shee weares good clothes, but never better; for shee finds no degree beyond *Decencie*." The "Fantastic Inns of Court Man" will "talk ends of *Latin*, though it be false, with as great confidence, as ever *Cicero* could pronounce an Oration, though his best authors for't, be *Taverns* & *Ordinaries*." But what precisely he says or what exactly will illustrate the good woman's framing outward things to her mind we can only guess. "A Courtier" (one of Overbury's most polished sketches), "A Wise Man," "A Reverend Judge," "A Virtuous Widow," "A Worthy Commander in the Wars," "A Noble and Retired House-keeper" are all drawn mostly by generalities, as often as not subjective, with the author's moral judgment woven into the description. This method obviously was not learned from Theophrastus. Instead, the reader will recognize its origin in Hall's Characters of Virtues (and also in his "Profane" and his "Unconstant") and, before that, in the homilists and the commentators on the Estates. As the model in Hall would imply, this method is most successful with virtuous types.

Another common method in the Overbury volume is the setting forth of a type by describing external, visualized conduct that reveals much of the man's inner nature. Along with such dramatic material there is a limited amount of analytical explanation of ideas and desires and motives. In addition to Theophrastus' "he is," "he sends," "he says," "he nails up," one finds in these Characters "he deems," "he prays," "his dream is," "his passions are." This combined procedure, for which Hall's Vices and Lodge's *Wits Miserie* could furnish models, can be seen in "A Very Very Woman," "An Old Man" (though here after the initial sentence, *they* supplants *he* as if out of respect for the long sequence, following Aristotle and Horace, of portraits of old men), "An Elder Brother," "A Fair and Happy Milkmaid," "A Mere Common Lawyer," "A Mere Scholar," and several more. A few of this sort, all now thought to have been written by John Webster—"A Drunken Dutchman Resident in England," "An Improvident Young Gallant," "A Roaring Boy," "A Puny Clerk"—are especially pungent. In these pieces some biography and a good deal of the data of dress and manners and favorite haunts and today's fashion in buttons and diet indicate that the Overbury authors were probably emulating the tart sketches in *Cynthia's Revels*[3] and the still more lavish and strongly-flavored type satire of Lodge. To be sure, the superabundance of vivid descriptive detail in *Wits Miserie* had to be pruned in order to achieve the neater design of the Characters, and Lodge's potpourri of quotation and preachment had to be discarded except for a residue of caustic, interpretive commentary. Jonson in learning from writers like Lodge had refined and cooled the tone of the pamphleteer; because his sketches were to be part of a play, he extracted from the satiric portrait the man's characteristic remarks and used them rather in the dialogue. The particular Overburian Characters of which we are speaking are a shade less moderate in tone than Jonson's sketches, and they occasionally utilize the revealing, typical remarks of the subject. Though I find no verbal evidence of indebtedness, the general resemblances between these Characters and the sketches in Jonson and Lodge seem too great to be entirely fortuitous.[4]

---

[3]C. E. Gough (*The Life and Characters of Sir Thomas Overbury*, Norwich, 1909, p. 111) called attention to a parallel between Jonson's *Poetaster*, IV, iii ("His tongue shall be gentleman-usher to his wit, and still go before it"), and a sentence in "A Mere Scholar." But our concern, of course, is with the question of indebtedness to the character-sketches in an earlier play.

[4]A good example of the closeness-without-identity in Lodge and Overbury can be found in a comparison of the latter's "Roaring Boy" and

A lively and representative character of the sort I have been discussing is the following, probably by Overbury himself.

An Affected Traveller

Is a speaking fashion; he hath taken paines to bee ridiculous, and hath seen more then he hath perceived. His attire speakes *French* or *Italian,* and his *gate* cryes *Behold mee.* Hee censures all things by countenances, and shrugs, and speakes his owne language with shame and lisping: he will choake rather than confesse *Beere* good drinke: and his pick-tooth is a maine part of his behaviour. Hee chooseth rather to be counted a *Spie,* then not a *Polititian:* and maintaines his reputation by naming great men familiarly. He chooseth rather to tell lyes then not wonders, and talkes with men singly; his discourse sounds big but meanes nothing: and his boy is bound to admire him howsoever. He comes still from great personages, but goes with meane. He takes occasion to shew Jewells given him in regard of his vertue, that were bought in *S. Martins,* and not long after, having with a *Mountebancks* method, pronounced them worth thousands, empawneth them for a few shillings. Upon festivall daies he goes to Court, and salutes without re-saluting: at night in an Ordinarie hee confesseth the businesse in hand, and seemes as conversant with all intents and plots, as if he begot them. His extraordinary accompt of men is, first to tell them the ends of all matters of consequence, and then to borrow mony of them; hee offereth curtesies, to shew them, rather then himselfe humble. He disdaines all things above his reach, and preferreth all Countries before his owne. Hee imputeth

Lodge's "Brawling Contention" (*Wits Miserie,* pp. 62-63). Clausen, "Beginning of English Character-writing," points out that Jonson and Overbury were at one time friends and argues that Jonson was the one who first showed an interest in Theophrastus. Clausen accepts literally Fuller's later remark that Overbury was "the first writer of characters of our nation" (*The History of the Worthies of England,* edited by P. A. Nuttall, 1840, I, 563) and assumes that the original Overbury Characters were written about 1607.

his wants and povertie to the ignorance of the time, not his owne unworthines: and concludes his discourse with a halfe period, or a word, and leaves the rest to imagination. In a word, his religion is fashion, and both body and soule are governed by fame, he loves most voices above truth.

Although this type of man was probably well known, Jonson's *Amorphus* (in *Cynthia's Revels*) seems to have provided the outline for this sketch, and Hall's "Hypocrite" and "Vainglorious" seem to have furnished several details.[5] The method often suggests that of Theophrastus: we are told much by mere items of behavior. The difference is, however, that only a part of the picture comes this way—the displaying of the jewels, the saluting strangers at court, the concluding his plaintive discourse in a meaningful half-period. But Theophrastus is always both

---

[5] "Behold me" in the second sentence echoes "Who sees me" in "The Hypocrite," and the jewels from St. Martin's may have originated in the "richest jewels, and fairest horses" somewhat differently introduced in "The Vain-glorious," the latter in turn deriving from Theophrastus' "Pretentiousness." Lodge's "Vainglory" is another possible source, and in the shrug, in the emphasis on fashion, and in his boasting of noble acquaintances the Overbury man recalls the picture of the traveler (and travelers) in Rich's *Faultes Faults* (1606), fol. 8.

Other Characters in which there are details probably adapted from Hall are "The Proud Man" (cf. Hall's "Vain-glorious," who when "well mounted thinks every man wrongs him, that looks not at him"), "A Golden Ass" (cf. "A bare head in the street, doth him more good than a meales meat" in Hall's "Vain-glorious" as well as the sentence just quoted), "A Covetous Man" (cf. Hall's "Covetous," who would hang himself "but that he is loth to cast away money on a cord" and who, if his servant break "but an earthen dish for want of light, . . . abates it out of his quarters wages," a detail in turn borrowed from Theophrastus' "Penuriousness"), "An Ignorant Glory-hunter" (cf. Hall's "Vain-glorious" and his acquaintance with the "honorable"). The resemblances noted by Paylor between the Overburian "Wise Man," "Worthy Commander in the Wars," "Devilish Usurer," and "Reverend Judge" and Hall's "Wise Man," "Valiant Man," "Covetous," and "Good Magistrate" may be due to actual imitation but are also almost obligatory by reason of the traditions of all these types. The Overbury "Noble Spirit," being so close to Hall's ideal for all good types, inevitably suggests several of his Characters.

objective and concrete; for the somewhat similar Man of Petty
Pride he tells us about the son's haircut at Delphi, the blackamoor
lackey, the jackdaw's ladder and shield, the ox-head displayed
over his door, the Melitean lap-dog's tomb, and so forth, and he
habitually begins his sentence with a participle to state the exact
circumstance (the *if* and *when* clauses of English translations).
But Overbury, who loved a witty generalization better than the
silent humor of a man's particular deed, could not keep to so
impersonal a style long. Instead he carried on the moralists' kind
of general, subjective attack ("Hee chooseth . . . to be counted
a *Spie* . . . his discourse sounds big . . . He disdaines all things
above his reach"); like Hall, Overbury starts with a bold metaphor and ends, as nearly as he can, with an epigram. In "An
Affected Traveler" there actually is much less of Theophrastus
than in the majority of Hall's Vices. Yet with the exception of
two Characters ("A Covetous Man" and "The Proud Man")
contributed by someone to the ninth impression (1616), the
"Affected Traveler" is as Theophrastan in construction as any
in the collection. "The Proud Man," as various scholars have
noticed,[6] may owe three of its list of actions to Theophrastus.
Otherwise I can see no cogent evidence that Overbury and his
"friends" had read the ancient Greek Characters.[7] But in the

---

[6]See Gough, p. 39; Karl Lichtenberg, *Der Einfluss der Theophrast
auf die englischen Characterwriters* (Weimar, 1921), p. 44; Paylor, *Overburian Characters*, p. 140.

[7]The Overbury "Country Gentleman" stares at everything in the city and
"casts his eyes upon gazing" as Theophrastus' Boor gazes at every ox or ass
(seeing nothing else in the streets), and the Overbury "Timist" "pleaseth
the children of great men" just as Theophrastus' Flatterer brings
apples and pears to the children of his patron. But it would be rash,
in lack of other evidence, to assert that the Overbury author got such
obviously typical details from reading the Greek or Latin Characters.
The "carracter" of a whore spoken by Monticelso in Webster's *White
Devil* (1612), III, ii, consists wholly of metaphors and is much less
Theophrastan than Webster's supposed contributions to the Overbury
collection.

light of their indirect dependence we can see how crucial Hall's work was for the development of the genre in England.

A few other variations in method are to be named. "A Quacksalver" and "An Arrant Horse-Courser" are constructed chiefly from the disreputable tricks of their trades. In the manner of the authors of coney-catching books, the writers of these pieces offered not a revelation of human nature but an exposure of dishonest occupations. Inevitably, too, in so varied a set of type portraits there are a few in which discursive and argumentative tendencies show themselves. In "An Excellent Actor," which was added to the sixth impression (1615), the challenge of an attack upon actors in John Stephens's *Satyrical Essayes Characters and Others* (1615) caused the defensive author (probably Webster) to forget his absolute authority as artist and to allude appealingly to what "you see" and "we see" and "some think" and "I observe" of the maligned group. The important Character of a prison—important because it provoked a number of other writers to try to Character institutions and places—is even more truly a form of essay. It affords no real picture of its subject; instead, it consists of a string of witty figures for prisoners, prison conditions, the immediate and indirect agents of imprisonment. Did the author's wit not fly off so continually on more or less thoughtful tangents, the piece might seem more like the other Characters. "An Hypocrite," twice as long as the longer sketches, carries to tiresome lengths a medieval figure of hypocrisy as a medicine and a disease of society before it turns to "Cleargy Hypocrites" and a sentence or two on "Clerke Hypocrites." Obviously an old-style homily has got among the Characters. It has less right to be there than Wotton's little poem on the Stoic-Christian wise man, which, though even less Theophrastan than some of the epigrams we were considering in Chapter III, is a consistently composed, subjective, general pic-

142

ture of a moral type; one can appreciate the publisher's giving it the inexact title, "The Character of a happie life."[8]

One cannot always separate the methods of development in the different Characters as exactly as I have tried to do. But certain non-Theophrastan habits of composition are apparent. The most striking feature of all, and one that compensates for the frequent absence of the particular pleasure that the classical Character provides, is the ubiquitous exaggeration of wit and fancy. In some of the Characters this wit seems to become the main method; an effect is achieved not by an accumulation of sentences that describe the habitual, revealing conduct of a representative individual but rather by a series of fantastic, astonishing figures and puns that merely have in common the same starting-point. "A Sailor," "A Whore," "A Sexton," "My Tailor" consist of very fancy embroidery upon simple designs; phrases and clauses are of the sort that Mr. Greenough labeled "syncopated conundrums." "An Host" is the "kernell of a signe: or the signe is the shell, and mine Host is the snaile." "A Sayler . . . is part of his own provision; for he lives ever pickeld . . . Hee . . . is well winded for hee tires the day and outrunnes darknesse." A soldier in charity "goes beyond the Clergy, for hee loves his greatest enemy best, much drinking." We know the subject little better for treatment like this. The striving for wit visible in Hall's writing has in these cases encouraged the author almost to abandon the idea of a portrait.

It is not uncommon for literary historians to describe the Overbury figures as conceits and to draw a comparison with the metaphysical wit contemporaneous in the poets. If a conceit is merely the "discovery of occult resemblances in things apparently unlike," the Overbury Characters are, except in the sketches of lofty moral types, lavishly conceitful. The sailor's life is "like

[8]See pp. 95, 129 above.

a *hawkes,* the best part mewed"; his "wisdome is the coldest part about him, for it ever poynts to the North, and it lies lowest, which makes his valour every tide oreflow it." A Welshman is "the Oyster, that the pearle is in, for a man may be pickt out of him." A tailor, "like a true Mungrell . . . neither bites nor barkes, but when your back is towards him." Unlike the pleasant and useful remark about the fair milkmaid that her breath is her own, "which sents all the yeere long of *June,* like a new made Hay-cocke," the former passages shed no light; they merely dazzle. Along with the numerous puns they lie on the surface, unlike the functional conceits of Donne and Herbert and Marvell. On the other hand one meets figures that are imbedded in the thought, that depend upon "dynamic" rather than sensuous or emotional comparison,[9] and that yet retain some of the logical agility of the syncopated conundrums: the virtue of the "Very Very Woman" is the "hedge of *Modestie,* that keeps a man from clyming over into her faults," and the soldier is the "husband-man of valor, his Sword is his plow: which honor and aqua vitae, two fierie mettald jades, are ever drawing." But such figures are scarce. The metaphysical effect in the Overbury Characters comes partly from the strong self-consciousness and psychological

---

[9]See Alice S. Brandenburg, "The Dynamic Image in Metaphysical Poetry," *PMLA,* LVII (1942), 1039-1045; Rosemond Tuve, "Imagery and Logic: Ramus and Metaphysical Poets," *Journal of the History of Ideas,* III (1942), 365-400.

A tie between Overbury's wit and that of the metaphysicals can perhaps be seen in a comparison of Overbury's "Courtier," whose "wit, like the *Marigold,* openeth with the Sunne," and the following lines in "Upon Phillis Walking in a morning before Sun-rising," written by that notorious metaphysical, John Cleveland:

> The Marigold whose Courtiers face
> Ecchoes the Sun, and doth unlace
> Her at his rise, at his full stop
> Packs and shuts up her gaudy shop

(printed in 1647). Cleveland, it may be remarked, wrote three pamphlet-Characters as well as this and other conceitful poems.

tendencies in viewing men and partly from the commingling of showy, superficial conundrum-wit and the exaggerations of humor (as in the remark that the devilish usurer "comes to Cathedralls onely for love of the singing Boyes, because they looke hungry," and in the assertion that the Puritan, where the gate stands open, "is ever seeking a stile"). Saintsbury has said that the mark of the true metaphysical is the habitual effort to "express something after, something behind, the simple, obvious first sense and suggestion of a subject." There is something of this in the figure about the soldier, but ordinarily Hall and Earle and even Stephens are deeper than Overbury. Though bitter, the Overbury authors do not feel or produce the "metaphysical shudder."[10] Most striking in this connection is the probability that Donne's "True Character of a Dunce," harmonious with the other pieces in the Overbury corpus, might never have been attributed to Donne had it always been published anonymously.

Before we leave the Overbury volume some notice should be taken of the breadth of material introduced into that collection and into Character-writing subsequently. Although few country types are included, the population of the city is before us—the true gentlefolk (one or two only) and numerous upstart pretenders, the learned professions, the military, the manual tradesmen, inn-people, the water-man and the pirate, prostitutes and sharpers, and, from the pen of Thomas Dekker, a set of prison types. Contemporary comedy and the lively work of recent epigrammatists presented a similar view, though scarcely a wider one, unless one excepts the realm of the nobility, about which the sharp tongues of Sir Thomas and the other contributors were tactfully silent. Some of the sketches are based upon moral character alone, but these sketches, whether of bad types like Theophrastus' or of

[10] See George Williamson, *The Donne Tradition* (Cambridge, Mass., 1930), pp. 90-98.

good types like Hall's, are inferior to their models and to the rest. It may be the effort to be clever that makes "An Intruder into Favor" less descriptive and less thoughtful than Hall's "Ambitious." The majority of the Overburian Characters are founded, as "An Intruder" is, on a combination of moral and social (including economic, national, occupational) features. This plan produces the most effective results, for the picturesque nature of Elizabethan life and the supercilious, strongly-biased minds of our authors made good collaborators. The Character of "An Elder Brother," one of the most penetrating of them all, dramatizes the effect of a particular position in a wealthy family upon the mind and principles and then the conduct of a man. Its suggestion of a whole life and milieu is so deft and satisfying that it must have done in small compass for the Jacobean reader what Addison and Fielding did for a later age at much greater length and less unpretentiously.

"An Elder Brother" is special enough to represent only one class of elder brothers. "A Drunken Dutchman Resident in England" carries the tendency towards individual portraiture still farther, because the man's nationality, his present residence, his three main vices (drunkenness, gluttony, greed), his business and business methods, his pronunciation of a new language, his religious affiliation, and something of his nation's history are all indicated. But in spite of so many differentiae he impresses one as only a type. The suggestion of Whibley[11] that Overbury's "Flatterer" represents himself and that the "Courtier" and "Amorist" represent his "friend" Rochester, and the remark of Gough[12] that the Overburian Characters contain veiled allusions to well-known people, including Sir Thomas More and Burbage, should not mislead us into putting any trust in the phrasing of a

---

[11]*Blackwoods' Edinburgh Magazine*, CLXXXV (1909), 760-761.
[12]Page 41.

title page inserted in the sixth impression (1615) of the volume: "New Characters (drawne to the life) of severall persons, in severall qualities." In such an ambiguous description of the contents, the publisher was less attentive to the artistic aims of his contributors than to the commercial advantage of hinting at the presence of exciting personal criticism. The Overburians appear not to have been attempting the Portrait-Character although their selection of small groups to Character tended in that direction. It is true that contemporary playwrights seem usually to have created their people to be individuals first of all, even if, mindful of the ancient doctrine of decorum, they also gave them the coloring of their type. But the Character-writer, starting with the whole group, aimed to compress the group into one perfect sample.

In some of the moral-social Characters one element or the other will be preponderant. In the pictures of certain occupational types, especially the low ones—"A Pedant," "A Sailor," "An Almanac-maker," "My Tailor"—the emphasis is all upon the occupation. In others the moral—or immoral—and psychological features of the social type are painted in, though they are taken for granted with a curious aloofness. The Serving Man's sloppy promiscuity is not deplored; the thoughts and feelings of a Country Gentleman in the city are much less interesting in Overbury's account than in the portraits of Sir Roger de Coverley. But the objectivity of such pieces is surprisingly Theophrastan.

It will be noted how often the Overbury Character represents a complex type of person without disturbing the formal pattern established by Hall—the witty beginning; the short, balanced rhythms; the rhetorical finale, often introduced by "lastly" or "to conclude" and enforced by an epigram, a tossing of the fellow to his proper fate, maybe by a spoken farewell. "A Mere

Pettifogger" ends: "Only with this, I wil pitch him o're the Barre, & leave him; That his fingers itch after a Bribe, ever since his first practising of Court-Hand."[13] The habit of beginning each Character with a figure instead of an exact definition in the fashion of Theophrastus may account, as Mr. Paylor suggests, for the lack of clear outline in many of the pieces. To say at the outset that a Flatterer is *"the shadow of a foole,"* that a "Tymist *Is a noune Adjective of the present tense,"* or that "A Fellow of a House Examines all mens carriage but his owne" is to talk around the subject and to delay, perhaps forever, a decision as to just what is the essence of any of those types. As for the sentence-patterns commonly seen in the Characters of Overbury and Webster, the Senecan ideal of Hall prevails. Hall employed verbal and logical antithesis more than they, and the short, jerky movement especially noticeable in the sententious Characters of Virtues, the sort of sentence not "above three inches long" which Milton objected to in Hall's pamphlets, is lengthened and loosened up slightly—by another half inch or so—in the Characters of Overbury and Webster. But the perpetually rocking rhythm of Hall's balanced phrases and clauses continues to appear. This sort of cadence is, in fact, one of the regular marks of the best early Characters. Dekker's additions to the Overbury collection lose something by neglecting it. How it sounds in Overbury can be illustrated in "An Affected Traveler," quoted on a previous page.

The Overburian Characters in general can be described as less exact than Hall's and less philosophical than Earle's, though furnishing abundant criticism of the ways of human society. The combination of social features and moral ones was not, to be sure, Overbury's invention. That feature of the English Char-

---

[13]For illustrations otherwise of the farewell fillip see "Her Next Part," "A Golden Ass," "My Tailor," "A Whore," "An Apparator."

acter in Overbury and others (Hall's "Good Magistrate" was his venture in this kind) as well as the types chosen for representation was due to men's acquaintance with many modern adaptations in drama, verse, and pamphlet of the old literature of Estates and of the literature of virtues and vices, all of which provided the dough, mixed, flavored, and ready for cutting.[14] Sometimes the material was brought very much up to date and place in the Character by allusions to the dress and comfits and romances lately in vogue; the merely moral types, on the other hand, are usually developed without local color. The fact that "A Puritan," "A Precisian," and "A Jesuit" were painted with contemporary allusions indicates that the classical Character and Elizabethan journalism were together preparing for the Civil War pamphlet-Character, for these three sketches were not written just for the fun of portraiture; they treated an important topic of public controversy with the intention of informing and persuading the reader. Dekker's group of prison sketches added in 1616[15] provided, furthermore, a looser form as well as dust and heat for the later pamphlet-Character.

Overbury and his group established the Character for the seventeenth century. To Hall's more careful and more thorough portraiture they were very much indebted, but to succeeding writers they offered a wider variety of subjects and methods. Complex social types, national representatives, women, and institutions; a strong sense of the local fact, perhaps at the expense of universality; the superficial Jonsonian "humor" rather than

---

[14] For example, that the social criticism in "An Engrosser of Corn" was traditional can be seen by comparing it with the material presented by Burton Milligan in "Sixteenth- and Seventeenth-Century Satire against Grain Engrossers," *Studies in Philology*, XXXVII (1940), 585-597.

[15] See p. 210 ff. for further discussion of these pieces. Paylor's Introduction offers information about their sources.

an ethical class; grotesque comparisons and "hard, presumptuous, unamiable wit" (to quote Saintsbury); a free commingling of external action, inner feeling, and author's interpretation; a reversion to the liberties of invective in the type-satire written before 1608—all these rode in the Overbury omnibus. No wonder the vulgar preferred it to Theophrastus and Hall. The sensitive reader may cry out against the lack of fairness in the pictures: the awkward and the ridiculous in men are exaggerated and usually made the object of jeers; the good types are often idealized without the earnestness and the devotion that win belief for Hall's lofty figures. But there are enough brilliant performances to please anyone—the famous "Milkmaid," who having delighted Isaak Walton continues to delight the rest of us, the terrifying "Very Woman," the rhetorically glittering "Courtier," the classical type of Puritan wittily drawn, the lamentable "Mere Scholar," the absurd "Ostler," the thoughtful "Elder Brother," and more. The Overburians, not excluding incarcerated but unchastened Thomas Dekker, are a fluent, irritable, droll set of men who maintain a good pretence of feeling only mirth or scorn and who describe their world of fraud and liveliness with just such tangy observation and extravagant fancy as the incredible world deserves. Obviously they are not concerned quietly and judiciously to study and then exactly to present the basic kinds of men; they are wits and men-about-town, not Aristotles. Their province is the interesting, not absolute and unchanging truth. Theophrastus necessarily relied upon common social standards for his categories, but the Overburians depend further upon the prejudices of themselves and their class. The particular intellectual and aesthetic satisfaction that the ancient Character provided is not, therefore, that which is mostly offered by the Overbury pieces nor by the broad current of seventeenth century Character-writing. But there are other rewards. These sometimes different pleasures, as well as the disappointments, are suggested by a definition, figurative as one would expect, which was added to the ninth impression of the Overbury collection:

> To square out a Character by our English levell, it is a picture (reall or personall) quaintlie drawne in various collours, all of them heightned by one shadowing.
> It is a quicke and softe touch of many strings, all shutting up in one musicall close: It is wits descant on any plaine song.

VI

THE

THEORY AND THE VOGUE
OF THE CHARACTER:
FROM CASAUBON TO EARLE

Queen Elizabeth once inquired of Nicholas Hilliard, the celebrated miniaturist, why it was that the Italian portrait painters, "who had the name to be the cunningest and to drawe best, shadowed not." The explanation he offered rested upon his opinion that the "principal parte of painting or drawing after the life consiste[t]h in the truth of the lyne . . . the lyne without shadow showeth all to a good judgment."[1] Shadows give greater visibility at a distance and may either conceal ugliness in the sitter or inexpertness in the artist; but shadows exaggerate. Elizabeth, with queenly faith in her beauty, proposed thereafter always to be painted outdoors in a full light.

Hilliard's remarks taken in connection with a sentence from the Overbury definition of the Character—"it is a picture (reall or personall) quaintlie drawne in various collours, all of them heightned by one shadowing"—bring us to the heart of the theory of our genre. The Character as Theophrastus created it is a picture of an imaginary person who represents the group of men possessed by that feature of character (ἦθος) which dominates him. He is to be imagined as alive and individual; but because he is to be seen only in those situations that reveal his dominant moral or psychological habit, the picture will be eclectic, the shadowing heightened. The Penurious Man may have been born in the country and be especially a judge of goats; he may once be plunged into black sorrow by the death of his first-born

---

[1] "A Treatise concerning the Arte of Limning," in *The First Annual Volume of the Walpole Society* (Oxford, 1912), p. 28.

son; he may be an oligarch or a democrat; but all these individual and necessary aspects of his humanity will be lost in the shadowing, which will conceal everything but his eagerness to collect his usury, to count the figs on his tree, to extract reimbursement for an old pot smashed by his servant, to discourage the habit of his neighbor of borrowing salt or lampwicks. He represents a large group of men, ancient and modern, and so, in a sense, is not an exaggeration of human nature. But the picture by shadowing will exaggerate him. The figures depicted in Theophrastus' Characters, with one or two exceptions, are not theoretical but real; in all cases they are types.

The logical basis of such a literary genre is, of course, Aristotelian rather than of the modern sort which George Boas has called statistical. The Aristotelian perceives the "self-identical essence in an apparent variety" while the statistical thinker considers the essence to be a mere metaphor, a convenience perhaps but a distortion of the irreducible variety of the actual world.[2] The logic of absolutes and dichotomies, Mr. Boas implies,[3] is outmoded; yet the very fact that Mr. Boas can classify kinds of logic demonstrates the power of survival in Aristotelian thinking. If the function of art is to render human experience in a fashion more intelligible, if the artist is to bring out of life a pattern, even a pattern of confusion, by virtue of which values of some sort emerge in our consciousness, there will be no need for a defense of the typical. Aristotle's pregnant saying that poetry, being concerned with the universal rather than the particular, is a more philosophic thing than history goes a good distance towards explaining the appeal of type-figures in art and the appeal of the Character. As long as our minds deal in absolute conceptions like redness, honesty,

---

[2] *Our New Ways of Thinking* (New York, 1930), pp. 146-147.
[3] This implication is repeatedly visible in his book even if he once insists (p. 141) that he is "merely noticing a tendency, not appraising it."

surliness, arrogance—and the statistical concept of the average becomes in some circumstances an absolute in effect—we shall visualize classes of men and recognize with satisfaction representatives of them in the society about us or in the creations of Terence and Chaucer, in the pages of Fielding and Dickens, Sinclair Lewis and John Dos Passos. In spite of the logical relativity required by modern scientific theory, many a respectable doctor still allows himself to allude to "the nervous type," Helen Hokinson continues to draw the recognizable dowager, and conversation would come to a stop if we could never employ such absolute concepts as "cheerful extrovert," "G. I. Joe," "Hollywood blonde," and "Hearst journalism." The choice of absolutes and the shadowing of art vary with the taste of the times, but the mind continues to envisage types. E. M. Forster has written persuasively in defense of "flat" characterizations in the novel, arguing that they contribute ease, speed, and a sense of permanence to a book—to good books, including Dickens' and Proust's.[4] Whether or not one agrees with Mr. Forster's assumption that all type-characters are flat—thinking of Meredith's work, I should disagree—one must acknowledge that the representative figure has by no means vanished from literature. Allardyce Nicoll ascribes to the theatre an actual requirement of stock types.[5] Furthermore, it must be true that many a modern man in his own life tries to achieve consistency in a kind of character which he has conceived to be his own, a pattern which is perhaps a better one, a less obvious one than the spectator may imagine, yet none the less a pattern. We try to resist the effect of circumstances on us; even with countless notions from psychology and

---

[4] *Aspects of the Novel* (New York, 1927), pp. 103-118.

[5] "[T]he theatre demands, not individualized and intimately observed personalities, but a series of stock types . . . In the theatre unconsciously we expect and fervently we welcome the old favorites" (*The Saturday Review of Literature*, XI [April 20, 1935], 630).

sociology to make us acquiesce in a fate that seems fortuitous and mechanical, we maintain, for example, the Elizabethan concept, drawn from a Stoic type, that that sort of man is admirable who

> Fortune's buffets and rewards
> Hast ta'en with equal thanks . . .
> Whose blood and judgment are so well commingled
> That they are not a pipe for Fortune's finger
> To sound what stop she please.

Neither the Romantic worship of the individual nor Darwinian biology nor voluntaristic philosophy has wholly destroyed the validity of types.

But there is a modern dilemma. In a brilliant entry in his journal Mr. Huxley's Anthony Beavis contrasts the "humors" characterizations of Jonson and the more fluid and individual creations of Shakespeare and remarks that for his own time Jonson's simplified people were "truer" than Shakespeare's because most Elizabethans saw themselves as well-unified "humors."

Hamlet inhabited a world whose best psychologist was Polonius. If he had known as little as Polonius, he would have been happy. But he knew too much; and in this consists his tragedy. Read his parable of the musical instruments. Polonius and the others assumed as axiomatic that man was a penny whistle with only half a dozen stops. Hamlet knew that, potentially at least, he was a whole symphony orchestra.

Mad, Ophelia lets the cat out of the bag. "We know what we are, but know not what we may be." Polonius knows very clearly what he and other people *are*, within the ruling conventions. Hamlet knows this, but also what they may be—outside the local system of masks and humours.

To be the only man of one's age to know what people may be as well as what they conventionally are! Shakespeare must have gone through some rather disquieting quarters of an hour.[6]

But we, writes Anthony Beavis, have come to believe in psychological atomism. Hamlet, the modern man, once more "casts a light."

> Polonius is much more obviously and definitely a person than the prince. Indeed, Hamlet's personality is so indefinite that critics have devoted thousands of pages to the discussion of what it really was. In fact, of course, Hamlet didn't have a personality—knew altogether too much to have one. He was conscious of his total experience, atom by atom and instant by instant, and accepted no guiding principle which would make him choose one set of patterned atoms to represent his personality rather than another. To himself and to others he was just a succession of more or less incongruous states. Hence that perplexity at Elsinore and among the Shakespearean critics ever since. Honour, Religion, Prejudice, Love—all the conventional props that shore up the ordinary personality—have been, in this case, gnawed through. Hamlet is his own termite and from a tower has eaten himself down to a heap of sawdust.

We are reminded of the implications of Mr. Boas's book; our new ways of thinking are not, among the informed, Aristotelian. There is little likelihood of a new popularity for the Theophrastan Character.

In James's day men could disagree on the relative propriety of Jonson's "humors" and the more protean effects of Shakespeare's characterization. (I ignore the possibility of reversing labels and describing certain of Shakespeare's creatures as "humors" and some of Jonson's as complex.[7]) But no Englishman of even ordinary education could have lacked indoctrination in the concept of social and moral types. The ancient view of the

---

[6]Aldous Huxley, *Eyeless in Gaza* (New York: Harper & Brothers, 1936), pp. 106-107. [7]See pp. 100-101 above.

universe as orderly, hierarchic, and fixed was already threatened, but its strength remained great. The disintegration of the feudal caste system under the contrary pressures of new economic arrangements might produce the most glaring social misfits; the bold guesses of scientific thinkers might endanger established astronomy and cast all in doubt. But Roman comedy, Galenic medicine, and Christian preaching still bore evidence of the fact that human nature can be classified. Aristotle continued to offer comfort, not yet dubbed false, to those who wished to believe in order and permanence.

The result is that wherever one looks in the publications of Shakespeare's day, classification of men greets one. The Seven Deadly Sins were merely a beginning for further subdivisions of drunkards, lechers, the greedy, the jealous, a "Bachelors Banquet" (1599; 1603) of wives. Bacon's *Essaies* in 1612 treated men as married or single, young or old, prince or suitor. The types of the morality plays became standard. Sometimes the catalogues of the old homilies were versified, repeating in a general way the century-old scheme of Barclay's *Ship of Fools*. Richard West's *Court of Conscience or Dick Whippers Sessions* (1607) had a full set, tiresome because in poor verse, of social-moral types, including the upright judge, the covetous man, the loyal subject, and the obedient child. Though stone-blind to what confronted him in the streets and halls and taverns of England, the Jacobean reader could readily become learned about the appearance, dress, stink, and babbling of the drunkard. No one who put pen to paper, seemingly, could resist describing this "swilswollower," this kisscup, Tom Tosspot, who is no man of fashion unless he can "drinke *super naculum*, Carouse the Hunters Hoope, quaffe Upsey-freese crosse, Bowse in Permoysaunt, in Pimlico, in Crambo, with Healthes, Gloves, Numpes, Frolicks and . . . by the Bell, by the Cards, by the Dye, by the Dozen, by the Yard."[8] The virtuous likewise could be classified, as the conduct-books and manuals of devotion demonstrate. On the title page of his translation of Guazzo's *Civile Conversation* (1586) George Pettie enumerated the divisions of society for whose conversations Book Two offered suggestions; they are young men and old, gentlemen and yeomen, princes and private persons, learned and unlearned, citizens and strangers, religious and secular, men and women. Elizabethan literature exhibits a passion for cataloguing.

As Miss Mohl has suggested, the ranging of the traditional Estates before the reader had been undertaken in medieval times in the hope that men might be persuaded by art as well as by Church and State to remain contented in their own rank and situation. The original division into three Estates—clergy, nobility, commons—was increased vastly even by Lydgate's time, his English version of the "Duodecim abusiones" listing king, bishop, lord, womanhood, the rich, the old, the true servant, and youth as separate Estates.[9] The usual charge to each group to fulfill its responsibilities and abide by its proper circumscriptions, which are either assumed to be known or are described for the reader, is usually kept. Gascoigne more than a century later subdivided still farther, distinguishing plowmen, roysterers, sycophants, courtiers, and gentlemen among the Estates. Actually he was bringing together the moral classes of the Virtues-and-Vices tradition, the social categories of Estates, and some of the favorite types of classical satire, but he applied to all his groups the method of the literature of Estates, which was to remind each of his proper moral and social obligations. Once the method was generalized, a multiplication of the older, basic groupings was certain

---

[8] Thomas Young, *Englands Bane* (1617), sig. D_1v-D_2. One may be reminded of Prince Hal's account of the art of drinking as practiced by the vulgar (*Henry IV, Part I*, II, iv).

[9] Mohl, *The Three Estates*, p. 123.

to follow; both the writer's need for fresh material and those very social and economic changes which the conservative author hoped to discourage would assure that. The second factor, a desire to preserve the *status quo*, also contributed to the persistence into the seventeenth century of the feudal literature of Estates. One sees that desire in Markham's *Booke of Honour* (1625), which is both a textbook on the ranks of nobility in England and a glorification of such an aristocratic system; one catches glints of the same attitude in the Character-books. Indeed in his scornful chapter on "*Dunghill,* or Truck-Knights" who buy their knighthood, much to the delight of their "gawdie Madames amongst their rude Dairy-maids," Markham duplicates the point of view and material of several Overburian sketches of spurious aristocrats, and the definition, late in the volume, of "An *Absolute King*" seems to have been shaped with some aid from the Character. The vogue of the Character must be understood as related both to the mental and literary habit of classification and to a conservative attitude towards new convolutions in society.

No break, then, will be visible between the Estates tradition and the Theophrastan genre. Joseph Hall drew his classifications from the Virtues-and-Vices literature or from Theophrastus, with the exception of his "Good Magistrate," a venerable Estates type considered with attention to the ancient question of its rights and duties. The Overbury collecton includes most of Lydgate's and Gascoigne's Estates—lawyers, soldiers, womanhood, age, and so one—but "A Reverend Judge" is accompanied by "A Fantastic Inns of Court Man," a "Mere Pettifogger," and a "Mere Common Lawyer"; a "Good Woman" is accompanied by two not so good; and a "Noble and Retired House-keeper" is supplemented by a ridiculous "Country Gentleman." Though the Estates attitude towards social hierarchy has survived, the old system of classification has been altered in favor of a new one which sees types not as necessary, numbered bricks in a venerable social arch but merely as picturesque and interesting parts of the giddy social scene. There are still Estates and solemn expositions of the moralistic, Christian view of life. But there is also a good deal of ordinary curiosity about the world of men as well as a delight in the wonders that social disintegration has wrought.

Today a casual reader of Theophrastus would be likely to attribute the composition of his sketches to a Hellenic impulse rather more than to a Hebraic one, to the mere fun of the game of providing amusing specimens for labels. But such an evaluation of them will not account for their being taken up by the Jacobeans. Casaubon's saying that Theophrastus' single purpose in writing his Characters was to improve morals[10] was precisely what was needed to link the objective, concrete pictures of Theophrastus to the English tradition in type-satire and homily, a tradition in which the pictures were more commonly analytic than objective and more commonly general than concrete. Casaubon gave permission to the still-moralistic Renaissance to adopt one more classical author. Most men knew nothing about him unless as a writer on scientific subjects; the accident that an even more shadowy man, maybe a Christian preacher of early times, whose words occasionally appeared in collections of wise sayings, bore the same name helped establish Theophrastus the Character-writer among the moral teachers.[11] His connection with rhetoric

---

[10] "Subiectum quidem est de moribus: quos emendare, unicus est auctori in hoc opere finis propositus" (ΘΕΟΦΡΑΣΤΟΥ . . . *Notationes Morum. Isaacus Casaubonus recensuit*, Lyons, 1612, p. 88).

[11] A Theophrastus, presumably not the Character-writer, is quoted in *Sententiae Ciceronis, Demosthenis, ac Terentii* (1603), pp. 128, 174, 342-343. Rich's *Faultes Faults* (1606) quotes "Theophrastus," fols. 13v, 25v. Lodge's echoing of Benedicti's use of aphorisms by a Theophrastus is mentioned p. 72. For suggestions about the reputation of our Theophrastus see Clausen, "Beginning of English Character-writing," especially pp. 34-35.

was also favorable: rhetoric, as Bacon said, existed in order *"to apply Reason to Imagination* for the better moving of the will"[12] just as school themes had as their purpose the training of boys to consider moral and political questions "especially concerning vertues and vices."[13] Still another mistake—the course of human affairs is not shaped by truth alone—assisted in the attaching of the Character to the ancient tradition of moralistic type-portraiture. In some period between the time of their composition and that of their rediscovery by the rhetoricians, seven of the sketches of Theophrastus were each given a sentence or more of moralizing or generalizing commentary that disguised or moderated the starkness of their technique and also made them look more edifying. These additions,[14] perhaps Byzantine in origin, were adopted as authentic in Casaubon's Latin translation and Healey's English version. To the Elizabethans and Jacobeans, who obviously relished the classics partly for the *sententiae* that could be found in them, this feature of the Characters constituted a distinct merit.

He that will "endevour to wipe away blemishes, must first lay them open."[15] What could serve better than the Character, with its concentration upon one human failing at a time, to expose blemishes? Even in ancient times, said Hall, "Charactery" enabled "the ruder multitude . . . [to] learne to knowe vertue, and discerne what to detest. I am deceived if any course could be more likely to prevaile; for heerein the grosse conceit is led on with pleasure, and informed while it feeles nothing but de-

---

[12]*The Advancement of Learning* (*The Philosophical Works of Francis Bacon*, edited by J. M. Robertson, London and New York, 1925, p. 127).

[13]Brinsley, *Ludus Literarius*, 1627 (edited by E. T. Campagnac, Liverpool, 1917, p. 175).

[14]See, in Edmonds' edition of the *Characters*, his notes on "Dissembling," "Flattery," "Garrulity," "Wilful Disreputableness," "News-making," "Late-learning," and "Friendship with Rascals."

[15]Rich, *Faultes Faults* (1606), fol. 13.

light."[16] So the new genre was either not seen to be new (for not even in Hall is there sure evidence that the precise nature of Theophrastus' technique was recognized) or it was perversely made over so that readers might continue to have what they were used to, the interpreted description of virtues and vices. The original Characters offered no comment beyond what a report on the concrete behavior of a typical man must say. But Rich and Lodge and Jonson and Hall, meaning to edify, broke into condemnation and praise. It was the much less earnest Overbury and other callous gentlemen his friends who tossed hope of reform overboard and made the Character amusing, thereby giving it the vogue it deserved.

But the solemnity and didacticism with which even the Overburians felt obliged to imbue a few examples of the genre was not soon to be abandoned. Thomas Adams, a fluent and literary preacher who incorporated in his sermons the Character form developed by Dr. Hall as well as many of that fellow-divine's ideas and phrases, is an instructive writer to watch, not only for his experiments with the Character but also for his preservation of another rhetorical device which, though he did not confuse it with the Character, probably explains why preachers could so readily adopt the latter. The device to which I refer[17] is the use of a well-known Biblical character to typify a whole group of men. "Soare not too high, yee *sonnes* of *Anak*," Adams warns; "strive not to attaine heaven by multiplying of earth, like *Babel*-builders." The busybody he compares to Jehu. His sermon on worldlings, *Politicke Hunting: or, A Discoverie of the cunning Esauites of our times* (1616), takes Esau as their type,

---

[16]*Characters of Vertues and Vices* (1608), "A Premonition of the Title and Use of Characters." See p. 174 below for a possible connection with a sentence in the *Advancement of Learning*.

[17]I am indebted to J. L. Lievsay for making me conscious of this feature of the Renaissance homily.

and in *Plaine-Dealing, or, A Precedent of Honestie* (1616) "Jacob is our exemplar, and patterne of *Plaine-dealing*. He was a plaine man, dwelling in tents." Furthermore, the medieval custom, noticed in Chapter III, of using one figure both as an allegorical symbol and an "historical" example continued to be used in the sermon. But Biblical type figures are not the same as fictitious types; Adams, fortified by frequent use of the former, may have felt freer to create the latter, but as an enthusiastic student of the new Character he could see and preserve the distinction. The relationships between the Renaissance art of preaching and the art of Character-writing were several, chiefly because the latter was generally misunderstood.

Aristotelian philosophy assumed the validity of absolute categories. The codified ethics of a revealed religion did the same. But there are some theoretical difficulties to be noted. Aristotle's conception of virtue, it is well known, implies a normal, fortunate degree between the excess and the deprivation of human impulses; the golden mean between rashness and cowardice, between prodigality and penuriousness, is what one should strive to attain. Stoics and Epicureans accepted, at least in theory, so reasonable an ethic. "If thou keepe a meane," said Epictetus in John Healey's translation (1616), "a meane will keepe thee." The ideal was popular among the Elizabethans. Theophrastus might be expected, as Aristotle's favorite pupil, to have intended the Characters to be the extremes of certain virtuous means, the latter for some reason not described. In the Characters of "Flattery" and "Surliness" there is perhaps just such a pair of opposite, vicious extremes.

But the Elizabethans, like their grandfathers and great-grandfathers, were in reality much better acquainted with the doctrine of their own religion that virtue and vice are two relentlessly opposed extremes. Abraham Fleming's *Monomachie of*

Motives in the mind of man [1582] bore the subtitle "a Battel betweene Vertues and Vices of contrarie qualitie," which correctly describes the arrangement of his book in discussing pride contrasted with humility, vainglory contrasted with the fear of the Lord, hypocrisy with true religion, and so on.[18] In truth, Aristotle seems to have encouraged just such an opposition of virtue and vice in a passage in his *Rhetoric* (I, ix). The good and evil types in Hall's *Characters*, we have seen, were drawn as absolute extremes, though he did not go very far in trying to pair them. On the other hand, the scheme of vicious extremes and virtuous mean Aristotle also illustrated in his *Rhetoric* (II, xii-xiv) in his careful analyses of the usual temperaments and behavior of old men, who are too calculating, of young men, who are too rash, and of middle age, which is the prime of life. These three sketches Daniel Tuvil paraphrased in *The Dove and the Serpent* (1614), but when Bacon considered the same subjects in his *Essaies* he clung to the usual Christian scheme of contrasting just two stages, youth and age. As we proceed, it will be noticeable that although Stephens, Lenton, and Saltonstall either mentioned Aristotle or made some use of his ethical pattern,[19] most of the Character-writers of the earlier seventeenth century set up the good and the bad as opposite extremes; in so doing, they were following what many supposed was the example of Theophrastus. Later, towards the middle of the century, when literary exhaustion and a closer scrutiny of men might have broken down this opposition, the chasm between the two main factions of Englishmen prolonged the division of all humanity into good and bad, black and white. It was still later that the

---

[18]Mr. Lievsay also called my attention to this book.

[19]See Stephens' *Satyrical Essayes Characters* (1615), p. 103; the contrast of covetousness and prodigality in Lenton's "Prodigal"; the reference to Aristotle in Saltonstall's "Scholar in the University."

Marquis of Halifax dared to offer his impressive *Character of a Trimmer* (1688), which projected a true mean.

That the Character should have become popular in the seventeenth century, once it was introduced, was almost inevitable, we can see, because of the prevailing Aristotelian and moralistic habits of mind. But the custom of regarding men as belonging to permanent types and the accompanying religious notion that men are either black or white had to face certain contradictory opinions—new anti-classical, heretical, skeptical tendencies. The Character was buoyed up on the stream of literature for a century by both classical and romantic currents.

The Characters in Casaubon's edition were, with three exceptions, representations of moral or psychological categories. Quite early in English writing the classifying of moral types and of social Estates became mixed, so that in addition to pictures of the honest man and dishonest there were sketches of the honest tailor and the (more usual) thievish tailor, the benign king and the tyrant, the incorruptible judge and the bribable judge. The result of this tendency was, of course, to make more and more classifications, so that in the Overbury collection, in which the subdividing has gone far, there is such a special and temporal type as the man who is Dutch, married, drunken, greedy, Protestant, and resident, we judge permanently, in England. He is still a type; but such insistent tracking down of the myriad small classes of men who have common features of character and milieu would lead to very remote ends; it would take us through the still classical categories of Square and Thwackum, Austen's "Sense and Sensibility," and the old-fashioned "Snobs" of Thackeray, to the special contradictions of Meredith's young Beauchamp and the complex discontents of Hardy's Eustacia Vye. Not all Character-writers after 1614 carried on the Overbury tendency toward smaller categories; it is noteworthy that some did not. But as one watches the variations upon favorite themes—the courtier, the fop, the scholar, the landed gentleman, the rustic—one observes that there are not many exits: unless a writer has unusual insight into human conduct he must either repeat tiresomely or decorate the old outline with witty surface arabesques or find new and inevitably less familiar types to portray. The latter exit, the door to individual portraiture, was happily opened and widened by the great eighteenth-century novelists.

Before we leave this topic, the anti-classical impulse to select individuals, we should examine again the bases of delineation in the four best Character-books of the earlier decades of the century. Of Hall's 26 Characters, only one, the "Good Magistrate," presents a type both moral and social (in which loose term I include economic, professional, occupational, and sociological features). Of the complete Overbury set of 82 Characters, about 15 treat moral (or psychological) types, about 20 present social classifications, but about 45 describe representatives of groups that have both moral and social characteristics, that have, in other words, a more complex framework than almost any of Theophrastus'. In John Stephens' set (1615) of 50 Characters the same proportion appears: approximately a quarter are moral, a quarter social, but about half are both. In John Earle's collection as printed in 1629 there were 76 Characters, of which, at first glance, about a third are of moral types, a third social, and a third both. But such a division is misleading. Earle could be so sensitive to the hidden nature of a man and also so thoughtful about his character in relation to the society in which it was formed that the resulting Character is hard to classify. A superficial count suggests that Earle was reverting to a more truly Theophrastan scheme; yet a careful reading of his Characters, of his "Vulgar-spirited Man" or his "Child" or "Paul's

Walk," indicates that even when he took a topic, a simple moral topic, from Theophrastus he investigated it with greater subtlety. Though he chose a few types according to their age as Aristotle did in his *Rhetoric*, Earle analyzed them with a finer social sense and a more poetic imagination. Yet classic typicalness is stronger in Earle than in Overbury or Stephens.

Character-writers sometimes passed off an individual for a type because of reasons other than the complexity of their classifications. Men were sufficiently agile of mind to understand Guazzo when he said that we consist of two persons, one common to all men as partakers of reason and another, because of the "diversite of mindes," peculiar to each of us.[20] Sir Walter Raleigh in the preface of his *Historie of the World* pointed out that "among those that were, of whom we reade and heare, and among those that are, whom we see and converse with; every one hath received a severall picture of face, and everie one a diverse picture of minde; every one a forme apart, every one a fancy and cogitation differing: there being nothing wherein Nature so much triumpheth, as in dissimilitude."[21] Even Ben Jonson, the great exponent of the type-character, observed that there are no fewer forms of minds than of bodies and that the "variety is incredible."[22] Perhaps Mr. Stoll is correct in asserting that in spite of Jonson's dramaturgic perversities and the modern interest in Elizabethan plotting and motivation of character, the success of Elizabethan drama lay in the individual, concrete, emotional, unmotivated characterizations.[23] Personal traits of character, the individual compulsion

[20] *The Civile Conversation*, I, 104. See also the discussion in Book II of the propriety of artificers, merchants, and gentlemen (and their wives) dressing in accordance with their class.

[21] *Sir Walter Raleigh Selections*, edited by G. E. Hadow (Oxford, 1917), p. 38.

[22] In *Timber* under the heading "Ingeniorum Discrimina."

[23] *Shakespeare and Other Masters*, pp. 92-94, 111-112.

of speech and style, immediate sympathy with a character—these, Mr. Stoll argues, gave to Shakespeare's plays their power. Othello and Hamlet must indeed have fascinated audiences by their specialness even if many another character succeeded because he fitted into a type long made familiar by Terence and Plautus and *decorum*. Cleopatra's attendants, sophisticates as Shakespeare realized they must be, know that the unpredictability of life sometimes renders doubtful the simple rules of rhetoric. All the more comic, then, is Iras's notion that an abandoned wretch like Alexas must have a cuckold's marriage if only to satisfy the rules of art: "Therefore, dear Isis, keep decorum, and fortune him accordingly."[24] In the spirit of comedy Shakespeare could follow the Horatian dictum of suitability to type: Jaques solemnly obeys it in his speechifying, Hamlet insults Polonius with a "satirical" description of old age so *decorous* that Polonius sees some method in it (II, ii), and Shakespeare amused his audiences with shrews, Thrasoes, and Plautean clever servants. But when he was serious he often perceived men to be many-sided and too complex for the ancient molds. The Character for its life had to resist the romantic "termite," the tendency towards individualism in Jacobean thinking. It did so, but there was some wavering. Though the Civil Wars checked this tendency, it triumphed in the portrait-Character of the Restoration.

The individualistic characterization of which we have been speaking is related to certain familar elements in the temper of the seventeenth century—the disillusionment and skepticism, the satiric tendency, as well as the rational, scientific impulses that variously showed themselves even before the end of Elizabeth's reign. Let us first take the satiric, analytic cast of mind and the accompanying revival of Roman epigram and satire near the

---

[24]*Anthony and Cleopatra*, I, ii. For later references to this doctrine see pp. 51-52.

turn of the century. Many explanations have been offered for this state of mind and heart. The political uncertainties of the royal succession; disillusionment following upon a period of national growth and accomplishment; economic dislocations and the lack of a proper means of caring for the new abundance of gold and silver; an intensification of Puritan earnestness; spiritual exhaustion after an enthusiastic effort to live life simultaneously on the basis of Christian, Stoic, hedonist, and Platonic doctrines; a recrudescence in bad times of medieval *memento mori* assisted by an increasing group of middle-class readers whose spiritual and mental condition had not ceased to be medieval; the disintegration of the old social ranks and the appearance about town of countless "new" people who flaunted their independence of old social taboos—these and other circumstances seem relevant for understanding the appearance in the 1590's of verse satire, caustic epigrams, the satiric drama of "humors," and satiric type-portraiture in prose pamphlets.[25] The verse forms continued to appear as late as 1620. As the Overburians composed it, the Character had much in common with these productions.[26] It took over "the mission of the Elizabethan anatomy of abuses"[27] and rather

---

[25]Oscar James Campbell in *Comicall Satyre* and Hoyt H. Hudson in his review of that work (*Journal of English and Germanic Philology*, XLIII [1944], 119-120) have much to say about the causes of the late Elizabethan spirit of satire.

[26]See my discussion pp. 91-99.

[27]Baker, *History of the English Novel*, II, 237. The prose anatomy of abuses can be seen turning into the Character-book in the anonymous *Man in the Moon*, published a year after Hall's book. Here a series of traditional social and moral types appear one by one. First Mockso describes the person's appearance; then Opinion, "somewhat criticall and taunting," sets forth the nature of the type; finally an old man, Fido, preaches to each. It is in Opinion's anatomizings of behavior and disposition that one comes upon passages that resemble Hall's Vices. See especially the opinions of the glutton and the lover. But the attachment to the framework and the insistent, fluent moralism keep the pieces out of the class of Characters.

gradually superseded the prose pamphlet. But it is the interplay of the prose Character and verse satire and epigram that concerns us here.

Roman epigrams usually castigated individuals, noting their special follies and crimes with relentless exactitude. Verse satire, on the other hand, might choose types but infrequently finished a picture, for its custom was to include several lamentable creatures in one poem with the purpose of seeming to discuss some general matter. Juvenal treated his type alternately in the singular and plural, slipping from description to damnation, from narrative to simile, from objectivity to subjective analysis, often speaking directly to his victim. His subject matter might be that of the Character, concrete and typical, but his method was not. As the verse forms and the Character continued to be written in the first decades of the century, the Greek form was sometimes Romanized—Overbury seems indebted to Jonson and Jonson to Martial —and later the Roman forms, satire and epigram, sometimes attempted to be Greek.

Though Joseph Hall carefully distinguished the method of his satires from the methods of his Characters, the differences were not always observed by English writers. Since Martial's epigram on Cotilus (III, 63) was practically a Character in verse, imitations of it by Sir John Davies and others had the same double affinity. The history of these forms before 1608, sketched in my third chapter, prepares us for what happened later, even to the continuing habit of petty thievery among authors. Samuel Rowlands, adept in the latter craft, published *The Knave of Harts* in 1612 containing a set of portraits in verse that employ the methods of the classical epigram though the knaves described came from the English books on virtues and vices. The "Busie Knave" and the "Covetous" were probably based on Hall's Characters; the "Hypocriticall Knave" was taken in large part

from Hall's "Hypocrite."[28] Here the Character fed the epigram
without altering its literary pattern. Indebtedness runs in the
opposite direction, however, in the case of *The Muses Sacrifice*
by John Davies of Hereford, published in the same year. "*The
Picture of an happy Man*," almost buried in this volume of pious
poems, is a long versified account of the ideal Stoic Christian
"That Makes a *Kingdome* of his *Minde*." It apparently inspired Sir Henry Wotton to write the much more compact poem
on the same subject which Lisle put into the fourth impression
of the Overbury *Characters* in 1614 with the heading "The
Character of a happie life."

Several of the collections of satires and epigrams published
after 1608 are not materially different from what any student
of Juvenal and Martial might produce. George Wither's *Abuses
Stript and Whipt* (1613), Richard Corbet's *The Times Whistle*
(1614?), Henry Fitzgeffrey's *Certain Elegies* (1620), and
Thomas Brewer's *Knot of Fooles* (1624) are, in the main,
Roman in manner. Discursiveness, a variation between singular
and plural, horizontal as well as perpendicular characterization of
a vice, and analysis mixed with items of behavior suggest Juvenal
as Wither's master. Corbet's picture in his second satire of a
"Vain upstart braggadochio" represents a type. This piece,
"Maddam Poppaea," and "Vain Epainnutus" may conceivably
have profited from the Character, but the usual accumulated list
of concrete actions as well as the antithetic prose style of Hall and
Overbury is conspicuously absent.[29]

The Charactering of the epigram can be seen in Richard

---

[28]Rowlands' indebtedness to Hall is pointed out in Lambert H. Ennis's
unpublished Harvard dissertation, "The Satire of Types in Elizabethan Literature."

[29]The vivid picturing of representative wrong-doers ("A Symonicall
Patron," a Jesuit, a drunkard, and so on) in John Taylor's *Water-
Cormorant His Complaint . . . fourteene Satyres* (1622) may also have
owed something to the Overbury volume.

Brathwaite's *Strappado for the Divell* (1615). His "Epigramme called the *Honest Lawyer*" and his "Epigram called the *Courtier*" begin and end like classical epigrams, and they are in couplets. But the former piece accumulates the actions and attitudes of an ideal type as Hall and Overbury would do in their preceptual Characters. And the second piece not only looks like an imitation of Overbury's caustic social pictures; it actually incorporates a great many telling phrases and ideas from Overbury's "Courtier." In Henry Hutton's *Follie's Anatomie: or Satyres and Satyricall Epigrams* (1619) there is further indication that the Character had made an impression on other literary forms. A "Timist" is drawn with some help from Hall's "Flatterer" and Overbury's "Tymist," though Hutton exercises the satirist's right to discourse as well as describe and to speak a warning to his man. The fraudulent gallant is also presented.

> Mounsier, *Bravado*, are you come t'out face,
> With your Mouchatoes, gallants of such place?
> . . . . .
> Wee'l not contest or squabble for a wall,
> Nor yet point field, though you us vassailes call.
> . . . . .
> Correct your frizled locks, and in your glasse
> Behold the picture of a foolish Asse.
> Barter your lowsie sutes for present gaine,
> Unto a Broker in rich Birchin lane.
> Compile a sonnet of your Mistresse glove.
> . . . . .
> Ride with your sweet-heart in a hackney coach.
> . . . . .
> Goe take a pipe of To. the crowded stage
> Must needs be graced with you and your page.
> . . . . .
> Where is your larum watch your Turkies Rings,
> Muske-comfits, bracelets, & such idle things?
> . . . . .

Dive in Mechanicks books, till in the streete
Seargeants arrest, convey thee to the Fleete,
And there in durance cag'd, consume with woe,
Beg with a purse, and sing *Fortune's my foe.*

As in a Character, the fellow is outlined by his actions. But the chronological ordering of the material and the scornful address to the poor victim as well as the use of verse justify the label "Satyricall Epigram." Seventeenth-century imitations of Juvenal and Martial gained amplitude, typicalness perhaps, and probably greater freedom in topical allusion from the example of Hall and Overbury. The epigram, on the other hand, must have helped create an audience for the Character and may have encouraged the bent toward tartness and individual portraiture. What one also notices is the identity of tone in satires, epigrams, and Characters of reprehensible types. Something is rotten in England, or so they seem to say; the times are out of joint. Overbury may be more cynical than Wither but not more so than Rowlands or Corbet. In this respect, perhaps, the Theophrastan genre was contaminated by Roman satire. Stephens and Earle did something, though not enough, to restore the original spirit of the amused philosopher-scientist.

The connection between the rational, scientific temper of the seventeenth century and the theory of Character-writing also deserves a word. The procedure of Theophrastus was deductive. He started with a one-sentence definition of an abstract quality and then assembled from concrete increments of behavior a picture of a man especially governed by that abstract quality. The public speaker, said Aristotle, must learn what the various kinds of men are, the kinds, it was assumed, being already established. In the second book of the *Advancement of Learning* (1605) Francis Bacon deplored the gaps in men's study of moral philosophy and asserted that before much could be done in that important field we should "set down sound and true distributions and descriptions of the several characters and tempers of men's natures and dispositions, especially having regard to those differences which are most radical in being the fountains and causes of the rest, or most frequent in concurrence of commixture."[30] For there are many kinds of minds, some disposed to great matters, as Aristotle said, and some to small, some pleased in others' good fortune and some displeased in it, some loving quiet and some loving action. Bacon's paragraph reminds one of many other Elizabethan classifications of men, and its opening sentence might be taken as an injunction to Character-writing, especially as an aid to moral philosophy and moral instruction.[31] Perhaps that is precisely how Joseph Hall and Nicholas Breton understood it. But we must not forget what Bacon a few pages before had said in distinguishing between the "Magistral" method in logic, which uses what is known without assisting the advancement of learning, and the method of "Probation," which has "progression" as its end. The latter is rarely adopted.

> For as knowledges are now delivered, there is a kind of contract of error between the deliverer and the receiver: for he that delivereth knowledge desireth to deliver it in such form as may be best believed, and not as may be best examined; and he that receiveth knowledge desireth rather present satisfaction than expectant inquiry; and so rather not to doubt than not to err; glory making the author not to lay open his weakness, and sloth making the disciple not to know his strength. But knowledge that is delivered as

---

[30] *The Philosophical Works of Francis Bacon*, p. 142. I am indebted to J. L. Lievsay for calling my attention to this sentence.

[31] Set off by itself at the end of Bacon's *Historie of the Raigne of King Henry The Seventh* (1622) is a concentrated account of the habits and character and policies of Henry. It is printed in italics and half of the paragraphs begin with the word *he*. If Bacon had a literary model, it probably was the portraits of Tacitus and Sallust rather than the Character.

a thread to be spun on, ought to be delivered and intimated, if it were possible, *in the same method wherein it was invented;* and so is it possible of knowledge induced. But in this same anticipated and prevented knowledge, no man knoweth how he came to the knowledge which he hath obtained.[32]

Which method does the Character adopt? The "Magistral," certainly, which Bacon said was widely enjoyed. For instead of documenting a picture with the fact that this detail about the Penurious Man came from a newly rich man and that detail from a man recently impoverished and this other from a man usually generous but, when we saw him, freshly disturbed by an extravagant wife—instead, in other words, of examining separate cases statistically and scientifically to see into the complex and variable roots of men's behavior, the Characterist assembles and blends in a Character all the data from many individual and necessarily dissimilar men and thus makes one typical figure of a man who never lived. The "Probative" method would present the details separately and analytically in an essay. Bacon's essays, even those on youth and age and on married and single life, are more "Probative" than the Character could be in that they adopt a comparative and piecemeal method and do not present universal representatives of human groups. But on the other hand, as John Stephens or Overbury or Earle contemplated society and broke it up into its multiform components, abandoning the simple moral classifications of Theophrastus (and Hall) for a subtler treatment of social-moral-local types, the process became increasingly scientific. "Shadowing" in the art of portraiture was being superseded by more exact line and color. But the Character had to continue to be "Magistral." That is why the polemic writers of the mid-century made so much use of it and why, after 1660, it was kept

[32]*The Philosophical Works of Francis Bacon*, p. 124.

alive by the satirists and moralists, by Tom Brown and Samuel
Butler and Joseph Addison, rather than by John Evelyn, Bishop
Sprat, or John Locke. It could not be hospitable to a "method
referred to Progression."[33]

But it need not lack truth. The comments of Joseph Hall
and John Earle strike one occasionally as deep and final. Perhaps
their knowledge of men's hearts was intuitive. Perhaps it was
one of the rewards of living in a troubled time when all Church-
men especially were bound to examine motives, in themselves and
in others. The Character, by its nature dependent upon classification and deduction, assumed the introspective cast, sought the
imaginative depth that can be found in other writing of the time.
It could not become really statistical, but it could become deeper
in its analyses. Earle went farther than a simple division into
good and bad, black and white. His "Downright Scholar," for
example, which was a protest against many previous sketches of
the pedant and don, presents a type, but a type in which black and
white are so combined that the white shines through the black
to produce an appealing gray. Occasionally the Characterist's
straining for greater truth within a logical framework that was
being rendered archaic, the tension between the necessity of treating recognizable types and a desire to express an individual discovery about human nature, a disharmony between the Theophrastan
precedent of dispassionate objectivity and the intense feelings
of disapproval that Hall and sometimes Earle and Overbury
wished to express gave to the Character under its glittering ornamentation of cadence, puns, metaphors, conundrums, paradoxes,
and alliteration a truly baroque effect. Even between the time
of Nashe and Lodge and that of Earle fresh and natural description, vigor and graphic invention yielded to a more psychological analysis, to a much more intellectual approach, and to a

---

[33]*Ibid.*, p. 24.

more self-conscious style. Sixteenth-century type-satire had become in a measure "metaphysical." It was almost never, therefore, to become merely Theophrastan.

An artistic genre may best be defined by what it does, by discovering what pleasure it has as its function to provide. Theophrastus' Characters offer the reader an account of the characteristic behavior of a plausible man who suggests an entire, special, familiar moral branch of the human family. Because of a simple style and a truthful, interesting selection of action and speech (dress would hardly serve in homogeneous Athens), Theophrastus has the extra effect of humor though he never smiles. He is dogmatic, not tentative nor theoretical nor in the least argumentative. Because it is the essence of the type, the efficient cause, that he is after, he ignores chronology and a fixed setting, usually, and goes backwards and forwards in time. And to retain the appearance of actuality he almost without exception uses the singular number and the objective third person. The whole piece covers not much more than a page. The pleasure obtained in an attentive reading of Theophrastus is so distinctive that, once having enjoyed it consciously, the reader is not likely to mistake other pleasures for it.

But to define the seventeenth-century Character, it must be apparent, is not so easy, partly because the writers and readers of the Character no doubt had heard of Theophrastus, were glad to have his classical blessing on their activities, but rarely could have read him. Not that there were not texts enough. Besides some nine editions, none complete, of the Greek text before 1599, and at least six Latin translations, there was in that year Casaubon's volume containing a Latin translation of twenty-eight Characters, followed by other Greek or Greek-Latin editions in 1604, 1612, 1613, 1617, 1618, 1628, 1632, 1633, 1638 and in later years. All but the puzzling 1604 and 1628 editions[34] were published on the Continent, not in England; but Casaubon himself was in London, Ely, and Canterbury from 1610 to 1614. The striking fact is that though the Character, recognized by name and form, began to flourish after Hall naturalized it, there are very few references to Theophrastus in the literature of the time, even in the Character-books. The English translation of Theophrastus by John Healey, who died about 1610, may have been done several years before his death and perhaps circulated in manuscript before it was finally printed in 1616 with his translation of Epictetus' *Manual*.

It has been asserted that Healey's translation "fell perfectly flat."[35] The truth of the matter is hard to discover. Healey's translation possesses in embryo several stylistic features that became permanent, conspicuous sources of delight in English Character-writing—tart and colloquial language, the choice of illustrative data from the meridian of London and the jargon of the moment, and a slightly Euphuistic shaping in the phrases ("Garlick is as sweet as gilliflower," "friends and familiars"). But these features may have come into the Characters of Hall and the rest by way of the pamphleteers of the 1590's. Whether Nashe or Healey accounts for these lively and artificial ways of writing, they must be incorporated in our definition of the seventeenth-

---

[34] A unique copy of ΘΕΟΦΡΑΣΤΟΥ ΗΘΙΚΟΙ χαραχτῆρες *Theophrasti Notationes Morum* (Oxford, 1604) in the Bodleian Library was briefly discussed in *The Athenaeum*, May 6, 1905. The suggestion was made that the book was privately printed for Scaliger's use. Two copies have been noted by Marian Harman (*Bibliographical Society of America Papers*, XXXII [1938], 98-101) of a book with the same Greek-Latin title published at Oxford in 1628. Both books contain only the Greek text, but they seem to have been printed from different plates. Harman's suggestion that the rarity of the books is to be explained on the ground of their being school texts strikes me, in view of the paucity of contemporary references to Theophrastus, as insufficient.

[35] H. B. Lathrop, *Translations from the Classics into English* (Madison, Wisconsin, 1933), p. 263.

century Character. John Stephens put a motto adapted from Theophrastus on the title-page of his *Satyrical Essayes Characters* (1615),[36] and in the essay "Of Poetry" which preceded the Characters he deplored the use of similes that were less familiar than the thing described and the use of mathematics and astronomy to illustrate "Grammer"; yet like everyone after Hall he wrote a figurative, witty language not authorized by Theophrastus. Richard Brathwaite in the dedicatory epistle in *Whimzies* (1631) condemned the "clinchings" and other affected and obscure wit of earlier Character-writers yet could himself hardly resist such decorations for as much as a page at a time. John Hoskins, the only English writer whom I have found discussing or even mentioning Theophrastus' Characters before 1608, attributed to the influence of the Characters Sidney's decorum, not his fancy manner of composing sentences. But a highly wrought, exuberant style became a *sine quo non* of the English Character, which was perpetually self-conscious. Not infrequently the manner ran away with the matter. We have noticed, for example, that the Overbury "Tailor" and "Sailor" are brittle constructions of wit. From those pieces and similar ones John Heath apparently drew the idea for the nine brief Characters printed at the end of his *House of Correction: or, Certayne Satyricall Epigrams* (1619). Each starts with a metaphor—"A Drunkard is a Master of Defense," "A Curtizan is a Musician"—which is expanded in enough puns to form a little picture. An artificial manner persisted in the Character, no doubt, because of the very nature of the genre: since the sketches had to be of types, after the first Character-books had explored the field the only originality attainable, especially because of the wealth of type-portraiture already in print in pamphlets and verse, would be in interpretation

---

[36]See p. 227 n.8. The motto did not appear on the title page of the "second impression" published in the same year.

or style. The usual non-Theophrastan emphasis on clothes and on local allusions had the same compulsion. Unlike the Greek master, the Jacobean Character-writers eventually faced the threat of exhausted material. It is a mark of their ingenuity that they kept the threat so well hidden.

The highly-wrought style that became a regular feature of the seventeenth-century Character and that accounts for part of its appeal was more than an accumulation of figures and wit. The texture and construction of the sentences are part of it. For the Character, from the beginning in Joseph Hall, assumed the Senecan manner. This Senecan prose style, adopted by Montaigne, Justus Lipsius, Francis Bacon, and others in a deliberate revolt against the suavity, copiousness, and empty formalism of the Ciceronian prose widely admired in the Renaissance, has been studied and described in an important series of articles by M. W. Croll and George Williamson.[37] It is characterized by a brevity in clauses or sentences, by a lack of symmetry in the parts of a sentence, by an omission of the usual syntactical connectives, and by a habit of "exploding" an idea abruptly in the first part of a sentence or sentence-group, allowing further aspects of the idea to emerge in later clauses. Obscurity, roughness, a natural but not always orthodox construction, antithesis of thought, a seesaw cadence—these are part of the style, as Mr. Croll and Mr. Williamson have pointed out. Derived from Seneca and Tacitus by writers who admired Seneca's moral philosophy, the style was associated at first with a Stoic point of view. In some of Montaigne's essays, in Justus Lipsius' Latin works, in Hall's Char-

---

[37] M. W. Croll, "Attic Prose: Lipsius, Montaigne, Bacon," in *Schelling Anniversary Papers* (New York, 1923); "The Baroque Style in Prose," *Studies in English Philology*, edited by Malone and Ruud (Minneapolis, 1929), pp. 427-456; George Williamson, "The Rhetorical Pattern of Neo-Classical Wit," *Modern Philology*, XXXIII (1935), 55-81; "Senecan Style in the Seventeenth Century," *Philological Quarterly*, XV (1936), 321-351.

acters of Virtues the style and the point of view are Senecan.[38]
The Overbury "Wise Man" and "Noble Spirit" preserve Hall's
manner as well as the Stoic ideal of virtue repeatedly presented in
Hall's first Book. John Stephens' "Complete Man"[39] and
"Contented Man," the latter opening with a figure that echoes
one in Hall's "Humble Man," are likewise Senecan. But Nicholas
Breton, who worked out a Euphuistic prose style of his own based
on Hall's Senecan manner, likewise departed from Hall in his
ideals: his conception of the "Wise Man" in *The Good and the
Badde* is pious and Calvinistic. John Earle, who drew no Stoic
types, his ideal being rational and regularly Christian, also moderated the Senecan style which he inherited. But as early as
1614 a satiric spirit had largely displaced the Stoic in the Character.

Both Mr. Croll and Mr. Williamson notice that the Senecan
kind of sentence, whether the short, jerky, syntactically discon-
nected sort ("période coupé") or the looser, longer kind employing antithesis and absolute constructions, was commonly employed
by Character-writers. The influence of Stoicism on Hall and of
Hall on subsequent authors and the influence of Bacon through
his essays explain how the style got a start in the Character.
There is another reason why it should have been kept there.
It has to do with the nonchronological order, the studied lack of
easy, flowing thought in the anti-Ciceronian compositions. The
third earl of Shaftesbury later said of Seneca's prose that "every

---

[38]Croll, p. 126, argues that Lipsius' Stoic Christianity probably influenced Hall's *Epistles* and *Meditations* even though he later opposed him
in sectarian controversy. That Hall satirized Lipsius in *Mundus Alter et
Idem* (cf. Rudolf Kirk's introduction to his edition of Lipsius' *Two Bookes
of Constancie*, New Brunswick, 1939, p. 12) he fails to notice.

[39]"*A Compleate Man Is an impregnable Tower:* and the more batteries
he hath undergone, the better able he is to continue immoveable. The time
& he are alwaies friends: for he is troubled with no more than hee can
well employ; neither is *that* lesse, then will every way discharge his Office;
So he neither surfets with *Idlenesse*, nor action . . ."

period, every sentence almost, is independent, and may be taken asunder, transposed, postponed, anticipated, or set in any new order, as you fancy."[40] These words can be applied to most portions of Theophrastus' Characters. But the *non sequitur* is not so much a literary style there as a technique employed to prevent a chronological sequence in the data assembled. It is true that a chronological arrangement appears in Lycon's "Drunkard" and in the sketch of the pretender to wealth in the *Rhetorica ad Herennium.*[41] But such a narrative tends to suggest an individual person on a particular day, whereas the Character should evoke any typical man of the group at any typical moment. The chronological order emphasizes the man; the Character-writer wishes to high light the essence of the man, which in any non-sequential order of events would still govern and form him. In this respect at least Ciceronian prose is wrong, Senecan prose is right, for the Character.

Among various features of the latter style, that which is most conspicuous in seventeenth-century Characters is one which I have previously mentioned for its attractiveness. I refer to the frequent use of a scheme of sentences beginning "He is . . . He does . . . He is . . . He acts . . ." with perpetual variation in the pattern of the rest of the sentence. Mr. Croll speaks of this "mannerism" of the Character to illustrate the concealed asymmetry often found in anti-Ciceronian prose. The last sentences of Hall's "Profane Man" show it thus:

> Hee cannot thinke of death with patience, without ter-
> rour, which he therefore feares worse than hell, because
> this he is sure of, the other hee but doubts of. Hee comes
> to Church as to the Theater, saving that not so willinglie,
> for companie, for custome, for recreation, perhaps for sleepe;
> or to feed his eyes or his eares: as for his soule hee cares no

---

[40] Quoted by Williamson, *Philological Quarterly*, XV, 323.
[41] See pp. 22-26 above.

more than if hee had none. Hee loves none but himselfe, and that not enough to seeke his true good; neither cares hee on whom hee treads, that hee may rise. His life is full of licence, and his practise of outrage. Hee is hated of God as much as hee hateth goodnesse, and differs little from a divell, but that he hath a body.

The other features of the "période coupé" can likewise be illustrated from Hall—the "exploded" idea in the first part of a sentence,[42] the misleading *and*,[43] the hovering, imaginative order. But they are less likely to appear in Overbury, Webster, Stephens, and Earle. Instead, the "loose" Senecan style, employing *and, for, nor* in its free but antithetic movement, suits these less Stoic writers. Stephens says of his "Ubiquitarie": "In his behaviour hee would seeme *French, Italian, Spanish,* or any thing, so he may seeme unvulgar; accounting it barbarous not to contemne his own Nation, or the common good; because he loves to bee more valued by seeming singularly pretious: His habite onely discovers him to be true *English*: and to be weary of the place, colours his emploiment." Earle's sentences are of the loose variety also, though they vary a good deal. The beginning of "A Tavern" has something of the broken, spontaneous effect of anti-Ciceronian writing:

A Tavern Is a degree, or (if you will), a paire of stayres above an Alehouse, where men are drunke with more credit and Apologie. If the Vintners nose be at dore, it is a signe sufficient, but the absence of this is supplyd by the Ivie-bush. The rooms are ill breath'd, like the drinkers that have been washt wel over night, and are smelt too fasting next morning; not furnisht with Beds apt to be

---

[42]"The Malcontent" is "a slave to envie, and loseth flesh with fretting, not so much at his owne infelicitie, as at others good; neither hath he leasure to ioy in his owne blessings whilest another prospereth."

[43]His "Honest Man" would "rather complaine than offend, & hates sinne more for the indignite of it, than the danger."

defil'd, but more necessary implements, Stooles, Table, and a Chamber-pot. It is a broacher of more newes then hogs-heads, & more iests then newes, which are sukt up heere by some spongie braine, and from thence squeazed into a Comedy.

More characteristic of Earle is a simpler construction, less asymmetrical, not particularly succinct, in which two or three independent clauses are linked by *and* and the Senecan seesaw and antithesis have been transmuted into a milder cadence. Thus he writes in "A Downright Scholar":

> He cannot kisse his hand and cry Madame, nor talke idly enough to beare her company. His smacking of a Gentle-woman is somewhat too savory, and he mistakes her nose for her lippe. A very Woodcock would puzzle him in carving, and hee wants the logicke of a Capon. He has not the glib faculty of sliding over a tale, but his words come squeamishly out of his mouth, and the laughter commonly before the iest. He names this word Colledge too often, and his discourse beats too much on the University. The perplexity of mannerlinesse will not let him feed, and he is sharpe set at an Argument when hee should cut his meate. He is discarded for a gamester at all games but one and thirty, and at tables he reaches not beyond doublets.

The cadence is so strong and regular that were the phrasing less natural one might suppose Earle to have been captured by the spell of the Euphuists and like them to have pursued the "sweet falling of the clauses" which Bacon deplored. Perhaps in fact he had. In the first edition of *Micro-cosmographie* (1628) Earle ridiculed the "Self-conceited Man" for preferring *"Lipsius* his hopping stile before either *Tully* or *Quintilian"*—an astonishing remark to come from a Character-writer. By the time the "fift" edition (1629) of *Micro-cosmographie* appeared, that remark had been deleted. Presumably Earle, like Bacon, changed his attitude toward Senecan style; but whereas Bacon at first approved of it and later (1623) decided that it was a "distemper of learning" artificially heavy and appealing only to the "meaner capacities" of his day,[44] Earle at first ridiculed it and then, possibly because he saw there was a good deal of it in his own Characters, decided to withdraw his criticism. Earle, like Breton, revealed a liking for suavity in prose; but Earle was too good a Character-writer to be able to do without some of Lipsius' effects. The theory of the genre rendered useful the rhetorical *non-sequitur* of Senecan prose and a sentence construction that follows the movement of thought (even if a mere tabulation of behavior). The short cadence was not necessary, but it attached itself to the Character and for twenty years at least became obligatory. All these features help account for the vogue of the genre.

Another appealing aspect of the Character, then and now, is the personal interest which a good collection of such sketches must inevitably have. The reader perpetually smiles as he sees his friends caught on one of the barbs in "The Pedant" or "The Malcontent" or "The Proud Man," and his enemies are everywhere. And, furthermore, not because the types are poorly defined but because human nature is so very hospitable to folly, a reader is bound to catch several unexpected glimpses of his own face in a Theophrastan collection. (The books of 1630-1632 are less amusing in this respect because more limited to local description than the earlier, more classical ones.) Theophrastus' appeal to our critical, if not to our malicious, faculties the earlier Character-writers banked on heavily, as an unidentified writer observed. In "A Character of one that writes Characters" he set forth the matter thus.

> Heres á Crittick that writes Animadversions uppon the fairest coppyes, & studyes Men as some study Bookes not to

---

[44]*De Augmentis* (*The Works of Francis Bacon,* edited by Spedding-Ellis-Heath, Boston, 1861, II, 127).

find out the notions but the errata; & pleaseth himselfe
more to looke upon the mote that Venus had, than uppon
her beauty; & take's himselfe to be extreame wise because
hee can see that in another which hee stood too neare to
see in himselfe.—If hee comes into company hee setts there
onely, as á painter doth to draw á picture; but hee doth
not as hee, whoe being to draw the picture of Venus, tooke
what was excellent in each person hee saw; but as if to draw
the Picture of á fury, takes that which is most deformnd.
He doth not like the Be goe to the Rose, but like the fingers
to the Thistles; & differs as much from á wise reprover as
a hand in the margent doth from the critticks nayle.—He's
a player whoe commonly reproves himselfe uppon the stage
for what constantly hee doth off from it.—His end is not
to make folks mend, but to make them laugh, & tells them
more what they are, than what they should be.—In á word
characters are commonly written by the Best witts, & the
Best men learn by them.[45]

This Character-writer proved his point by his own example, for
in ignoring all the Characters of good types he likewise went
only to the thistles. Joseph Hall offered as many Vices as Virtues. Breton did the same in *The Good and the Badde*. Against
the good types of people the Overbury volume set about 15 types
drawn with relative impartiality and about 55 regarded as
lamentably bad or foolish. Whenever Thomas Adams imitated
the Character in his sermons, it was to damn a type. John
Stephens found 8 types to praise, 10 about whom he was non-
committal, but 32 whom he ridiculed. John Earle, nearer to
Theophrastus in spirit than the previous writers, none the less
described with open hostility some 28 types, wrote with something like Theophrastus' kind of objectivity about 40 types, and
offered only 7 types of the elect. The Character was found to
be best adapted to giving satiric pleasure.

---

[45]Bodleian MS Add. A. 301. Abbreviations have been expanded in the
transcription.

But the idealistic sketches, by no means inconspicuous in the gallery of seventeenth-century Characters, were managed, as I have already pointed out,[46] not by the method of Theophrastus so much as by the similar methods of Seneca, the Bible, and Christian exhortation—all powerful forces, in the early years of the century, lending support to the vogue of the Character. An ideal figure possesses more virtues than one. Joseph Hall's "Wise Man," "Honest Man," and "Faithful Man" have much in common, and all were embraced in Hall's later Character of "An Happy Man." Furthermore, though a man's actions speak louder than his words, his heart alone declares his quality. Subjective analysis, an anti-Theophrastan method, was necessary for reliable depictions of the "Wise Man," the "Worthy Commander in the Wars," Earle's beloved "Child," the "Fair and Happy Milkmaid," and all other good moral types. None of the authorities dealing with the rhetorical figures *descriptio*, χαρακτηρισμός, *notatio*, nor Casaubon writing on the Character had forbidden this serious modification of Theophrastus' method.

With a handful of other explanations of the vogue of the Character we shall end this part of our discussion. Of fashionable court wits like Overbury and Lovelace and Suckling and Francis Lenton the composition of slight pieces only could properly be expected. The Character, like the lyric, would be assumed to call for just such a momentary and ingenious concentration of mind as might amuse a gentleman. The author of *Choice, Chance, and Change* (1606) gives us a hint of how in fiction and maybe at James's court the composition of a Character might come about. In a conversation with Tidero a fine lady speaks: "Lend me your little Table book in your pocket: for I did a little overlooke you the other daie and I am much mistaken, but I sawe you writing of verses."[47] "In deede Mistresse," replies

---

[46]See pp. 130-131 above. [47]Sig. I₃.

Tidero, "it is true, upon some certaine idle notes that I took out of my observation of certaine Creatures, I wrote a fewe idle odde lines." His compositions, each "a kinde of Epigramicall sonnet," describe a "finicall Asse," a "shamfast clown in gaie clothes," a minx called a "cunning Tit," and several other interesting creatures. Some are types, some individuals; the sketches are part sonnet, part epigram, and even part Character. The implication is that such exercises served merely to amuse oneself and one's friends. A. C. Benson adopts this notion for his pleasant picture[48] of John Earle among the learned and intellectual visitors to Lord Falkland's hereditary estate, scribbling off Characters on random pieces of paper and dropping them over someone's shoulder or leaving them on the table in one of the rooms at Great Tew. The picture is vivid and appealing, but its authenticity is seriously shaken by our discovery that Earle's Characters repeatedly echo the words and ideas of Theophrastus, Hall, and Stephens. Characters may have been casually composed at Great Tew in the manner Mr. Benson suggests, but not those in *Micro-cosmographie*. I know of no evidence that Character-writing ever became a parlor game. There is probability, nevertheless, in the argument that its small compass drew authors into attempting it. One should observe also that the form had not only classic authority but also the respectability given it by the reverend Dr. Joseph Hall and the court associations lent by Sir Thomas Overbury, whose "untimely and much lamented death" is variously alluded to on the title pages of the early editions of the collection. To the latter fashionable interest was soon added the exciting and terrible revelation that Sir Thomas, the author of an attractive, earnest poem on marriage as well as of the keen sketches of contemporary society, had been murdered,

---

[48]*Essays* (1896), p. 21. See below p. 238 n.25 for further discussion of this matter.

probably at the instance of the wife of his patron, the king's favorite. If the spirit of satire was abroad, here was assurance that it would not immediately die. The fact that the 1664 edition of the Overbury collection was labeled the seventeenth proves that it did not.

There were many reasons, then, philosophical, religious, social, literary, and personal, for the emergence and development, during the Jacobean period, of the Character as a self-conscious literary form. Behind or beside all the causes stood the example, not always seen, and the theory, always and necessarily preserved, of Theophrastus.

VII

THE
CHARACTER IN RELATION
TO THE
ESSAY AND THE SERMON

I f there were scattered before one on a table copies of the first
editions of the Character-books of Hall, Overbury, and Earle,
Breton's *Characters upon Essaies* (1615), Bacon's *Essayes. Religious Meditations. Places of perswasion and disswasion* (1597)
and his later *Essaies* (1612), Stephens' *Satyrical Essayes Characters and Others* (1615), and Mason's *Handful of Essaies. Or
Imperfect Offers* (1621) one would notice that they look a good
deal alike. All are little books; some—Earle's and Mason's and
the first edition of Bacon's—are really tiny.[1] They seem to have
been designed to slip pleasantly into the hand, then into the pocket
or under the girdle, whence to be readily extracted in an idle
moment. They are made up of many short, pithy pieces, miscellaneous but on traditional topics, *utile et dulce.* In the title
pages the prominent word is sometimes "Character," sometimes
"essay"; often both appear. In the minds of many people the
two terms were never to be precisely distinguished.

The difficulty was that because the essayist often wrote on
topics belonging to the Character-writer, even treating them for
a sentence or two in his manner, and conversely because the English Character-writer inevitably indulged the Renaissance pro-

---

[1] The first editions of Bacon's, Earle's, and Mason's collections are thin
volumes, approximately 3 inches wide and 5 tall. Hall's, Stephens', and
Breton's books and Bacon's second edition (1612) measure roughly 4 by 6
inches. Overbury's first edition, packed with miscellaneous matter in addition to the Characters, is slightly over 5 by 7 inches—a giant in this
company. It shrank in some later editions. Lenton's, Brathwaite's *(Whimzies),* and Saltonstall's volumes reverted to pigmy proportions, all being
less than 3 by 5 inches.

pensity for moral generalization, the two literary forms were often not seen to be, as they truly are, different—different in literary pattern and in function or theory.[2] The idea of the type and the objectifying of it in a single being whose actions and perhaps whose thoughts are cumulatively assembled—these are obligatory for the Character, merely sporadically useful to the essay. Succinctness, a definite bias, and a persistent following of the same subject (almost of the same grammatical subject) must also be present in the Character, whereas the essay may omit them.

Bacon's name was early associated with the Character, and it is to his influence that the characteristic epigrammatic sentences, antitheses, and short rhythm of the genre are often attributed. It is more probable, however, that both Bacon and Hall were drawn to this fashion of prose by their admiration for Seneca and by their familiarity with a similar style in relevant passages in English Bibles. Something rather like this style had already been established for type-portraiture by sixteenth-century moralists and satiric pamphleteers and fell as a legacy to Hall and his successors. Nicholas Breton by dedicating to Bacon his *Characters upon Essaies* brought Bacon's name into the history of the genre when the latter was still new and could profit from so dignified an association. "I have read," wrote Breton in his dedicatory epistle, "of many Essaies, and a kinde of Charactering of them, by such, as when I lookt into the forme, or nature of their writing, I have beene of the conceit, that they were but Imitators of your breaking the ice of their inventions." What Bacon thought these words meant I do not know. Hall's, Overbury's, and perhaps Stephens' collections were then in print, but the evidence suggests that Breton was thinking principally of Hall's. Actually Bacon's essays, in spite of their treating old men and young, parents,

---

[2]See my earlier remarks, pp. 81-83, and Hugh Walker, *The English Essay and Essayists* (London, 1928), pp. 94-114.

princes, married and single people, and a few other classifications sometimes chosen by Character-writers, have little of the Character about them. The title "Of Young men and Age" used in the 1612 *Essaies* for the essay which in the 1625 volume was headed "Of Youth and Age" indicates correctly the mixed and discursive manner of Bacon's writing. Usually his titles mention an abstract topic, and in view of Bacon's generalized treatment such titles are more appropriate. The Latin meditation "De Hypocritis" in his 1597 volume is also an essay. Since his purpose was to consider both or all sides of a question, he could not be satisfied with a type figure but would instead use the method of "Probation."

Except, then, for a common choice of the problems of ethical and social conduct to discuss and of a Senecan style to imitate, Bacon's and Hall's pieces are not alike. Breton attempted to bridge the gap though conscious that "Characters are not every mans construction." In a sense he copied Hall's method: the subject of the sketch—wisdom, peace, knowledge, fear—is kept as the grammatical subject of most of the sentences, and its acts, desires, appearances, effects are listed. But the subject in Breton is a personified abstraction, not an abstracted person. What it does or is or seems Breton perpetually couches in a metaphor (that is, he doubles the abstractness) so that the result is remote from the Character as Hall wrote it and hardly recognizable as akin to the sketches of Theophrastus.[3] Instead, Breton's first sketch, "Wisdom," looks like an extension of the essay on wisdom in the seventh and eighth chapters of the Apocryphal "Wisdom of

---

[3]What this sort of personification would be if the extra metaphors were not added can be seen in a passage in Daniel Tuvill's *Essayes, Morall and Theologicall* (1609), p. 173: "True valour is not headstrong; Obstinate opinions are not of her company; nor selfe-will'd Resolutions of her counsell: Shee stands not upon Termes of honour and reputation with her Fortune, but willingly treades the path to which necessity doth drive her," and so on.

Solomon." His accumulating of metaphors is no doubt in imitation of Hall's opening and closing flourishes. Hall's "Humble Man" is a "lowly valley sweetly planted, and well watered; the proud mans earth, whereon he trampleth," and his "True Friend" is "the comfort of miseries, the guide of difficulties, the ioy of life, the treasure of earth; and no other than a good Angell clothed in flesh." Breton petrifies Hall's cadence of four and, in Mr. Greenough's phrase,[4] becomes a quadrumaniac.

> Peace, is a Calme in Conceit, where the Senses take pleasure, in the rest of the Spirit: It is Natures holy day after Reasons labour, and Wisdoms musique in the Concords of the minde: It is a blessing of Grace, a bounty of Mercy, a proofe of Love, and, a preserver of life: It holds no Arguments, knowes no quarrells, is an enemie to sedition, and a continuance of Amitie: It is the root of plenty, the Tree of pleasure, the fruit of Love, and the sweetnesse of life . . . It is a grace in a Court, and a glory in a Kingdom, a blessing in a Family, and a happinesse in a Commonwealth: It fills the rich mans cofers, and feeds the poore mans labour: It is the Wise-mans study, and the Good-mans ioy: who love it, are gracious, who make it, are blessed, who keep it are happy, and who breake it, are miserable: It hath no dwelling with Idolatry, nor friendship with falshood, for hir life is in Truth, and in hir, all is *Amen*. But lest in the Iustice of Peace, I may rather be reproved for my Ignorance of hir worth, then thought worthy to speake in his prayse, with this only Conclusion, in the commendation of Peace, I will draw to an end, and hold my peace: It was a message of Ioy at the birth of Christ, a song of Ioy, at the imbracement of Christ, an assurance of Ioy, at the death of Christ, and shall be the fulnesse of Ioy, at the coming of Christ.

Reading just one of the Characters in this first collection by

---

[4] Nicholas Breton, "Character-Writer and Quadrumaniac," *Anniversary Papers . . . of George Lyman Kittredge* (Boston, 1913); reprinted in *Collected Studies by Chester Noyes Greenough.*

Breton is enough; abstraction, an obsession with figures, and quadrumania have led him into monotony and occasionally into meaninglessness. (The emptiness of his work can be exposed by shifting about the nouns in his sets of four without serious damage to the sense: why may we not write, concerning Peace, "Who love it are blessed, who make it are happy, who keep it are gracious"; "It hath no dwelling with falsehood, nor friendship with idolatry"?) Breton has adopted in exaggerated and mechanical fashion those elements in Hall which are not Theophrastan but which may be expected, though not in such mad persistence, in Bacon or any essayist. Some crossbreeding of the two genres was to be expected, but Breton forced the union and got a grotesque product.

A more natural conjunction of the essay and Character can be seen in the discussion "Of Ambition" in *Horæ Subsecivæ. Observations and Discourses* (1620), probably written by Sir William Cavendish.[5] The piece begins, as Hall's "Ambitious" does, with a set of descriptive phrases: "It is an unlimited desire, never satisfied. A continuall proiecting without stop. An undefatigable search of those things wee wish for, though not want. No contentment in a present state, though fortunate, and prosperous." Next comes a development of the idea, utilized in Hall's Character and in Bacon's "Of Ambition" in the 1612 *Essaies,* that the ambitious man is dangerous when thwarted. Cavendish seems to draw on both authors and both literary forms, but the main effect is certainly that of the essay.[6]

The gradual emergence of the Character form and idea within the essay can also be traced in a volume that appeared only a year after Hall's. This work, Daniel Tuvill's *Essayes, Morall*

---

[5]See Douglas Bush, *English Literature in the Earlier Seventeenth Century* (Oxford, 1945, p. 508), for evidence that Cavendish wrote this work and the *Discourse Against Flatterie,* mentioned below p. 199.
[6]In other essays in the collection there are debts to Overbury.

and Theologicall (reissued in 1629 as *Vade Mecum*) has at least three passages[7] that personify a moral quality and describe it in a half-allegorical style common in earlier homiletic writing. Another passage, on showy pretenders to philosophy, would seem closer to the subjective variety of Character were it in the singular. Finally in another passage Tuvill writes as follows: "A generous and heroicke spirit will yeelde to Fortun, as he sees occasion. He will not strive to swim against the wave, to sayle against the winde. The greatnes of his minde gives place to the weakenes of his meanes: when he cannot what he would; he wils but what hee can: & thinks those plots and counsels to be best, which though they be inglorious, & want that lustre, which prosperitie might lend them, are yet convenient to bee followed in regard of circumstances."[8] Here we have a simpler, shorter, less figurative copy of Hall's Characters of Virtues.

If the essayist sometimes depended upon the Theophrastan genre for point and vividness, how much more defensibly might the writer of a treatise do so. In the case of Robert Burton's *Anatomy of Melancholy* (1621), since the matter was going to be identical often with that of Theophrastus and Hall and Earle, the appearance from time to time of something resembling a Character is not surprising. Burton's purpose, it is well known, was to set forth in detail the causes, symptoms, and remedies for various states of mind and feeling. He assumed, of course, that men could be diagnosed in groups, whether cases of head melancholy or wind melancholy, whether scholars, "Temporizing Statesmen," Puritans, the rich, Formalists, "politick Machiavelians," or what not. His method therefore often seems "magistral," in Bacon's phrase, and he can state the symptoms of the covetous man as they were "elegantly expressed by *Theophrastus* in his

---

[7] Pages 1-3, 22-23, 174-175.
[8] Pages 177-178.

character of a covetous man."[9]   But so serious a scientist as Burton had also to be "probative"; hence he describes groups in the plural rather than in one representative figure, and he piles up descriptive data from many and even contradictory authorities. (Plautus, Horace, Lucian, and others supplement and document Theophrastus on the covetous.) Because he related physical health to one's social and moral being, Burton easily ran off into moral discussions, where of course a Character-like passage would lend persuasion.   In an account of the fearful man whose trouble is jealousy Burton writes as if he were thinking of Hall's Character of the "Distrustful" or of Earle's "Suspicious or Jealous Man."[10] Apropos of scholars' melancholy Burton anticipates Earle's wry defence of the poor scholar:

> How many poor scholars have lost their wits . . . in the world's esteem they are accounted ridiculous and silly. . . . Or if they keep their wits, yet they are esteemed scrubs and fools by reason of their carriage . . . Because they cannot ride an horse, which every clown can do, salute and court a gentlewoman, carve at table, cringe, and make congies . . . Thus they go commonly meditating unto themselves . . . his wits were a woolgathering, as they say, and his head busied about other matters . . . Your greatest students are commonly no better; silly, soft fellows in their outward behaviour.[11]

---

[9]Bohn's Library edition (1923), I, 331 (I, ii, mem. 3, subs. 12). Besides the English in the text Burton gives a Latin version of Theophrastus' words in a footnote.

[10]"*Suspicion* and *jealousy* are general symptoms: they are commonly distrustful, timorous, apt to mistake, and amplify . . . peevish, and ready to snarl upon every small occasion, *cum amicissimis* . . . If they speak in jest, he takes it in good earnest. If they be not saluted, invited, consulted with . . . they think themselves neglected and contemned: for a time that tortures them. If two talk together . . . or tell a tale in general, he thinks presently they mean him . . . Or if they talk with him, he is ready to misconstrue every word they speak, and interpret it to the worst" (I, iii, mem. 1, subs. 2).

[11]I, ii, mem. 3, subs. 15.

But Burton was too endlessly fascinated by his subject ever to compose a shapely, final Character.

Yet what the word meant in its technical sense he must have known. So did Breton, who after developing an unfortunate idea that he could Character[12] the Baconian essay went on in *The Goode and the Badde* (1616) with other adaptations of the form. The word had various significances for various people. A pamphlet printed in 1627 with the title *The Character of A Christian As hee is distinguished from all Hypocrites and Hereticks* has nothing of the literary Character in it; instead, the word in the title was intended to have the ordinary meaning, *nature*. George Herbert tells the reader of *A Priest to the Temple* (dated 1632, printed 1652) that there he meant to set down "the Form and Character of a true Pastor." Again the word has the ordinary, non-technical meaning; Herbert was writing an extended manual, not a little piece of Theophrastus' or Hall's sort. Richard Brathwaite warns us that even among the "literary" the term was used loosely. When in 1620 his *Essaies upon the Five Senses* appeared, it included "The Authors Opinion of Marriage: Delivered in a satisfying Character to his friend," in which the essay plan and style triumph; yet Brathwaite also wrote into the piece brief Character-like accounts of a faithful wife and a devoted wife. Just afterwards he put a perfectly sustained and correctly labeled Character of a shrew, Overburian in manner though extremely long. The "expressive Character of a reall friend" and other sections entitled "Characters" which appear in his *English Gentleman*, published ten years later, again show him ignoring completely the Theophrastan meaning of the term. And

---

[12]Breton appears to have been the first to use this verb in our special sense. The complimentary verses of "I. B." printed in *Characters upon Essaies* suggest two ways of accenting it:

"While I Essay to character this Booke,
And these charactered Essayes o'relook."

the Characters which he collected in *Whimzies* (1631) were a compromise: they belong in the classical tradition, but they honor it as much in the breach as in the observance. None the less, it is safe to say that the label *Character* as early as 1616 had a particular value.[13] The vogue of the genre was established.

The fusions and confusions of the Character with other prose forms in the first two decades of the century do not suggest that the Character was unimpressive. On the contrary, as one goes through book after book of this period, one is surprised to see how many people who were plainly not writing Characters succumbed to the impulse to imitate the method occasionally, to choose the same subjects, and to steal a phrase from Hall or Overbury. If their model was Hall, they usually merged the Character into a work of spiritual exhortation, and the essay or the sermon on an abstract topic remained the dominating form. If something in the Overbury collection was the model, the social scene is likely to be anatomized. It is from this collection that many of the more easily recognizable fugitive Characters derive. Let us examine first the near-Characters inspired by Hall.

The reader will remember about the Characters of Hall that in the Vices there are passages of the concrete, dramatic sort that Theophrastus habitually wrote, as well as general, condemnatory remarks and florid sets of metaphors. In the Virtues there is a

---

[13]See p. 294 for further discussion of the meanings intended by the word "character." How the Character gradually was taking shape can be seen by comparing the first edition of George Webbe's *Practice of Quietness* (1615) and the third edition of 1618. The former describes quietness abstractly: "To be *Quiet* is to iudge charitably, to speake lovingly, to converse freindly, to put up wrongs patiently," and so on (pp. 9-10). The latter offers "The character of a quiet man," making a representative man who is shown "settling himselfe alwaies to iudge charitably, to speake lovingly, to converse friendly, to put up wrongs patiently, and to wrong no man willingly." The preceptual Character thus is developed out of the preceptual essay. (Notes on the 1615 edition were kindly supplied by Fredson T. Bowers.)

persistently analytical and general method, more searching than Theophrastus', in addition to the conspicuous figures; one may be reminded of classical discussions like Plutarch's diffuse account of the flatterer or the statement of the "conditions of a wise and worthy woman" in Proverbs, in which appear the data of behavior and spiritual tendencies as well as striking figures. It is not surprising, in view of these connections, that one finds here and there in moralistic prose of these decades discussions of problems of conduct carried on in a fashion rather like that of Hall's Virtues. In Owen Felltham's *Resolves. Divine, Morall, Politicall*[14] the sections on "the *envious man*" (I, lxiii), the valiant Christian (I, xiii), and the "*covetous* man" (I, lxx) resemble Hall's work, though in fragments only. The same sort of general resemblance is heightened by actual verbal thefts in Sir William Cavendish's *Discourse Against Flatterie* (1611). The thefts, from Hall's "Flatterer," appear at widely separated points (pages 5, 44, and 87-88) and are from Hall's figurative sentences and also from his more or less Theophrastan sentences. Cavendish's flatterer is essentially Hall's, but Augustine, Chrysostom, the Psalms, Martial, Terence, his own previous remarks, and doubtless many other authors assisted him in amplifying the discourse. The Character as such is lost in the homily. The thefts from Hall were carefully deleted when the work was reissued in a briefer, better form in *Horæ Subsecivæ* (1620), but at the same time Cavendish offered a new essay "Of Arrogance," which sounds at times like Hall's "Malcontent," and an essay "Of Affection," which freely pillages Overbury's "Affected Traveler." Yet all are still discursive essays.

There are two books in which Hall's influence seems marked. The first, Brathwaite's interesting work called *The Schollers*

---

[14] I have used the 1628 edition; the date of first publication was perhaps 1623.

Medley (1614), addresses itself at one point[15] to "Maister Miser"
to tell him what a wretch he is and then, changing to the third
person, sets forth "The Character of a Liberall Man" in the
analytical, descriptive style of Hall. In spite of a shorter compass
and decorative scraps of Latin, this Character of generosity, a
virtue not treated by Hall, recalls Hall's work and some of his
ideas. The other book, a tiny volume by William Mason aptly
called *A Handful of Essaies* (1621), brings us back to the cross-
ing of Bacon and Hall. The table lists essays "Of Sermon-
hearers," "Of Parents," "Of Covetousnes," and on flatterers,
the commonalty, bribing, usury, pride, bad company. The
couching of the topic sometimes in an abstract noun and sometimes in the name of a class of men correctly implies that both
Hall's and Bacon's manners of writing appealed to Mason. All
the pieces are truly essays; they move from analysis to anecdote
to general opinion to a quotation from Seneca or Socrates to a
simile from the animal world to a momentary report on what
this sinner or these sinners habitually do. The long essay "Of
Covetousness" could be so ample because there was stuffed into
it a diffuse Character concocted of thefts from Hall's "Covetous"
and his "Distrustful" and peppered with Latin quotations.

The employment of the Character to nourish, enliven, and
enforce a moral discussion is especially interesting in the sermons
of Thomas Adams, who as a city preacher addressed those very
types that Jonson and Overbury and Dekker depicted. Being the
possessor of a sprightly mind, he made good use of the liberty
allowed by Calvinist doctrine to the minister who wished to appeal
directly to his auditory.[16] In consequence, some of his sermons,
witty, vivid, eloquent, deepened by a sense of man's fearful situation, are still remarkable. His experiments with the Character
began, at least as far as I know, in a sermon preached at Paul's

---

[15]Page 89. [16]See Mitchell, *English Pulpit Oratory*, pp. 197-224.

Cross in 1612, entitled *The White Devil, or The Hypocrite Uncased.* In the course of the discussion Adams says of flatterers that they

> eate like moths into liberall mens coats, [are] the bane of Greatnes, are theeves, not to be forgotten in this catalogue. These rob many a great man of his goodnes, & make him rob the Common-wealth of hir happines. Doth his Lord want money? he puts it into his head, such fines to be levyed, such grounds inclosed . . . Be his maintainers courses never so foule, either he furthers them or he smothers them: sin hath not a more impudent bawd, nor his master a more impious theefe . . . He would raise himselfe by his Great-one, and cannot contrive it, but by the ruine of others. He robs the flattred of his goods . . . of his soale: is not this a thiefe? *beneficia, veneficia:* al their good is poysen. They are *Dominis arrisoris* . . . their Masters Spaniels, the Commonwealths wolves, put them in your Pater-noster, let them never come in your Creed: pray for them, but trust them no more than theeves.[17]

A comparison of this much of the sketch and Hall's "Flatterer" will reveal the origin of Adams' method and of several of his descriptive details. But the shifting from singular to plural, the Latin tags, and the pious conclusion joining the sketch to the larger plan of the sermon should remind us of the moralistic type-portraits that preceded Hall's more sophisticated art. Adams remarks at one point that all the sons of Adam possess some hypocrisy but that hypocrisy possesses only certain men; as a preacher Adams was obligated to treat his topic horizontally, examining the sin in all forms in all frail men, though he might also try a vertical embodiment of it in The Hypocrite. The same sort of imitation of Hall, only more frequently and also more piece-meal, Adams carried out in the second sermon of *The Divells Banket* (1614). The flatterer, the drunkard, the covetous are

---

[17] *The White Devil* (1614), pp. 49-50.

made interesting by sentences in Hall's manner and by figures or descriptive details from his "Flatterer," "Unthrift," and "Covetous." The idle man, described in Hall's phrase as "the Devils Cushion,"[18] is given a more old-fashioned, allegorical depiction than in Hall's "Slothful," but there are echoes of Hall and he is mentioned in a marginal note. Adams in *The Divells Banket* demonstrated that he was learning eagerly and trying his wings. The psychologist rather than the literary historian can explain why he felt moved to remark, following these tentative, fragmentary Characters, that "All *stollen* things are accountable for; the law of all Nations hath provided, that (*cuique suum*) every man may enioy his owne."[19]

Parson Adams experimented with the Character further in the second sermon of *Mystical Bedlam,* printed in 1615. In addition to employing the Character adulterated with allegory (the "Usurer") and the Character broken into fragments (the "Drunkard"), he chose a plan for this sermon—a description of the world of spiritual madmen—which allowed him to run through a list of twenty of the usual vicious types—the epicure, the proud, the lustful, the hypocrite, and so forth. The ample and effective account of "The Busie-Body" is clearly based upon Hall's "Busy-body," especially upon the general and figurative parts rather than the Theophrastan sentences. More interesting as a variation on the form is the description of the epicure in a Charactered catechism.

> I would faine speake (not onely of him, but) with him. Can you tend it, Belly-god? The first question of my Catechisme shall be, *What is your name? Epicure. Epicure?* What's that? speake not so philosophically; but tell us in plaine dealing, what are you? *A lover of pleasure, more then of God.* One that makes much of my selfe;

---

[18]See p. 128 above.   [19]Page 84.

borne to live, and living loving to take mine ease. One that would make my *belly* my executour, and bequeath all my goods to consumption, for the consummation of my owne delights. Hoh! a good-fellow, a merry man, a *mad-man*. What is your *summum bonum? Pleasure*. Wherein consists it? Rehearse the Articles of your beleefe. I beleeve that delicacies, iunkets, quotidian feasts, suckets & marmulads are very delectable . . . I beleeve that midnight revels, perfumed chambers, soft beds, close curtaines, and a *Dalila* in mine armes, are very comfortable. I beleeve that glistering silkes, and sparkling Iewels, a purse full of golden charmes . . . gardens, orchards, fish-ponds . . . is a very heaven upon earth. I beleeve, that to sleepe till dinner, and play till supper, and quaffe till midnight, and to dally till morning . . . the most absolute and perfect end of mans life.[20]

A description of the contentious man is constructed of verses from Proverbs fitted together in the way that Hall in *Salomons Divine Arts* (1609) had fitted together a Character of the slothful man.[21]

In *Diseases of the Soule: A Discourse Divine, Morall, and Physicall* (1616) Adams adopted his most ingenious scheme for exploiting his (and Hall's) skill in Character-writing. The plan is to range before the reader—for surely Adams was not intending to *speak* such a composition—nineteen diseases of the body, each being mentioned and identified only in order to introduce a figuratively parallel disease of the soul. Twelve of the nineteen topics are identical with twelve of Hall's fifteen topics in his *Characters*. For each there is a description, a section on the cause, another on the "Signes and Symptomes," and a fourth on the cure. The Character-method may appear, at length or

---

[20]*Mystical Bedlam*, pp. 48-49.
[21]See p. 128 above. The contentious man is described in *Mystical Bedlam*, pp. 67-68.

briefly, in any or all of the four sections but is most conspicuous in "Signs and Symptomes." The accounts of at least eight of the types—the brainsick novelist, the unconstant, the envious, the idle, the covetous, timorous suspicion, and the vainglorious— have verbal debts to Hall, and three—the vainglorious, the proud, and the flatterer—draw from a new stealing-place, Overbury. Now Adams imitates the concrete and graphic parts of Hall's and Overbury's work as well as the analytical, general, and figurative passages, and he rivals both authors in tart wit and psychological insight. The best-sustained Characters are of the proud man (under "Signs and Symptomes"; a lively imitation of the best Overburian manner), of the covetous man (which, under "Signes," though preceded by Latin verses and ancient authorities and though interrupted by quotations, is still often concrete and vivid), and the vainglorious (under "Signes").

> You shall easily know a *vaine-glorious* man: his owne commendation rumbles within him, till he hath bulked it out; & the ayre of it is unsavory.[22] In the field, he is touching heaven with a launce; in the street, his eye is still cast over his shoulder.[23] He stands up so pertly, that you may know he is not laden with fruite. If you would drinke of his wisedome, knocke by a sober question at the barrell, and you shall finde by the sound, his wits are emptie. In al companies, like chaffe he will be uppermost: hee is some surfet in natures stomake, & cannot be kept down. A goodly Cipresse tree, fertile onely of leaves. He drinks to none beneath the salt; and it is his Grammar rule without exception, not to conferre with an inferiour in publike. His impudence will over-rule his ignorance to talke of learned principles; which come from him, like a treble part in a base voyce, too bigge for it. Living in some under-staire

---

[22]Cf. Hall's "Vain-glorious": "All his humor rises up into the froth of ostentation; which if it once settle, falles downe into a narrow roome."

[23]Hall's "Vain-glorious" looks "over his left shoulder, to see if the point of his rapier follow him with Grace."

office, when he would visite the countrey, he borrowes
some Gallants cast sute of his servant, and therein (Player-
like) acts that part among his besotted neighbours. When
he rides his masters great horse out of ken, hee vaunts of
him as his owne, and brags how much he cost him.[24] He
feeds upon others curtesie, others meat: and (whether
more?) either fats him. At his Inne he cals for chickens
at spring, and such things as cannot be had; whereat angry,
he sups according to his purse with a red Herring.[25] Farre
enough from knowledge he talkes of his castle (which is
either in the aire, or inchanted) of his lands, which are
some pastures in the Fairyground, invisible, no where. He
offers to purchase Lordships, but wants money for earnest.[26] He makes others praises as introductions to his
own, which must transcend; and cals for wine, that he may
make knowne his rare vessell of deale, at home: not for-
getting to you, that a Dutch Marchant sent it him, for
some extraordinary desert. He is a wonder every where;
among fooles, for his bravery, among wisemen for his
folly.[27] He loves an *Herald* for a new *Coate,* and hires
him to lye upon his Pedigree. All Nobility, that is ancient,
is of his allyance; and the Great man is but of the first head,
that doth not call him, *Cousin.* When his beames are
weakest, like the rising and setting Sunne, hee makes the
longest shadowes: whereas bright knowledge, like the
Sunne at highest, makes none at all; though then most
resultance of heat, and reflection of light. He takes great
paines to make himselfe derisory; yet (without suspecting
it) both his speech and silence cries, Behold mee. He dis-
commends earned worth with a shrugge, and lispes his

---

[24]Hall's "Vain-glorious" is "proud of another mans horse; and well
mounted thinks every man wrongs him, that looks not at him."

[25]Hall's "Vain-glorious" "picks his teeth when his stomacke is emptie,
and calles for pheasants at a common Inne."

[26]Hall's "Vain-glorious" prices "the richest iewels, and fairest horses,
when his purse yeelds not money enough for earnest."

[27]Hall's "Vain-glorious" is "a Spanish souldier on an Italian Theater
. . . a fooles wonder, and a wise mans foole."

enforced approbation.[28] Hee loves humility in all men, but himselfe, as if hee did wish well to all soules but his owne.

There is no matter of consequence, that Policy begets, but he will be Gossip to, and give it a name; and knowes the intention of all projects, before they be full hatched. Hee hath somewhat in him, which would bee better for himselfe, and all men, if he could keepe it in. In his hall, you shall see an old rusty sword hung up, which he swears killed *Glendower* in the hands of his Grand-sire. He fathers upon himselfe some villanies, because they are in fashion; and so vilifies his credit, to advance it. If a newe famous *Courteghian* be mentioned, he deeply knowes her; whom indeed he never saw. He will be ignorant of nothing, though it be a shame to know it. His barrell hath a continuall spigot, but no tunnell; and like an unthrift, he spends more then he gets: His speech of himselfe is ever historicall, histrionicall. He is indeed admirations creature, and a circumstantiall Mountebanke.[29]

In such writing Adams proves himself the artist, both in his expert mosaic-work and in his abandoning, for the moment, any preachment.

But in most of the descriptions in *Diseases of the Soule* Adams subordinates the delights of the Character to the solemn ends of the homily. The habit of sprinkling the page with Latin phrases, anecdotes, Biblical allusions, and authorities which we noticed in various essayists—Mason, Cavendish, Brathwaite—persists in

---

[28]Overbury's "Affected Traveller Is a speaking fashion; he hath taken paines to bee ridiculous . . . His attire speakes *French* or *Italian*, and his *gate* cryes *Behold mee*. Hee censures all things by countenances, and shrugs, and speakes his owne language with shame and lisping."

[29]*Diseases of the Soule* (1616), pp. 61-62. Lambert H. Ennis has described (*PMLA*, LVI [1941], 141-150) a manuscript collection of nineteen Characters in the British Museum, apparently written by Margaret Bellasys in the 1620's, which consists almost entirely of rearrangements of Characters in *Diseases of the Soule*. Except for curious substitutions of polysyllabic and strange words, the additions to Adams are entirely taken from Hall's Characters.

these sermons. The rhetorical license of the pulpit and the example of Biblical passages like the account of the virtuous woman in Proverbs weaken Adams's art by leading him to introduce descriptions that are more symbolic than real; though it is suggestive to remark of the Inconstant that "He knowes not whether he should say his *Pater noster* in Latin, or English; and so leaves it and his prayers unsayd," it is better when Theophrastus reports of the Distrustful that "His cloak is put out to wash not where it will be fulled best, but where the fuller gives him good security."[30] Theophrastus' detail is suggestive and also plausible; Adams' we can hardly believe literally. The fluent heaping-up of figures tends, even more than a similar habit did in Hall, to dissipate the actuality of the type-figure, and we become aware that Adams is attacking his material horizontally again, checking the vice in all of us.

After the bold and brilliant work in *Diseases of the Soule* the rest of Adams' adoptions of the Character idea are anticlimactic An abstract Character of a good man he introduced into *The Spirituall Navigator* (1615);[31] some allegorical sketches he put into *The Souldiers Honour* (1617);[32] and in "The Foole and His Sport" there are brief Characters of the ambitious fool (based upon Hall) and the "Glad foole"[33] (somewhat indebted to Overbury's "Roaring Boy") which are rather general and abstract. In his address to the reader prefixed to *The White Devil*, the first sermon in which he attempted a Character, Adams defended himself against the charge of being "too merry," arguing that the gravity of his material prevented his being guilty of lightness. If not merry he was certainly sprightly, and this quality of his mind and temper shows in the figures and odd remarks that

---

[30]Edmonds' translation.   [31]Page 21.
[32]In Adams' *Works* (1841), I, 81-87.
[33]In Adams' *Happiness of the Church* (1618), p. 77.

enliven his pages.[34] It led him also into the usual preference for bad types to Character. That he had ever seen a sketch by Theophrastus is doubtful. If he had, his genuine earnestness as well as his fanciful, witty nature would probably have kept him loyal rather to the examples of Hall and Overbury, whose work, like his own, strikes one as perfectly suited to the Jacobean temper.[35]

As we are now to study the imitators of the Overbury Characters we may occasionally have to leave saintly company and join the rough, the ribald, and the wrathful. Not that all the writers who echoed a phrase or a topic of Overbury's were undignified or unrestrained. The *Characters* were originally a mere appendage to *The Wife*, Overbury's sober and moderately thoughtful poem on marriage, and *The Wife* provoked several imitations.[36] None of these is a Character, to be sure, but they suggest that Overbury's influence extended to the earnest as well as to the facetious.

One feature of the Overburian Characters that caught everyone's fancy was the frequent choice of current social types, recognizable London folk of the year 1614, to portray unsparingly and wittily. Not that this sort of writing was altogether new; perhaps, indeed, it was an already established taste that caused this particular emphasis in the Overbury collection and in the imitations. Take, for example, the popular type of affected, shallowminded traveler. Thomas Lodge in *Wits Miserie* fitted him

[34]A fair sample is his matching the gospel (God's spell) with the devil's spell, "either *Lucian* his olde *Testament*, or Machiavell his new" (*The Divells Banket*, p. 2).

[35]That Adams could be moving, eloquent, splendidly rhetorical after the manner (perhaps literally) of John Donne and even prophetic of Sir Thomas Browne can be seen in his *Sinners passing-Bell. Or A complaint from Heaven for Mans Sinnes* (1614).

[36]John Davies of Hereford, *A Select Second Husband for Sir Thomas Overburies' Wife* (1616); Richard Brathwaite, *The Description of a good Wife* (1619); Patricke Hannay, *A Happy Husband or Directions for a Maide to choose her Mate* (1619).

(with his thirty thousand crowns in eggshells at a Venetian banquet, his band heroically won in Transylvania, and his hat given him by Henry II of France) into the more capacious category of vainglory. Jonson, who especially dealt in such social enormities wittily organized, called him Puntarvolo and then Amorphus.[37] In *Faultes Faults* (1606) there is a vivid account (in the plural, but none the less Character-like) of lying travelers who go abroad "to see fashions, but none at all, to learne vertue."[38] In 1614 Overbury's "Affected Traveler," a specialized, heightened adaptation of Hall's "Vain-glorious" (itself based upon Theophrastus' "Petty Pride") was put into print and became a classic. Possibly the vague resemblance between it and the discursive consideration in Brathwaite's *Schollers Medley* of both *"Commenting Travailers"* and *"Phantasticke Travailers,"* who cross Alps and deserts "for what end Heaven knowes, save onely to wrest out a phantasticke behaviour of superfluous wit," resulted from Brathwaite's having seen Overbury's sketch in manuscript.[39] Other explanations of the resemblance are, of course, possible. After Overbury's Character was printed, Thomas Adams took a phrase from it for his vainglorious man (in *Diseases of the Soule*), and Barnabe Rich, who had done very well with bright, objective type-descriptions in *Faultes Faults* two years before the Character had been officially Anglicized, was moved to revise that earlier work (in general for the worse), adding to his sketch of the malcontent a paragraph partly taken from Overbury's "Traveler." (The surprising thing about Rich's revised work, called *My Ladies Looking Glasse* (1616), is that though he borrowed

---

[37]See p. 104 above.   [38]Fol. 8.

[39]Compare Overbury's saying that his traveler "hath seen more then he hath perceived" and Brathwaite's saying of the commenting travelers that they publish "more then they have seene" and, of the fantastic travelers, that they publish "lesse then they have seene" (p. 9). Brathwaite's extensive thefts from Overbury's "Courtier" for a Charactered epigram in *A Strappado for the Divell* (1615) are mentioned above, p. 172.

from Overbury for his malcontent and courtier and for two new Overburian Characters of a "Formalist" and "Ninihammer,"[40] the book is no more definitely a Character-book than was the earlier version. Rich preferred to remain a moralist and type-satirist of the old school.) Finally to be mentioned, though not final, among the progeny of Overbury's "Affected Traveler" is an essay "Of Affectation" in *Horæ Subsecivæ* (1620). After a Theophrastan definition at the beginning, it considers among affected types those that travel not to observe "governments of Nations, situations of Countryes, dispositions of People" but "fashions of behaviour . . . a *Peccadill*, or a *Picadevant*" (they seem, indeed, to be those we have met in *The Schollers Medley*); they shudder at native beer, hope to have forgotten the English tongue and accent, yet try to pass themselves off as "Statesmen" on the basis of having read *Gallo-Belgicus*. The whole thing (it runs from page 33 to page 49), obviously indebted to Overbury for matter and manner, shows how the Overbury Character could be torn apart, stuffed, expanded, pluralized, and made into a descriptive essay.

Another influence exerted by the Overbury collection came from those Characters which treated serious public abuses, the dangers seen in "An Engrosser of Corn," "A Jesuit," "A Precisian," "A Puritan," and especially the six pieces on prisons, now attributed to Thomas Dekker. It was these sketches which, not long after, were to lead to the strenuous, intensely argumentative, shapeless pamphlet-Characters. It is true that there is a connection also between these nine pieces and both the old, personified descriptions of national dangers in such work as *Piers Plowman* and the more recent handbooks on coney-catchers. But the former precedents are allegorical and horizontal in method, and the latter treat not the moral nature of the rascal

---

[40] *My Ladies Looking Glasse* (1616), pp. 53, 50, 51.

discussed but his professional habits and criminal devices. The Character must depart from both, and for the nine Overbury pieces the label "Character" seems correct. What is said about the "Precisian," who "hath nicknamde all the Prophets & Apostles with his Sonnes, and begets nothing but *Vertues* for Daughters," makes that least heartfelt sketch the most amusing. But there is cold dislike in the "Engrosser of Corn" and a warning against treachery in the "Jesuit."

Dekker's special adaptation of the Character in the six prison pieces had been prepared for in his earlier work. His two pamphlets, *Iests to make you Merie* (1607) and *The Belman of London* (1608), contained the sort of technical exposés of thieves and other rascals, sometimes by way of an amusing anecdote, that I have described in Chapter III. Near the end of *Iests* Dekker put a "description of a Prison," which is "the very next doore to hel . . . It is a mans grave . . . it is a Sea wherein he is alwaies shipwrackt . . . a wilderness . . . It is an unsatiable gulfe . . . the cave where horror dwels." Later there is an extended comparison of a prison to a military camp. In *Worke for Armorours* (1609) and in *A Strange Horse-Race* (1613) he presented several allegorical figures, including Hospitality, Parsimony, a Niggard, and Blasphemous Insolence, none of them resembling the creations of Theophrastus or Hall very closely. But when he constructed the six prison pieces that Lisle added to the Overbury collection in 1616 he had a new model. Yet, being confined for debt in the King's Bench Prison in Southwark, he could not escape from the mood or the recollection of his earlier work. So in his first sketch, "A Prison," he expanded the smoldering, figurative sort of description he had published in 1607, now comparing a prison to a ship rather than a camp; by adding figures to suggest what a prison does (it brings an arrant coward in three days to an admirable stomach; it teaches

men to sing—*Lachrymae*), Dekker shaped the descriptive essay
into a Character of an institution, a new thing in Characters.
Perhaps he had forgotten his school rhetoric, but he once must
have learned that *prosopopoeia* might dramatize an inanimate
thing as well as a person. In the five other sketches, "A Prisoner," "Creditor," "Sergeant," "His Yeoman," and "Jailor,"
Dekker used the Overbury models of humble and contemptible
types, about whose lives and characters the Overburians usually
offered odd puns and sarcastic imagery rather than useful description. Dekker's pity for the prisoner and his burning hatred
of creditors and jail-keepers and all their tricks and heartlessness
distinguish these Characters from the rest in the book. They
are not to entertain; they are to arouse indignation.

During the next year, 1617, one William Fennor was incarcerated in the Compter in Southwark. One result of his experience was a pamphlet, *The Compters Common-Wealth,* written,
as Dekker's sketches seemingly were, to bring both money to
himself and public attention to the conditions in debtors' prisons.
After one night in "this *Infernal Iland*" and in "the middest of
melancholy" he wrote a "character of a prison" which he printed
in his pamphlet: "It is a Fabricke built of the same stuffe, the
Keepers of it are made of, stone and iron: It is an unwholesome
full-stuffed humorous body . . . It is a booke where an honest
man may learne and reade a lesson of bettering himselfe . . . A
Bankrupts banquetting house . . . a Prodigals purgatory . . . a
dicing house" and so on. Fennor had read Dekker's Characters,
but his inspiration here is not only they but also Dekker's "description" in *Iests to make you Merie.* In succeeding chapters
he discussed his whole experience and the experiences of others.
In Chapter Five "spent-Gallants" are described, those fellows
who prey on Overbury's sort of "Golden Ass," and the marigold
figure from Overbury's "Courtier" ornaments the account. "A

Character of a Iaylor," really of jailors, in Chapter Ten begins with a Character-like passage but quickly turns into an essay and a coney-catcher exposé-with-anecdotes. The Character, a sophisticated literary form, could no more maintain itself here than in the equally mean, fearful, and angry surroundings of a better-known but less interesting work, Geoffrey Mynshul's *Essayes and Characters of a Prison and Prisoners,* published the following year.

To explain Mynshul's book we must return to Thomas Dekker, who in 1616 had issued *Villanies Discovered.* This was a fifth edition of his *Lanthorne and Candlelight,* augumented by a new section containing six chapters: "Certaine Discoveries of a Prison by way of Essayes and Characters, written by a Prisoner; Of Prisoners; Of Creditors; Of Choice of Company in Prison; Of Visitants; Of Jaylors."[41] In spite of the label "Characters" the additions are essays; the topics but not the method duplicate those of the prison Characters in the Overbury volume.

In 1618 Dekker was apparently still in the King's Bench Prison. One of his fellow-sufferers at the time was Geoffrey Mynshul, who early in the year gave to the press *Certaine Characters and Essayes of Prison and Prisoners* and later in the year a revision called *Essayes and Characters of a Prison and Prisoners.* Both volumes were subscribed from the King's Bench; the second one, having dropped a section on jailors that offended Mynshul's keepers, supplied further matter on prison life.[42] Like Fennor, Mynshul called the place "this infernall Iland," and like him he hoped to purge melancholy by gathering "a few Essayes and Characters" of the hideous place. The book consists of an alternating sequence of essays and Characters, often

---

[41]My account of this work, including the chapter headings quoted, is based on the description of it in Mary L. Hunt's *Thomas Dekker* (New York, 1911) and her article, "Geffray Mynshul and Thomas Dekker." *Journal of English and Germanic Philology,* XI (1912), 231-243.

[42]See Gwendolyn Murphy, *A Bibliography of English Character Books* (Oxford, 1925), pp. 31-32.

with one of each on a topic. The topics, titles, and their order
came from the new section of *Villanies Discovered*, and the
essays in the first two thirds of the book (I am speaking of Mynshul's revised edition) were to an astonishing extent filled up
with thefts from his fellow-prisoner's pages, the phrasing only
slightly altered.[43] It is in the Characters that one is to look for
Mynshul's own work—that is, if one can believe Mynshul capable of original effort. The first, a Character of a Prison, consists
entirely of figures of speech, some borrowed from Dekker's
metaphors for a prison in *Iests to make you Merie*, some from
Fennor; but the whole is less descriptive than the Overbury
"Prison." Among the others only four properly should be called
Characters: the "Character of a Prisoner," the third little sketch
under "Characters of Companions in Prison," the "Character of
Visitants," and "A noble understanding Prisoner," the Stoic
ideal of which suggests Hall's in his Virtues. Of the remainder,
the "Character of a Creditor" moves away from describing representative behavior to narrating an interesting trick or two as
Fennor did in his pretended Character of a jailor. Some of the
sections are merely or mostly factual description. The section
hopelessly labeled "Essayes and Characters of Iaylors and Keepers
of Prisons," with nothing of the Character in it and not much on
the announced subject, exposes Mynshul's confusion, his literary
ignorance. Very much concerned to inveigh against abuses and
abusers, he was not concerned to distinguish the typical features
of each class of offenders. Presumably he knew what he was
talking about, but his visual imagination was poor and he needed
constant literary stimulation.[44] Even his best Characters are

---

[43]Paylor, *The Overburian Characters*, p. xxxi, suggests that Mynshul's
second preface was written by Dekker.

[44]An exact list of Mynshul's other borrowings seems not worth while.
Fennor's first, second, and tenth chapters and Overbury's "Worthy Com-
mander," "Affected Traveler," and "Jailor" were particularly useful to
Mynshul.

therefore quite inferior to Dekker's, and his exposition of prison
life is inferior to Fennor's. There was some propriety, then, in
Fennor's decision (or a publisher's) to reissue his pamphlet, the
year after Mynshul's appeared, with a new title, *The Miseries
of a Iaile . . . With many speciall Characters of Serieants, Key-
turners . . . and other Officers.* One effect of the Overbury
volume, obviously, was to demoralize the classical Character.

We can conclude our discussion of the vogue of the Character among the essayists of the early seventeenth century by noticing
a few more appearances of the full-grown Character in works
that were chiefly occupied with other matters.

The moralistic essayist, as we have frequently observed, could
enliven his abstract discussions with type-portraiture. Richard
Brathwaite, genuinely interested in the new genre as Thomas
Adams was, could do a good deal with it, especially since his
spirit—again a resemblance to Adams—was both merry and
solemn. In his *Essaies upon the Five Senses* (1620) he talked
about marriage seriously, using a few Character-like passages for
ballast, and then added a long, amusing Overburian Character
of a shrew. His merry humor, in fact a Rabelaisian humor, pre-
vailed in the twelve-page Character, inserted in *A Solemne Ioviall
Disputation . . . briefely Shadowing The Law of Drinking*
(1617), of Cornelius Vandunk, a "sou'd Gurnet," no peripatetic,
for whom the whole street is too strait, who so long as "hee is
his owne man . . . keepes a just accompt, in scoring everie dozen
by unloosing a button: but falling backe in his chaire, hee referres
the reckoning to his Hostesse and her unconscionable chalke:
which scores him on for sleeping, though he drinke nothing."[45]
Cornelius becomes a heroic figure of the drunkard; but though
Brathwaite's method is like that of Overbury, the satisfaction
derived by the reader from this ample picture is not so much

---

[45]Page 68.

that of the compact, witty individualizing of a type as it is that of scene-painting—scene-painting like Breughel's.

Among the other essayists to explore the uses of the Character was Thomas Young, who published an even more comprehensive report on the causes, temptations, habits, results (you might commit murder, you might smell like a brewer's apron) of this same evil in a booklet called *Englands Bane: or, The Description of Drunkennesse* (1617). Less familiar with the new Overburian genre than Brathwaite, he tried much more hesitatingly to adopt its methods. His most noticeable attempt is the insertion, re-punctuated, of the latter two-thirds of Breton's Character of a drunkard (from *The Good and the Badde*), not inaptly labeled a "description." More expert than most of the Characters inserted singly in moralistic prose is Thomas Tuke's "Pictur of a Pictur, Or, The Character of a Painted Woman," printed in his *Discourse Against Painting and Tincturing of Women* (1616).[46] Tuke's book is as solemn as inclusive (poisoning and witchcraft somehow come into it); one may be surprised how well Tuke nevertheless observes the rules of style of the English Characters, even to such phrasing as "Her trade is tinckturing, and her lustre is her life." The explanation is that he had studied the Overbury and Stephens collections and perhaps others. He steals phrases from both writers,[47] but his joiner's work is good, and he outdoes the Overburian timeliness by inserting among Overbury's remodeled phrases a reference to the Mistress Turner who helped kill him.

The relationship between the Character and both the courtesy-book and the phrase-book as it appeared in the sixteenth century was pointed out in Chapter III. I have just referred to the use-

---

[46]The "Pictur" appears pp. 57-62.

[47]From Overbury's "Fine Gentleman," "Very Very Woman," "Her Next Part," "Good Wife," and Stephens' "My Mistress."

fulness of the Character to the painter of manners. An interesting bringing together of all four kinds of writing occurs in *The
Rich Cabinet Furnished with varietie of Excellent discriptions,
exquisite Charracters, witty discourses, and delightful Histories*
(1616), a work partly taken from Giovanni della Casa and
usually attributed to Thomas Gainsford. The main, earlier
part of the volume is organized like a phrase-book—"Affinity,"
"Anger," "Atheism," and so on, with miscellaneous quotations
and sentences for each. By the time the author has reached
"Courtiers" he has slipped into the Characterist's manner, though
he does not maintain it long nor organize his material properly.
The important heading for us is "Gentery," which after three
pages on "Generosity" provides a complete Character of the
English parasite of high degree.

> A Gentleman without meanes, is a painted bardge without
> oares; faire to looke on, but there is no use of him . . .
> While hee is tied to his post, and stayes at home, hee
> either rots . . . or else takes in such foule water of everie
> vice . . . as either in short time corrupts within him, or
> speedily sinks him.
> But if you untie his rope . . . [he may land in the lap of a
> rich widow or rot in a ditch] . . .
> A Gentleman without meanes is a prettie plant, but without
> rinde, without roote . . . He is a tender creature that
> can weare his clothes in good fashion, if his Mercer &
> Teylor will trust him. Hee can borrow with as plausible
> and pittifull perswasion, and put off payment with as
> pretty invention . . . as any man . . .
> Hee is a loving and frequent friend to his wealthy neighbor
> or country-man . . . He feeds as choicely & freely,
> drinks as sweetly and soundly, and talkes as boldly and
> bravely as any in the roome . . .
> He shall weare a cloake, & a paire of boots as long, borrow
> your horse as often, and ride him as well as the best . . .
> Hee can hold up the lower salt, with festivall and timely

> table talke . . . and (barre distinction, and orderly
> speaking) he wil over-argue a scholer in his owne pro-
> fession . . .
> He can hold a trencher hansomely for neede . . . None shall
> sooner spy out a fit match for your sonne, or daugh-
> ter . . .
> Take him to a play, and trouble not his cogitation with the
> water-man, entrance, or sitting: hee shall laugh as
> hartily, observe as iudiciously, and repeat as exactly for
> nothing, as another man shall for his halfe crowne.

There is much more in the same ironic vein on the gentleman's
capacity for gambling and for living a smug country life at someone else's cost and for ivy-like clinging to "some substantiall
rich oake." "For conclusion, this beggerly Gentleman, is too
proud to be a servingman, to poore to be a Merchant-man, too
weake to be a husband-man, too wastfull to be a tradesman . . .
For full and finall description . . . he is a rationall creature,
potentially apt for any thing, but actually good for nothing."

Utile et dulce the Character early proved itself to be. Regardless of Casaubon's notion that Theophrastus wrote in order to
make men better and in spite of the evidence in Hall's volume
that the Character could be an elevating and even eloquent means
of instruction, its capacities for giving pleasure seemed its true
forte. The vogue of the Character resulted from its nature, and
its nature Theophrastus showed was especially to portray not
perfection in mankind but the many and picturesque kinds of
imperfection. English writers repeatedly tried to make the genre
"practical." George Wither, for example, thought he could
make two Characters,[48] one of the Honest Stationer and the
other "A meere Stationer," lend weight to his argument that
the Stationers Company had outrageously mistreated him as well

---

[48]Not so labeled but almost certainly intended to be Characters. They
appeared in *The Schollers Purgatory* (1625), and are reprinted in Gwendolen Murphy's *Cabinet of Characters*, pp. 151-156.

as other deserving poets. But the two pieces are not impressive. The idea that the genre might be employed in moral and theoretical discussions may have been fostered by Aristotle's inclusion of the discursive, comparative analyses of young men, old men, middle-aged men, and so forth in his *Rhetoric* and by two or three similar discussions in his *Nicomachean Ethics*. The former analyses as well as the briefer sketches in Horace's *Art of Poetry* were paraphrased by Daniel Tuvill in the ninth chapter of his *Dove and the Serpent* (1614); the analyses of youth and age appeared also in John Reynolds' translation of *A Treatise of the Court or Instructions for Courtiers* (1622) by Denys de Refuges.[49] Earlier, in 1606, Lodowick Bryskett copied Aristotle's description of the magnanimous man as well as Horace's passage on the youth into his *Discourse of Civill Life*.[50] But Aristotle's analyses are not Characters: the varying of the subject in Reynolds' version from "wee" to "they" to "young men" demonstrates one difference. Nor is the description, the exposé of prison conditions, the sermon, or the dispersed, meditative essay a Character, even if writers tried to incorporate the latter in the former.

Of the Characters and near-Characters surveyed in this chapter, those that best remain in the memory are the graphic and stylistically pointed ones; but of these, many stay in the mind less with the effect of a Character than simply as good imaginative description, sharply phrased. The Character at its best is at least partially objective; it also is compact, carefully typical, and well set off from other writing. Because of Hall's and Overbury's books and to a lesser extent because of Stephens' and Breton's, the genre pushed its way into many places in the first two decades of the century, almost always to the profit of the literary work that gave it shelter. The most artistic Characters, none the less, will be found in the Character-books.

---

[49] I, xxvii.   [50] Pages 232-233.

VIII
THE
MAIN CHARACTER-BOOKS
AFTER OVERBURY

1. JOHN STEPHENS

The third Englishman to offer a book of Characters was neither a divine nor a courtier but, rather, a member of Lincoln's Inn.[1] He was John Stephens, a gentleman of a Gloucester family, whose recorded associations were with inns-of-court men but who also could boast that a play of his, the tedious *Cynthia's Revenge* (1613), had won commendation from Ben Jonson. He had no great gift for letters, but because of his interest in the world about him his Characters are worth reading. The first edition bore the title *Satyrical Essayes Characters and Others. Or Accurate and quick Descriptions, fitted to the life of their Subiects* (1615) and carried mottoes on its title page from Juvenal and Theophrastus. It contained, first of all, three verse satires on cowardliness, written after Juvenal's manner with brief comments on current vices and vicious classes. Then came four prose essays, Baconian neither in method nor style, which allowed Stephens to consider his subjects in leisurely fashion, to apply to them the wisdom of Solomon and Aristotle, and to add his individual judgments. Since he included both an essay "Of Discontents" and a bona fide Character of "A Contented Man," one can see that, though Stephens (like apparently everyone else) thought that Characters and essays and satires might properly be bound together in one pair of covers, he was clearer than many on what the artistic distinctions were between them.

---

[1] It is possible that Breton preceded with *Characters upon Essaies*, which seems to have been entered in the Stationers' Register May 4, 1615 (Arber's edition, III, 567). Stephens' book was not entered.

Of the forty-three Characters in the little book, there are three near the beginning that present virtuous moral types ("A Complete Man," "A Good Husband," "A Contented Man"); there is one, "A Good Emperor," that treats an Estate topic and suggests that Stephens may have seen in manuscript Breton's forthcoming collection, *The Good and the Badde;* there are half a dozen types from Stephens' own legal profession and three from the writers' guild; and, especially novel, there are some rural types. As has been pointed out in Chapter VI, about a quarter of the types are moral, another quarter social or occupational, but about half combine moral and social features, as in "A Worthy Poet" and "A Crafty Scrivener." In general Stephens ranged among bourgeois and humble folk, not courtiers.

When the volume was published, the Overbury collection had already reached its fifth edition (containing thirty-two Characters). It was a matter of course that the third Character-book should have ties with the first and second. Stephens defined a worthy poet as one that "hath more debtors in knowledge among the present Writers, then Creditors among the ancient Poets" and that "paies back all his imitation with interest." On the whole it must be said that Stephens had fewer debts than most Character-writers. His "Complete Man," however, resembles Hall's sketches of the virtuous in its generality and subjective evaluation as well as in its ideas. His "Good Husband" perhaps echoes a phrase of Hall's.[2] His "Churl," "Gossip," "Farmer," and "Humorist" may have taken hints from Theophrastus,[3] though Stephens' debts to the Greek Characters are nothing

---

[2]Hall's Wise Man "loves to be guessed at, not known," and Stephens' man "seekes rather to bee well knowne, then commonly noted." Compare also, for possible debts, "A Parish Politician" and Hall's "Unconstant," a "Churl" and the first part of Hall's "Malcontent." The alchemist figure in his "Jailor" had been used in Hall's "Covetousness," Adams' *Divells Banket*, and Overbury's "Tailor."

[3]The "Humorist" from Theophrastus' "Late-learning."

compared with Hall's and fewer than Earle's. The greatest influence was that of the Overbury collection. Stephens' selecting types from the current social scene, his tart way of speaking of them (thus, the Country Bridegroom "hath no vaine-glory; for he contemnes fine cloathes with dropping pottage in his bosome"), the occasional construction of a Character out of a set of brittle puns and witticisms that really tell little about the type—all these features show that Stephens had taken lessons from Overbury. The disrespectful "Mere Common Lawyer" inserted in the latest edition of the Overbury collection may have encouraged Stephens to go into the field of law more carefully, judiciously separating the good and the bad. Possibly there were other debts.

These dependences Lawrence Lisle, the publisher of the Overbury collection, did not accept placidly. The cause of his excitement was, no doubt, as Mr. Paylor divines,[4] not that Stephens should have borrowed ideas from his book but that he should have presumed to write Characters at all and thus reduce Lisle's market. Whatever the reason, Lisle's sixth edition, published later in the year (1615), included a caustic allusion to the "imitating Characterist"; this allusion was embedded in a laudatory portrait of an "Excellent Actor" which was meant to silence or at least combat the ridicule aimed at the acting profession in Stephens' "Common Player." The probability that John Webster, the dramatist, wrote the new Character (and many more) for the sixth edition makes the controversy doubly interesting and suggests that some sort of feud was in progress.[5]

---

[4] *The Overburian Characters*, pp. xx-xxi. This theory should not be pushed too far; for Lisle was one of the publishers this same year of Hall's *Recollection of such Treatises*, containing his *Characters*.

[5] The feud seems to have lasted until 1620, in which year Henry Fitzgeffry's *Certain Elegies* contained commendatory verses by John Stephens (whom Jonson had praised in 1613) and an attack on "Crabbed (Web-

But the debts were not all contracted nor the insults all paid. Let us take the debts first. Stephens' collection presented a Character of a jailor which, if not a very Theophrastan report on the conduct of a type, is at least more descriptive than the emotional Character of a jailor introduced in the ninth (1616) edition of the Overbury collection (and written probably by Thomas Dekker, another friend to the profession of acting that Stephens had ridiculed). Perhaps Lisle's six prison Characters were in a measure due to Stephens. Another tie comes by way of the rustic types. Lisle had published two such Characters, the "Country Gentleman," based perhaps upon a hint from Theophrastus' "Boorishness," and the "Elder Brother"; both are mildly sarcastic and represent the upper classes. Stephens put into his *Satyrical Essayes Characters* sketches of "A Warrener," "A Huntsman," "A Falconer," "A Farmer," "A Country Bride" and "Bridegroom," none of which can be called hostile though they do not falsify, not even in the case of the "Bride." The boorish farmer that Theophrastus had presented was a more offensive creature. For Stephens' pictures the word *realistic* is perhaps appropriate, and it points out a new tone in English Charactery.

The sixth edition of the Overbury volume contained not only the "Noble and Retired Housekeeper" and the "Franklin," both admiringly drawn, and the sarcastic "Engrosser of Corn," but also the famous "Fair and Happy Milkmaid," who is as humble as Stephens' rustics but refined into a quite different, idyllic sort of being. When we learn[6] that the "Milkmaid" was constructed with the help of sentences from Sidney's *Arcadia*, we can see

sterio)," the playwright-critic. Perhaps the first Character in Stephens' volume, "An impudent Censurer," was understood by Webster, properly or improperly, to be a caricature of himself.

[6] See the article by H. Dugdale Sykes, *Notes and Queries*, 11th Series, XI (1915), 335-337.

that if Stephens was less the artist in two senses (for his "Bride" and "Bridegroom" are imperfect Characters in being too nearly fixed in place and time), he was more original and in the latter pieces a better observer. He was favorably impressed, however— and who is not?—by the idealistic "Milkmaid" even as Lisle (or Webster) seems to have been stimulated by Stephens' realistic sketches. So to the second edition of his book Stephens added "An Honest Shepherd," which was a fairly successful attempt to match the "Milkmaid" with a male counterpart of equal innocence and pastoral charm. We need not try to balance the ledger in this account, but one may speculate on the possibility that the rivalry between the Overburians and Stephens led to the assembling of the "Milkmaid." It is possible, too, that that Character in turn intensified the pastoral atmosphere of the delightful scene in *The Compleat Angler* (1653) in which Walton blessed the obliging country girl with "Sir *Thomas Overbury's* Milk-maids wish" only a few pages after his fishermen found a high hedge to defend them, just as "the next groave" defended Stephens' Shepherd, from a gentle shower.

Stephens' style in these pieces can be illustrated by the following example.

A Farmer

Is a concealed commodity: his worth or value is not fully knowne till he be halfe rotten, and then he is worth nothing: he hath Religion enough to say, *God blesse his Maiesty; God send peace, and faire weather;* So that one may picke Harvest out of him to be his time of happines: but the Tith-sheafe goes against his conscience; for he had rather spend the value upon his Reapers and Plough-men, then bestow any thing to the maintenance of a Parson. Hee is sufficiently booke-read, nay a profound Doctor, if he can search into the diseases of Cattell; and to fore-tell raine by tokens, makes him a miraculous Astronomer. To

speake good English is more then he much regards; and for
him not to contemne all Arts and Languages, were to con-
demne his owne education. The pride of his housekeeping
is a messe of Creame, a Pig, or a greene Goose, and if his
servants can uncontrowled finde the high-way to the Cup-
boord, it winnes the name of a bountifull Yeoman. To
purchase Armes (if he æmulates Gentry) sets upon him
like an Ague . . . and he can never be quiet till the *Herald*
hath given him the Harrowes, the Cuckow, or some ridiculous Embleme for his Armory. The bringing up, and
Mariage of his eldest sonne, is an ambition which afflicts
him so soone as the boy is borne, and the hope to see his
sonne . . . placed above him, drives him to dote upon the
boy in his Cradle: To peruse the Statutes and preferre them
before the Bible, makes him purchase the credit of a shrewd
fellow, and then he brings all adversaries to composition . . .
Meane time, he makes the prevention of a dearth his title,
to be thought a good Common-wealths man: And therefore
hee preserves a Chandelors treasure of Bacon, Linkes and
Puddings in the Chimney corner. Hee is quickely and
contentedly put into the fashion, if his cloathes bee made
against Whitsontide or Christmas day: and then outwardly
hee contemnes appearance: he cannot therefore choose but
hate a *Spaniard* likewise; and (hee thinkes) *that hatred*
onely, makes him a loyall subiect: for benevolence and sub-
sidies be more unseasonable to him, then his quarters rent.
Briefly, being a good house-keeper, hee is an honest man;
and so, hee thinkes of no rising higher, but rising early in
the morning; and beeing up, hee hath no end of motion,
but wanders in his woods and pastures so effectually, that
when he sleepes, or sits, hee wanders likewise. After this,
he turns into his element, by being too *ventrous* hot, & cold:
then he is fit for nothing but a checkered grave: howsoever
some may think him convenient to make an everlasting
bridge; because his best foundation hath been (perhaps)
upon wool-packes.

As for the insults, those aimed at Stephens in the sixth edition of the Overbury collection were sent back, with corrections and additions, in Stephens' later edition, to which he gave the title *Essays and Characters, Ironicall and Instructive* (1615).[6a] The front-matter includes sneers at the author of the Overburian "Excellent Actor" and a claim by "I. Cocke" that he had written three Characters (the "Tinker," "Apparator," and "Almanac-Maker") stolen by Lisle for his collection. Stephens also printed a new verse satire in defense of lawyers, written as a rebuttal probably to the Overburians and also to a play by George Ruggle called *Ignoramus*.[7]

It is not Stephens' method that makes him interesting, for his combination of general and particular, of analytical commentary and graphic revelation through behavior we have met before in Hall and Overbury. In some of the Characters he either had not exactly defined his type or was presenting a remarkably complex one: his "Spendthrift" is stupid and dreamy and good-natured, unfeelingly hopes his father will die soon, longs to have a fair mistress and to become Lord Chief Justice! Hall's "Unthrift" is much more recognizable. Sometimes in his determination to be original Stephens was already feeling the restrictions imposed by the nature of Character-writing: there are certain obvious types of people and certain obvious things to say about them; refusing to duplicate previous work and being limited in inventiveness, Stephens was forced to select more elusive types, such as a "Rank Observer" or a "Ubiquitary," or to talk *around* a familiar type, as when he writes of a "Common Player," "If hee cannot beleeve, hee doth coniecture strongly; but dares not resolve upon particulars, till he hath either spoken, or heard the *Epilogue;* unless he be prevented." Stephens strikes one

---

[6a]Besides making several changes in the text and titles of the original forty-three Characters, Stephens here added seven new Characters. Harvard has a volume containing the title page and front matter of the first edition and part of the front matter and all the text of the second.

[7]Paylor, p. xx.

occasionally as being deeper than Overbury, but he does not write so well. A moralist, he seems unwilling merely to report a significant action, leaving it to speak for itself.[8] Although in his "Atheist" and "Liar" he almost sermonizes, he is more likely to be thoughtful than pious or eloquent. In his "Worthy Poet" his Aristotelian way of thinking,[9] the balancing of self-love against prodigality, of snarling against flattery, of conservative instincts against a taste for novelty, of form against matter, and of essence against "efficient" heightens the form of the Character. He is perhaps at his best when describing the "Worthy Poet" in his moral elevation, the young "Page" in his precocious corruption, and the "Novice" and the country types, whom he seems neither to praise nor to condemn.

Senecan prose and witty figures Stephens took over from Hall and Overbury along with their methods of development, but as one might expect, with some abatement. In the earlier pieces Senecan compression and short rhythm are more conspicuous than in the later ones. In his essay on poetry Stephens objected to "crabbed stile and forme," to "rough harshnesse, and all mystery" and "Phylosophicall questions" in poetry, and to the use of similes drawn from mathematics, astronomy, and other sciences less familiar than the thing interpreted. Such a dislike of the "metaphysical" in poetry would not necesarily extend to the Character. In his own work Stephens indulged in puns and similes but not of a profound sort. His efforts to duplicate Hall's pregnant first sentences and Overbury's dazzling ones had an

---

[8]It is significant that the Greek motto printed on the title page of Stephens' first edition and attributed to Theophrastus came from the late additions. The motto, which can be rendered "It is more necessary to guard against those of this disposition than against serpents," was added to Theophrastus' "Dissembling," and its obvious moralism does not fairly represent Theophrastus' artistic method. But it does fit Stephens'.

[9]See the references to Aristotle in *Satyrical Essayes Characters*, pp. 103, 119.

indifferent success: *"A Worthy Poet Is the purest essence of a worthy Man,"* and *"A Lawyers Clarke Is his Masters right hand, except hee writes with his left."* Stephens' only contribution to the art of Character-writing was his impartial representation of rustic types, but his fifty sketches made a meaty addition to the growing body of Theophrastan literature.

2. NICHOLAS BRETON

The relative importance of technique and substance may be considered in connection with Breton's second, England's fifth, Character-book.[10] Neither the title, *The Good and the Badde, or Descriptions of the Worthies, and Unworthies of this Age* (1616), nor the preface uses the word *Character*, as if Breton had been rebuked for the liberties he had taken with it in his earlier *Characters upon Essaies.* Yet here again he was experimenting with the genre, employing an idea furnished by the literature of Estates, not by Bacon. Once more he varnished everything with his shiny style, his figure of four, which at first blinds the eye and stupifies the mind. Underneath it, however, one can discover that the fifty Characters in the collection are divisible, with only occasional difficulty, into four kinds differentiated often by both matter and manner. A novel scheme gradually yields to the older, better one.

The first thirteen Characters and several others[11] present good and bad exemplars of the old Estates—a Worthy and an Unworthy King, A Worthy Queen (without an opposite), a Worthy and Unworthy Prince, and similarly contrasted pairs of councillors, bishops, judges, and so forth. Following the old way of such writing, Breton considers each type not for its habitual character but for what its duties and opportunities are and for

---

[10]See p. 191 for a discussion of Breton's *Characters upon Essaies* (1615); see also note 1.   [11]Numbers 30, 31, 34, 38, 45, 48.

what a good or bad performance within those limits will mean for the rest of the nation. Hall in Charactering a "Good Magistrate" had also treated the duties and privileges of that Estate, but so concretely that the abstract division of a theoretic social scheme became something nearer to an actual man doing what he typically would in particular circumstances. Breton, on the contrary, clings to the abstractness of the older tradition; he sees the figure from the outside and at a distance, in general and preceptually.

A Worthy Iudge

A Iudge is a Doome, whose breath is mortall upon the breach of Law, where Criminall offences must bee cut off from a common-wealth: Hee is a sword of Iustice in the hand of a King; and, an Eye of Wisedome in the walke of a kingdome: his study is a Square for the keeping of proportion, betwixt command, and obedience, that the King may keepe his Crowne on his head, and the Subiect his head on his shoulders. Hee is feared but of the foolish, and cursed but of the wicked; but, of the wise honoured, and of the gracious beloved: Hee is a surveier of rights, and revenger of wrongs, and in the iudgement of Truth, the Honor of Iustice. In summe, his word is Law, his power Grace, his labour Peace, and his desert Honour.

Miss Mohl has suggested [12] that Breton perhaps drew his scheme of Estates from the *Steele Glas* of his stepfather, George Gascoigne. One would like to believe that he got something of value (Breton must have thought the scheme valuable even if the modern critic may not) from the man who stole his patrimony of land.[13] It is at least equally probable that the plan of the book came from *The Philosophers Banquet . . . The second Edition . . . By W. B.* (1614), the second section of which

---

[12]*The Three Estates*, p. 229.
[13]See F. Flournoy, *Review of English Studies*, XVI (1940), 262-273.

contains a few anecdotes or classical episodes on twenty-six different Estates, beginning with emperors, kings, and princes and ending with several female conditions.[14] Twenty-four of Breton's fifty types could have been suggested by the list.

The manner of expression in Breton's abstract Characters of Estates is that with which we became familiar in *Characters upon Essaies:* metaphors are assembled in fours, not always with much exactitude in their application, and tied together by some form of the verb *to be*, often unexpressed. There is some appropriateness in the style here, for what Breton has to say is well known to the reader, and the rippling pattern of words carries him over many a dull place with some pleasure. Also there is just enough imagination and just enough recollection of Biblical precedents in the accumulation of metaphors to prevent the reader's giving up.

The reader is held, too, by the appearance in the fourteenth Character and often afterwards[15] of a slightly more concrete tendency. A third of these sketches present Estates, the rest Virtues and Vices. It is as if Breton had glanced back at Hall's sketches, from which he had developed his cadenced, figurative, abstract style, and had noticed a forgotten element in Hall's work. So in his "Worthy Knight," "Worthy Soldier," "Usurer," and the others he allowed a word or two for such tangible matters as dress, diet, exercise, rendezvous.

A third variety of Character starts to appear in "An Unworthy Lawyer" (No. 19), who is "better read in *Pierce Plowman,* then in *Ploydon,* and in the Play of *Richard* the Third, then in the Pleas of *Edward* the Fourth." The sketch of an "Honest Poor Man" likewise tends toward the graphic; it seems

---

[14]I am indebted to H. Adelbert White for calling my attention to this volume.

[15]Numbers 15-18, 20, 24, 27, 28, 32, 35, 42, 46, 49, 50. It is hard to say whether Numbers 36 and 37 belong here or in the first group.

so sincere and meaningful that one may again seek an explanation in Breton's biography. In the "Fool," "Beggar," and "Parasite" a similar Overburian impulse to be specific begins to exert itself.

Finally, in the "Untrained Soldier," "Unworthy Merchant," "Unworthy Physician," "Coward," "Bawd," and "Effeminate Fool" the concrete, allusive, caustic style of Overbury triumphs, and even the cadence of fours is, here and there, pleasantly disturbed. In "An Effeminate Fool" the catalogue of the man's actions surpasses in completeness that of Martial's "Cotilus." Weary apparently of the abstract subjects and treatment that he had taken over from Hall, Breton has become more nearly Theophrastan, though the break with his past is not complete; when he begins by saying of the "Unworthy Physician" "An unlearned, and so Unworthy Physician" we see the habit of Estates literature of reminding each class of its responsibilities and of scolding it for its present failure to carry them out.

It would be interesting to know what Bacon's response was to the dedication to him of Breton's earlier *Characters upon Essaies*, for though a complimentary poem in the volume spoke of its *"Lipsian stile, terse phrase,"* there was far more mellifluousness in it than Lipsius or Bacon would be likely to approve. The seesaw cadence of Bacon's 1597 "Of Studies" and of Hall's *Characters* Breton adopted again in *The Good and the Badde* but in the majority of cases with little of the Senecan asymmetry, even reverting to Euphuistic similarity of sounds in parallel constructions; if the "Honest Poor Man" be married, "Want rings in his eares, and woe watreth his eyes: if single, he droopeth with the shame of Beggery, or dyes with the passion of penurie." The artificiality of figure and cadence that Joseph Hall attached to the English Character reached its extreme point in the early work of Breton. It is usually a pleasant feature of the Character, and when Breton's mind moved beneath his word-patterns, it is pleasant in his sketches, too.

Beyond question Breton made his mark on the seventeeth-century Character. We shall see that though John Earle emulated the best work of his other predecessors in respect to positive, substantial comment on men's motives, his cadence often assumes a relaxed, regular flow that reminds one of Breton's rather than Overbury's or Stephens'. Much later, in the sketches of Sir Roger de Coverley, Will Honeycomb, and Will Wimble, one imagines at moments that one hears the same soft movement; Hall started the pendulum, Breton and Earle and Addison kept it going.

Some readers liked Breton for what he said. Nine years after the publication of *The Good and the Badde* Alexander Garden issued through an Aberdeen publisher his *Characters and Essayes,* which is little more than Breton's book versified. Without revealing his source, Garden declares that the intention of his work is moral edification. He goes through forty-eight of Breton's fifty Characters, preserving titles, subject matter, figures, and, in spite of adopting blank verse, Breton's quadrumania, with odd ambiguities in the rhythmical effect. Garden commonly inserts new matter, moralizings and jejune figures, and he rearranges nouns and epithets in the way that I have suggested one harmlessly could.[16] The Character in verse is perhaps an admissable variety, but Garden's doggerel manipulation of Breton proves nothing.

Henry Parrot was also interested in Breton, adapting the matter and style of his "Good Wife" in a Character which he placed among the quite dissimilar ones in *Cures for the Itch. Characters. Epigrams. Epitaphs. By H. P.* (1626). Of the other twelve Characters, the "Tapster," "Drunkard," "Humor-

---

[16]See p. 194.

ist," and "Common Fiddler" are based upon sketches in Stephens'
Essayes and Characters. Hall provided a hint for "A Jovial
Good Fellow," but that Character is of the Overbury-Stephens
kind. The main part of the volume consists of short epigrams,
and the individualizing habit of the epigram exerted an influence
on the Characters. "A Rectified Young Man" is noteworthy for
its point of view; in previous sketches young men are either evil
or ridiculous. The "Young Novice's New Younger Wife," designed with the aid of Overbury's second and third Characters to
be a good match for Stephens' gullible, good-hearted, but im-
mature "Novice," is an individualized type:

> *A young Novices new yonger wife*
> Is a Codling in Iuly that comes not to be ripe before
> September, howsoever sooner pluckt for wantonnes more
> then of taste . . . Its the same Thing in her minoritie which
> we call a woman, who no sooner entring into the yeare
> of teene, but then begins to bloome and burnish much like
> the Strawberry the first fruit thats gathered. Time hath
> not taught her yet the dues of Matrimony: but well shee
> woteth . . . the summe or portion which her father gives
> her . . . is able to keepe two maids at least . . . She . . .
> makes choice of such a Taylor as best can tell how to put her
> to charges . . . Shee knowes not how to chide her man
> without laughing, having beene so childishly familiar with
> servants before her mariage. The most she wanteth, are
> those tearmes to gossip it, being thereto nere accompanied
> with her Mother, and that which grieves her, is not to have
> beene at womans labour, no not so much as her eldest
> sisters, not knowing how soone shee may (unexpert) bee
> thereto occasioned: her shoomaker vexeth her . . . who
> maketh her foot seeme so unfashionable or over-pinching
> as is not possible to be endured. If her new husband grant
> not what she asketh him, twenty to one but she falls a
> weeping, or will not arise the next day to dinner. Shee
> hates that woman of what sort soever, that weares a Beaver

or a Ruffe so curious as may compare with hers for comlinesse . . . Her care is next to have her Picture drawne, could she but meet that cunning Painter who drew my Lady being great with child. Her chiefest solace is to sit at door, and that on Sundayes commonly after Evensong, when being in her best and handsomest habit . . . Theres nothing could content or pacifie her after the cat had kild her Sparrow, untill she had a Parraquito bought her, which lik't her not a moneth till shee was weary of. Her second choice shee hopes, shall prove a Gentleman. If this content her not which now she hath, or things fadge otherwise then are expected, let them thanke her father for it, that made the match, and theres an end.

But we have not done with Nicholas Breton. In 1626, twenty-two years after it was registered and ten years after the publication of *The Good and the Badde*, his *Fantasticks* was issued, conceivably for the first time.[17] Consisting of bright, pictorial sketches of "The World," "Love," "Money," the four seasons, the twelve months, the twelve hours of the day, *Fantasticks* might seem to be offering Characters; at least its procedure is to concentrate on a subject to describe its characteristic behavior within the limits of a page. But the subjects being what they are, Breton must report what the whole compound—of men, beasts, sun, air, streets, soil, schoolbooks, shops, children—does, and one may be reminded less of the Theophrastan genre than of old sets of drawings of the months and seasons. Here is "Five of the Clocke."

It [is] now five of the Clocke, and the Sunne is going apace upon his iourney: and fie sluggards, who would be asleepe: The Bels ring to Prayer, and the streets are full of people, and the high-wayes are stored with Travellers: the Schollers are up and going to schoole, and the Rods are ready for the Truants correction: the Maids are at milk-

[17]See p. 111, n.103.

234

ing, and the servants at Plough, and the Wheele goes merrily, while the Mistresse is by: the Capons and the Chickens must bee served without doore, and the Hogges cry till they have their swill: the Shepheard is almost gotten to his Fold, and the Heard beginnes to blow his horne through the Towne. The blind Fidler is up with his dance and his song, and the Alehouse doore is unlocked for good fellowes: the hounds begin to find after the Hare, and horse and foot follow after the cry: the Traveller now is well on his way, and if the weather be faire, he walkes with the better chéere: the Carter merrily whistles to his horse, and the Boy with his Sling casts stones at the Crowes: the Lawyer now begins to look on his Case . . . In briefe, not to stay too long upon it, I hold it the necessity of Labour, and the note of Profit. Farewell.

The word "Descants" in the subtitle, perhaps reminiscent of the Overbury definition of the Character, perfectly suits these little rhapsodies on common themes. Breton, who in this case wrote delightfully, probably did not intend this work to be a contribution to the Theophrastan genre. But the literary state of affairs in 1626 was such as to make him look like a Character-writer of an agreeably experimental turn.

3. JOHN EARLE

Although it was the Overbury collection that made the greatest impression in the seventeenth century, the Character-book that strikes the modern reader as the most humane and the most rewarding is John Earle's *Micro-cosmographie* (1628). Earle was the son of the registrar of the archbishop's court at York. He was sent to Oxford, where he became probationers fellow of Merton College in 1620, "aged 19 years or thereabouts."[18] Remarkable in his youth for "oratory, poetry, and witty fancies," he impressed Isaak Walton many years later by

---

[18]Wood's *Athenae Oxonienses*, edited by P. Bliss (1817), III, 716.

his "sanctified learning," his "pious, peaceable, primitive temper."[19] Lord Clarendon wrote that he was "of a conversation so pleasant and delightful, so very innocent, and so very facetious, that no man's company was more desired and more loved . . . He was amongst the few excellent men who never had, nor ever could have an enemy, but such a one who was an enemy to all learning and virtue, and therefore would never make himself known."[20] In his late twenties or early thirties Earle was a particular friend of Lucius Cary, Viscount Falkland, and as a favorite guest at Falkland's country estate he mingled with men of peculiar excellence—Chillingworth, Selden, Clarendon, Suckling, Waller, Kenelm Digby, and others. We know a good deal about his later career. He served as one of the proctors of the University, as tutor to Prince Charles, and when his graceless charge became king, as Dean of Westminster. He soon became Bishop of Worcester and then of Salisbury, in which position he "dealt very tenderly with the nonconformists." But the only conclusion relevant to our study which can be drawn from these interesting circumstances is that the man who at the age of twenty-seven or less[21] wrote the Characters seems to have been possessed of unusual judgment and insight. The wit and the humanity of *Micro-cosmographie* were fixed elements in his nature.

There were several issues of Earle's collection in 1628, all

---

[19]Walton's Life of Hooker.

[20]*The Life of Edward Earl of Clarendon . . . Written by Himself* (Oxford, 1827), I, 57-58. Although Clarendon spelled the name *Earles*, there is at least as good contemporary authority for *Earle*.

Philip Bliss's edition (*Microcosmography*, 1811) and S. T. Irwin's revision of it (Bristol, 1897) contain a good deal of information about Earle and his work.

[21]The date of Earle's birth is assumed, on the basis of Wood's report, to have been 1600 or 1601. The Durham manuscript of his Characters is dated Dec. 14, 1627. See *Notes and Queries*, 4th Series, VIII (1871), 363-364.

containing the same fifty-four Characters. Exactly how many issues and editions preceded the "fift Edition" of 1629 and precisely which of them should be called the first has not yet been established beyond question. According to Gwendolen Murphy,[22] the first edition was one issued by "W. S." (William Stansby) for Edward Blount bearing the title *Micro-cosmographie. Or, A Peece of the World Discovered: In Essayes and Characters. Newly Composed for the Northerne parts of this Kingdome.* Mr. Greenough, on the contrary, gave precedence to a more carelessly printed volume, likewise issued by " W.S." for Blount, the title page of which lacked the legend "Newly Composed for the Northerne parts of this Kingdome."[23] For our purposes the variants in these and the other issues of 1628 are not important, and since it is not certain that Earle had anything to do with any or every one of the issues, the obscure significance of the "Newly Composed" legend in some of the title pages, though tantalizing, need not detain us. Earle's name was not introduced in the publication until 1732. Instead, the Characters were sometimes ascribed to Edward Blount, the publisher of all but one of the 1628 editions. In an epistle "To the Reader" which appeared in all the editions of 1628 Blount explained that the author had written the Characters one by one merely to pass away the time in the country and to please his friends; because the Characters passed from hand to hand in numerous transcripts, "some very imperfect and surreptitious [copies] had like to have past the Presse, if the Author had not used speedy meanes of prevention." Here, then, were the true versions, issued with the "unwillingly willing" permission of the author. Blount, the self-

---

[22]*Bibliography*, p. 38.

[23]Huntington Library copy, no. 60210. An issue by Stansby for R. Allot (Harvard copy, no. 14465.40.5) Mr. Greenough thought might be the last one preceding the "fift" edition (1629), which latter contained important changes in the text.

styled friend of Christopher Marlowe and co-publisher of Shakespeare's first folio, had something of a literary flair, as his prefaces show, but he patently disclaimed authorship of these Characters. Whether it was he or Earle who invented the title for them is uncertain.[24] Clarendon implied that Earle's authorship of the volume was common knowledge soon after its publication. In 1871 J. T. Fowler reported that among the manuscripts in the Durham Cathedral Library was a collection of forty-six of Earle's Characters, subscribed December 14, 1627, and, in another hand, "Edw. Blunt Author," which appears to be one of the "sundry dispersed Transcripts" to which Blunt referred in his preface. The wording of the manuscript differs extensively from the printed text in some of the Characters. The edition of 1633 also made excisions and additions. But the variations do not materially alter our conception of Earle's work.

That the Character is a separate and sophisticated literary type might well be argued from the fact that Earle is both one of the best and one of the most imitative of Character-writers.[25] Theophrastus and Hall and Overbury and Dekker and Donne and Stephens he read appreciatively and analytically, noticing a

---

[24]Possibly the title was borrowed from ΜΙΚΡΟΚΟΣΜΟΓΡΑΦΙΑ : *a Description of the Body of Man . . . out of all the best Authors of Anatomy* (1615), a medical treatise written by Helkiah Crooke, physician to King James. Arber in his edition of Earle's *Micro-cosmographie* (1868, p. 8) supposes that the base-word is *microcosmus* and that *micro-cosmographie* means " 'a description of the little world' (i.e., man)." It is at least possible that the hyphen is significant and that the phrase means "a little picture of the world." Certainly the book was physically little.

[25]I have previously mentioned (p. 188) A. C. Benson's appealing picture ("A Minute Philosopher" in *Essays*, London, 1896) of Earle moving among the other guests at Great Tew and amusing them with casually scribbled Characters. But most of the Characters printed in *Micro-cosmographie* are too obviously studied to have been produced quite in the way Benson suggests. And since Cary did not retire to Great Tew until at least a year after the publication of Earle's book (see Kurt Weber, *Lucius Cary Second Viscount Falkland*, New York, 1940, pp. 3, 22-23), Earle could not have written the Characters in *Micro-cosmographie* there.

happy phrase or suggestive gesture here, a useful procedure there, a provoking mixture of two distinguishable human types somewhere else. The art behind the pleasure of the Character was what he was after. Almost always he seems the sort of imitator John Stephens had once approvingly mentioned, the sort that "paies back all his imitation with interest." The interest Earle paid came in the form of greater precision in conceiving his subjects as well as in an increment of wit and of penetration into men and society. Remembering the Aristotelian theory of the genre, we can say that Earle's Characters are often more correct than his English models.

His return to classical certainty of design is not surprising in a man known, at least at Great Tew, for his scholarship in Greek. Theophrastus, whom Earle (unlike the Overburians and Stephens and Breton) can be seen to have read attentively, teaches the art of developing a Character upon a small and precise moral basis, and this instruction Earle had sufficient sharpness of mind to profit from. Theophrastus may also have made him more eager than the Overbury authors were to attempt moral and psychological types. To the same influence as well as to the Christian's charity may be attributed the attitude of mild disapproval that is much more common in him than the scornfulness which in the Overbury Characters perpetually comes out in exuberant exaggerations.[26] The most nearly Theophrastan of his pieces in respect to method is perhaps "A Pretender to Learning," but the clearest debts in subject-matter appear in the "Plausible Man," which is essentially Theophrastus' "Self-seeking Affability," the "Meddling Man," based on Theophrastus' "Officiousness," the "Too Idly Reserved Man," reminiscent of Theophrastus' "Dissembling," and the "Sordid Rich Man," reminiscent of Theophrastus' "Meanness." Earle's "Flatterer," mostly based on

[26]See p. 186.

Hall's, and his "Detractor" have one detail each from Theophrastus' "Flattery" and "Backbiting" respectively; his "Plain Country Fellow," mostly derived from Stephens, introduces one idea from Theophrastus' "Boorishness." Although his specific debts to the Greek come to a smaller total than his debts to Overbury or Stephens, they should be noticed, because among all the Characterists in our period only Hall exceeded Earle in visible dependence upon Theophrastus and only Hall rivaled him in depth. Earle said that the Pretender to Learning "talks much of *Scaliger* and *Causabone,* and the Iesuites, and prefers some unheard-of Dutch name before them all." Did he mean that even in 1627 more people talked of Casaubon's *Theophrastus* than read it?

Earle's particular debts to Hall can be found in "A Detractor," seemingly based upon Hall's broader "Malcontent," and in "A Discontented Man," "A Flatterer," and "A Self-conceited Man." But more important, Earle resembles Hall in his discursive, analytical way of proceeding, in his witty, figurative style, and in his habit of pronouncing judgment on each type.[27]

Earle's response to the Overbury collection was extensive and various. The courtier's sneers at scholars undoubtedly provoked him to write that delightful, backhanded defense of the don, "A Downright Scholar." Overbury's cruel "Old Man" moved Earle to denials and sympathetic reinterpretations in "A Good Old Man." Earle's "Younger Brother" complements Overbury's "Older Brother" realistically but not without compassion. Dekker's "Prison" Earle matched with a less striking "Prison" of his own, and then he wrote three more Characters of institu-

---

[27]There was a hint for Earle's view of the "Child" in Thomas Adams' remark about ambition: "He is a child in his gaudy desires, and great Titles are his rattles, which still his crying, til he see a new toy" (*Diseases of the Soule,* 1616, p. 41). Adams, it will be remembered, was a student of Hall's Characters.

tions. Altogether there are at least eleven sketches for which the Overbury volume undoubtedly supplied the topic and nine more that may have been suggested in the same way.[28] Sometimes the resemblances do not go beyond the topic: witness the Overbury "Purveyor of Tobacco" and Earle's "Tobacco Seller." Sometimes several of Overbury's sketches contribute to one of Earle's: "A Mere Common Lawyer" and "A Mere Pettifogger" are echoed in Earle's "Attorney"; and Overbury's "Very Woman," "Her Next Part," "Precisian," and "Puritan" appear to have made suggestions for "A She Precise Hypocrite." In "A Discontented Man" Earle agrees fairly closely with Overbury's "Distaster of the Time," but he sees deeper into the type, takes him much more seriously, and regards him as a real threat to the commonwealth.

How Earle restored Theophrastan simplicity to the English Character, now broadened and corrupted by moralistic and satiric purposes, can be illustrated by comparing "A Mere Formal Man" and "A Plodding Student" with their common source, John Donne's "True Character of a Dunce," printed in the eleventh edition of the Overbury collection (1622). Donne's Character, inadequately labeled, represents a dull, soulless clod who stupidly moves only in imitation of other folk. Donne also reveals, rather to our surprise, that this inanimate thing has somehow become "intangled amongst bookes and papers" and cultivates (in vain) both poetry and society; his works are rubbish; he anguishes out his words, uses old jests and stale proverbs, gets lost in his stories, assents to all men's opinions. He is a dunce, but a bookish, scribbling, nightcap-wearing, utterly conventional dunce placed in

---

[28]Besides those mentioned in the text, Earle's "Surgeon" and "Mere Dull Physician" were suggested by Overbury; and Earle's "Cook," "Handsome Hostess," "Staid Man," "Mere Great Man," "Church Papist," "Carrier," "Upstart Country Gentleman," and "Alderman" perhaps were suggested by the same volume. Gough's *Overbury*, pp. 134-145, lists some of these debts.

good society. Seeing the complexity in the piece, Earle extracted
the single element of a desire to follow conventional good form
and built on that basis a clear picture of the "Mere Formal Man."
Parallels in phrasing indicate the origin of Earle's figure. The
other, more conspicuous part of Donne's man, his unnatural and
hopeless addiction to books and writing, Earle put into "A Plodding Student." Earle's man shares with Donne's an appetite
for learning odd in such a lump of flesh; the two are alike in
spending long hours in gown and cap pouring over books; they
plod on constantly and in the dull pace of a work-horse; they
adopt apothegms to simulate wit; and their final effect is to make
others "feare Studying as a cause of Duncery."[29] Earle's Character, though thoroughly derivative, is more exact than Donne's,
less given to exaggeration, and more vivid.

To the characters of John Stephens Earle's debts are less
numerous but still important. Both writers appear to have ven-
erated Artistotle. Both could treat a ridiculous or base type with
some allowance for the conditions of his being. Both interspersed
analysis and opinion among concrete descriptive details rather than
preserving Hall's usual way in his Vices of separating subjective
generalization and graphic representation. Stephens was a more
thoughtful writer than Overbury, though he was not always
perspicuous. Earle's kind of sentence, the "loose" rather than
succinct and obscure Senecan construction, is more graceful often
than Stephens', but it sometimes is the same sort of thing basically.

From Stephens Earle took hints for at least six of his Characters; elsewhere one imagines he catches an echo of Stephens in

---

[29] My quotation from *Micro-cosmographie* are from the issue "by Wil-
liam Stansby for Edward Blount" (Harvard copy, no. 14465.40.6).
Murphy lists such an issue as "(b)." Edward Arber's text in his edition
(English Reprints, 1868) came, he explains, from a Stansby-Blount issue,
but his printed text does not agree in all particulars with that of the
Harvard copy.

the turn of a phrase or the expression of an opinion.[30] What
Earle did in deriving Characters from Overbury he also did
here: from a combined set of features he drew the one or two
that appeared to him to be basic in a familiar human type, and
then he built a Character upon them. His "Plain Country Fellow" took its topic and method from Stephens' "Farmer."[31] A
close comparison of the two pieces reveals that some of the best
strokes in Earle's sketch were suggested by the earlier writer. It
reveals also how by ignoring the parental emotions and social
ambition of the "Farmer" (feelings that many types would
share) and by making the man a tenant rather than a land owner,
Earle could accentuate and clarify his rusticity. That Earle increased the social distance between himself and his subject is also
noticeable; he is always the aristocrat, whereas Stephens suggests
that he has a friendly feeling for his middle-class types. In re-
shaping Stephens' "Novice," an interesting sketch of a young
fellow of twenty-one ready to trust his goods and his honor to
any smooth "friend," Earle was less successful; by shaving off
most of the social features Earle produced a figure ("A Weak
Man") that is simpler and a strictly moral type but also less concrete. Earle's "Player," on the other hand, stresses the profes-

---

[30]Besides the debts mentioned in my discussion, Earle owed something
for his "Poor Fiddler" and "Trumpeter" to Stephens' "Fiddler," for his
"Blunt Man" to Stephens' "Churl," and for his "Tavern" to Stephens'
"Drunkard." His "Acquaintance" may have been suggested by the earlier
"A Friend" and his "World's Wise Man" by Stephens' "Sick Machiavell
Politician." It is perhaps worth noting that Stephens' "Contented Man" has
a sentence ("Events therefore cannot oppresse him; for he propounded
all, before he undertooke *some;* and saw the extreamest poynt of danger,
before he did imbarke") that may have shaped one in Earle's "Discontented Man." Stephens' remark about his "Honest Lawyer" that "hee
makes the cause, and not his Client, the obiect of his labour" reminds one
of one of Earle's comments on his "Grave Divine."

Since Stephens' "Fiddler" appears to have been known to Earle we may
conclude that Earle used the second edition of Stephens' collection, in which
that piece first was published.

[31]Quoted pp. 224-225.

sional and public aspects of Stephens' social-moral "Common Player." In Stephens' "Base Mercenary Poet" Earle may have found the elements of the tavern wit which he incorporated in "A Mere Empty Wit" and those of the journalist-poet which he incorporated in "A Pot Poet." Stephens was verbose and careless, but his view of society was neither superficial nor narrow; Earle could profit from both his weakness and his strength.

Not all of Earle's debts were to the main Character-books. His "Affected Man," though owing something to Hall, seems in its first sentence and elsewhere to echo the essay "Of Affectation" in *Horæ Subsecivæ*, published by Blount in 1620.[32] Henry Morley noted[33] that the opening of Earle's "Prison" resembles the first words in Mynshul's "Character of a Prison." Earle's description of "A Self-conceited Man" as preferring Ramus before Aristotle and Paracelsus before Galen may echo Thomas Lodge's remark about Vainglory in *Wits Miserie:* "In his hood and habit hée will proove *Ramus,* to be a déeper Philosopher then Aristotle, and presume to read the *mathematiques* to the studious, when he knowes not what either *Axis, Equator,* or *Circulus* is." There may be recollections in *Micro-cosmographie* of other outlying works. But the main debt was to the Character-writers, whose art Earle seriously strove to master and develop.

Classification of Earle's Characters according to subjects is instructive. There are three Characters based upon age—"A Child," "A Young Man," "A Good Old Man." There are five, all substantial and well-wrought, of religious and ecclesiastical types. The "Young Raw Preacher" and "She Precise Hypocrite" are triumphant in comic satire. As we should expect, there are several representatives of university life—three scholars,

---

[32]See especially pp. 30, 37.
[33]*Character Writings of the Seventeenth Century* (London, 1891), p. 217 n. A connection with Burton's *Anatomy* has been suggested on p. 196.

two undergraduates, and two servants. The court is passed over, and the two pictures of rural types are wholly unsympathetic. Business and professional and city people Earle presented fairly often, the largest group being from the humble and menial and morally low ranks. These latter sketches—of a carrier, a trumpeter, a cook, a shark, a fiddler, and some ten more—often glitter in the highly figurative style of the many Characters of base folk in Overbury, and they have a similar unfriendly tone. In the sketches of professional and city types one sees a frequent continuation of Overbury's and Stephens' habit of developing the social and moral attitude along with description of the tricks of the trade. Sometimes the professional practices are more important, sometimes the point of view. But Earle always indicates his dislike of social upstarts, especially of oily, sober aspirers to gentility; in this matter Overbury, Lenton, and Saltonstall were his fellows. "A Mere Gull Citizen" with its ridicule of the prosperous, sentimental shopkeeper whose commercial and social relationships ambiguously fuse, is one of the best of many seventeenth-century attacks on the type. Moral and spiritual qualities are really the main concern in this sketch, but moral and spiritual qualities in relation to economic, social, occupational circumstances. A great many of Earle's Characters depict moral or psychological types; though of varying degrees of complexity and elusiveness they rest upon the sort of universal human bases that Theophrastus habitually built on. There are about thirty of these in *Microcosmographie*—more than in any other Character-writer after Hall. Finally are to be mentioned the four characters of social institutions—"A Prison," "A Bowl Alley," "A Tavern," and "Paul's Walk."

In his choice of topics Earle several times paired off opposites, thus exercising a right which the Aristotelian background of the Character had bestowed upon the genre but which almost no one had made much use of. "A Partial Man" is said in the first sentence to be the opposite extreme of a "defamer," whom Earle duly described in "A Detractor." "A Young Raw Preacher" and "A Grave Divine," "A Mere Formal Man" (good outside, empty within) and "A Downright Scholar" (rough outside, a diamond within) constitute approximate extremes. As one proceeds, the oppositions become finer. "A Blunt Man," whose coarse, rough style comes not out of ignorance so much as humor, and "A Plausible Man," whose sole and mild endeavor is not to offend, are alike in their choosing a manner consciously, but they are opposed in the manners selected and in the reasons for their choices. Some Characters constitute a chain of contrasts: the "Modest Man" has a low opinion of his own quality and expects others to share that opinion; the "Bold Forward Man" also has a low opinion of himself but hopes to persuade the world to think him impressive; the "Insolent Man" has a lofty view of his new and adventitious virtues and will browbeat the world into admiring him; the "High-spirited Man" really has solid merits, thinks well of himself, and demands strict justice of the world's opinion. Theophrastus in drawing "Meanness" and "Penuriousness" made a similarly fine distinction. Earle keeps on with such work in contrasting the "Plausible Man," who is courteous and cool, and the "Mere Complimental Man," who is excessively courteous and falsely warm; a "Formal Man" and a "Vulgar-spirited Man" both follow the crowd, but the former copies their polite manners and is a zero whereas the latter adopts their errors in thinking and becomes a troublesome fool. Earle had studied the species of men so carefully that he could distinguish not only the varieties that have grown from one moral or social or psychological kernel but also the varieties that, resembling each other superficially, have developed from quite different seeds.

Some of his types are broad, easily recognizable, and permanent, but some are not. Furthermore, the resemblances between Clarendon's descriptions of his friends Earle and Chillingworth and Earle's Characters of "A Downright Scholar" and "A Skeptic in Religion" might lead one to suppose that Earle may on occasion have passed off a portrait of an individual as a Character of a type. An ingenious attempt has been made to identify "A Pot Poet" with Waller.[34] (Earle's "Epitaph on the Living Sr. Lorenza Carew"[35] might in its first lines be taken as a Character of any courtier.) But the probability is that the sketches were all intended to be Characters—that is, typical. What Earle did in separating the mixed elements in Donne's "Dunce" and Stephens' "Farmer" shows him moving away from the complexity of portraiture, not toward it. Several of his Characters are subtle, even difficult, but the cause seems to be their minute basis and theoretical consistency. As for the argument from Clarendon, the probability is that the historian copied the Character-writer, not that Earle copied history. Of course the Characterist may be assumed to have observed many individuals before he writes, but his final picture is of no one in particular. Possibly Shakespeare's Coriolanus helped form Earle's "High-spirited Man" and his Roman citizens Earle's "Vulgar-spirited Man" (for both measure the happiness of the kingdom by the cheapness of corn). Possibly Earle's "Blunt Man" and the self-consciously blunt fellow whom Shakespeare's Cornwall imagines he sees in Kent[36] also had specific models. But in these instances and regularly in *Micro-cosmographie* the typical appears to be what the author intended to present.

It is not merely the minuteness of the kernel nor the theoretical consistency of the development that sometimes creates an

---

[34]Henry Wood in *American Journal of Philology*, XI (1890), 62-69.
[35]Printed from a Bodleian manuscript in Weber, pp. 43-45.
[36]*King Lear*, II, ii.

effect of individuality in a Character. The keenness and freshness of Earle's observation often impart sufficient vitality to his work to cause the reader's imagination to call up particular visions. All that Theophrastus and Hall and Overbury and Stephens could teach, Earle learned, and his technique became perfect. But he mastered several methods and styles. In "A Young Raw Preacher," in "A Pretender to Learning," and in "A Mere Dull Physician" he enumerated the revealing actions of the type, showing him from the outside, as Theophrastus customarily did, but at the same time passing' judgment wittily. This latter, Overburian feature we cannot deplore because the result is often very satisfying. Here is an illustration.

A Pretender to Learning

Is one that would make others more fooles then himselfe; for though hee know nothing, he would not have the world know so much. He conceits nothing in Learning but the opinion, which he seekes to purchase without it, though hee might with lesse labour cure his ignorance, then hide it. He is indeed a kind of Scholler-Mountebank, and his Art, our delusion. He is trickt out in all the accoutrements of Learning, and at the first encounter none passes better. He is oftner in his study, then at his Booke, and you cannot pleasure him better, then to deprehend him. Yet he heares you not til the third knocke, and then comes out very angry, as interrupted. You find him in his Slippers, and a Pen in his eare, in which formality he was asleep. His Table is spred wide with some Classicke Folio, which is as constant to it as the carpet, and hath laid open in the same Page this halfe yeare. His Candle is alwayes a longer Sitter up then himselfe, and the boast of his Window at Midnight. He walkes much alone in the Posture of Meditation, and ha's a Booke still before his face in the fields. His pocket is seldome without a Greeke Testament, or Hebrew Bible, which hee opens only in the Church, and that when some stander by lookes over. He has his sentences for Company, some scatterings of *Seneca* and *Tacitus*, which are good upon all occasions. If *hee* read any thing in the morning, it comes up all at dinner: and as long as that lasts, the discourse is his. Hee is a great *Plagiarie* of Taverne-wit: and comes to Sermons onely that hee may talke of *Austin*. His Parcels are the meere scrapings from Company, yet he complains at parting what time he has lost. He is wondrously capricious to seem a iudgement, and listens with a soure attention, to what he understands not. He talkes much of *Scaliger* and *Causabone*, and the Iesuites, and prefers some unheard-of Dutch name before them all. He has verses to bring in upon these and these hints, and it shall goe hard but he will wind in his opportunity. He is criticall in a language hee cannot conster, and speaks seldome under *Arminius* in Divinity. His businesse and retirement and caller away is his Study, and he protests no delight to it comparable. Hee is a great Nomen-clator of Authors, which hee has read in generall in the Catalogue, and in particular in the Title, and goes seldome so farre as the Dedication. Hee never talkes of any thing, but learning, and learnes all from talking. Three incounters with the same men pumpe him, and then hee onely puts in, or gravely sayes no thing. He has taken pains to be an Asse, though not to be a Scholler, and is at length discovered and laught at.

But the subjective method Earle adopted, perhaps more commonly. His "Skeptic in Religion" and "A Self-conceited Man," both admirably sharp sketches, demonstrate his skill with it. They perpetuate Hall's blending of subjective analysis and witty figures. Because Earle was especially interested in men's points of view and in the psychological and emotional sources of their attitudes he selected a great many types that we could loosely catalogue as types of mind. The skeptic, the self-conceited, the "Partial Man," both the vulgar-spirited and high-spirited men, the "Mere Complimental Man," and the "Staid Man" all require a subjective method. The interweaving of objective and inner description, something that was common in English Characters by 1628, Earle effected beautifully, as in "A Mere Gull Citizen" and the following piece:

A Shee-precise Hyprocrite

Is one in whom good Women suffer, and have their truth mis-interpreted by her folly.

She is one, she knows not what her selfe if you aske her, but shee is indeed one that ha's taken a toy at the fashion of Religion, and is enamour'd of the New-fangle. Shee is a Nonconformist in a close Stomacher and Ruffe of Geneva Print, and her puritie consists much in her Linen. Shee ha's heard of the Rag of Rome, and thinkes it a very sluttish Religion, and rayles at the Whore of Babylon for a very naughty Woman. Shee ha's left her Virginity as a Relique of Popery, and marries in her Tribe without a Ring. Her devotion at the Church is much in the turning up of her eye, and turning downe the leafe in her Booke when shee heares nam'd Chapter and Verse. When she comes home, shee commends the Sermon for the Scripture, and two houres. She loves Preaching better then Praying, and of Preachers Lecturers, and thinkes the Weeke-dayes Exercise farre more edifying then the Sundaies. Her oftest Gossipings are Sabaoth-dayes iourneyes, where (though an enemy to Superstition) shee will goe in Pilgrimage five mile to a silenc'd Minister, when there is a better Sermon in her owne Parish. Shee doubts of the Virgin Marie's Salvation, and dare not Saint her, but knowes her own place in heaven as perfectly, as the Pew shee ha's a key to. Shee is so taken up with Faith, shee ha's no roome for Charity, and understands no good Workes, but what are wrought on the Sampler. She accounts nothing Vices but Superstition, and an Oath, and thinkes Adultery a lesse sinne, then to sweare by my Truely. Shee rayles at other Women by the names of *Iezabel* and *Dalilah:* and calls her owne daughters *Rebecka* and *Abi-*

gail, and not *Anne* but *Hannah.* Shee suffers them not to learne on the Virginalls, because of their affinity with the Organs, but is reconcil'd to the Bells for the Chymes sake, since they were reform'd to the tune of a Psalme. She over flowes so with the Bible, that she spils it upon every occasion, and wil not Cudgell her Maides without Scripture. It is a question, whether shee is more troubled with the Divell or the Divell with her: shee is alwayes challenging and daring him, and her weapons are Spels no lesse potent then different, as being the sage Sentences of some of her owne Sectaries. No thing angers her so much as that Woemen cannot Preach, and in this point onely thinkes the Brownist erroneous: but what shee cannot at the Church, shee do's at the Table, where she prattles more then any against sense, and Antichrist, till a Capon wing silence her. Shee expounds the Priests of *Baal* Reading Ministers, and thinkes the Salvation of that Parish as desperate as the Turkes. Shee is a maine derider to her capacitie of those that are not her Preachers, and censures all Sermons but bad ones. If her Husband be a Tradsman, shee helpes him to Customers, how soever to good cheere, and they are a most faithful couple at these meetings, for they never faile. Her Conscience is like others Lust never satisfied, and you might better answere *Scotus* then her Scruples. Shee is one that thinkes shee performes all her duty to God in hearing, and shewes the fruits of it in talking. Shee is more fiery against the May-pole then her Husband, and thinkes he might doe a Phinehas his act to break the pate of the Fiddler. She is an ever-lasting Argument; but I am weary of her.

Whether in objective or subjective description, concrete and specific details contribute to vividness. Occasionally (and in "A Downright Scholar" steadily) Earle enumerates precisely what the type does *not* do. Direct speech, a favorite or striking phrase can be used tellingly also, as in "A Detractor" and "A Younger Brother." But the particular illustrative act

251

Earle liked to supplement with generalizations that broaden the effect, as when he says of the "She Precise Hypocrite" that she is so taken up with faith she has no room for charity. The less local and less social types are sometimes presented almost wholly by generalizations, which, because Earle struck to the roots of things for himself, are neither vague nor dull. The "High-spirited Man" who is more "sensible of a neglect then an undoing" and "strives more to bee quitte with his friend then his enemy," the "Lascivious Man," and the "Plausible Man" are successful though general in method.

Earle is thorough and consistent. When he built on a small, clearly defined base, completeness was perhaps not difficult; yet in "A High-spirited Man" or "An Antiquary" there were temptations to digress or include the irrelevant which Earle expertly avoided. In several of the Characters of moral types added in the 1629 edition only thoroughness and consistency save the work from failure. In these pieces—"An Insolent Man," "A Meddling Man," "A Rash Man," "An Affected Man," and a few more—the topics are simple, familiar moral types, in some cases already treated by Theophrastus. But being general and subjective they lack the vividness that Theophrastus' method would have supplied, and they possess little wit. If the more successful "Good Old Man," "Mere Gull Citizen," "Poor Man," and "Ordinary Honest Man" (as special a type as most of these are common) were not among the lot, one might say that the whole group did not appear in the first collection because Earle or Blount rightly judged them less interesting.

The really dangerous tendency in Earle's writing is one we have seen before—the inclination to offer "dispersed meditations" on subjects, in a word, to write essays. In the four Characters of institutions he clung to his subject persistently and thus managed to suggest its essence (if such institutions as a tavern or Paul's Walk can be imagined to have essences) by a selection of metaphors and concrete data. Such Charactering is hard to do. Where we see the disintegrating influence of the essay-impulse is rather in the occasional spreading out of an individual representative person into a vision of the whole group, as in "A Mere Empty Wit," "A Lascivious Man," and "An Insolent Man." In the bittersweet Character of "A Child" the older, much less innocent spectator is almost as clearly and constantly envisaged as the child. In "A Poor Man" the reflective spectator is again introduced, and we notice that the subject is really the effect of poverty on both the poor man and his richer neighbors. In "Acquaintance" the concrete method of the Character yields entirely to the abstract and comparative method of the essay, indeed of many previous essays similarly concerned with an evaluation of friendship.[37] Yet the word *Essayes* printed in the descriptive title of Earle's collection meant, if we are to be accurate, less than it did in the title of Stephens' book.

For didacticism was less central in Earle's nature or, at least, less dynamic, than an analytical cast of mind, an instinctive sense for psychology, and an interest in the configurations in the appearance of society that come from the mental and emotional impulses within individuals. Of course Earle perpetually expressed moral sentiments, but when his disapproval became sharp as in "A She Precise Hypocrite," "A Mere Gull Citizen," "A Skeptic in Religion," or "A Poor Country Fellow," it appears to have been the ecclesiastic or the aristocrat, not the moralist, who was excited. His professed ideal was Christian humanism. Like his "Grave Divine" he counted it not profaneness "to bee polisht with humane reading, or to smooth his way by *Aristotle* to

---

[37]In addition to the method of Bacon's essays Earle seems almost to be adopting Bacon's style in his saying "for it is with men as with pictures, the best show better a far off and at distance; and the closer you come to them, the courser they are."

schoole-divinitie," and a good deal of classical reasonableness shows in the majority of his Characters. Errors in morality moved him to thoughtfulness and melancholy, even to cynicism, but not to anger. How the Idols of the Cave twist and thwart people he repeatedly pointed out. Self-deception is everywhere, and the ruling passion encourages and fortifies extravagance. More than most Character-writers Earle suggested the unhappiness locked up in men—in the young man, in the self-conceited man, in the modest man, even in the high-spirited man. Earle's sole picture of a generally admirable man, the "Staid Man," suggests a broader ideal than the extreme Stoic type presented by Hall. Earle was too much the artist not to give each Character a "slant," but he was too truly the scholar to conceal the doubleness of men.

Yet that subtle penetration into the difficulties of men's relations with each other and with their own egos which he was able to achieve he did not always attempt. Tradesfolk and servants did not interest him, except as peculiar social phenomena; so he made up for a lack of psychological depth in his pictures of them by an application of decorative figures to the surface. Hence the number of puns and surprising quibbles in "A Player" (whose life is not idle, for it is all action), "A Carrier" (no unlettered man), "A Trumpeter" ("the Elephant with the great Trunke, for hee eates nothing but what comes through this way," and who, though humble, is puffed up), "An Old College Butler" (a man of reckoning), and so on. Such chatter is mostly for the fun of it. When his interest was really engaged, Earle's wit still played with words (the "Church Papist" brings in his body to save his bail; the "Upstart Country Knight" when justice of the peace will do wrong with more right) and still spoke in contradictions (the "Contemplative Man" comes "not in Company, because hee would not be solitary"), but rhetoric here has a serious function. And since Earle delighted in irony, paradox and antithesis were more than stylistic devices in his better compositions.

His wit is best when combined with humor. The exaggerations of respectable human instincts and capacities that render absurd the antiquary, the downright scholar, the merely formal man, the farmer, the young man, the official of the College of Heralds moved Earle to interesting laughter, as did the excesses of less tolerable human propensities. The Herald, "like some shamelesse Queane," fathers more children on the gentry than they ever begot. The She Precise Hypocrite, who "knowes her own place in heaven as perfectly, as the Pew shee ha's a key to," the Antiquary, who reads only those inscriptions which are illegible, the "Skeptic in Religion," who "could like the gray haires of Poperie, did not some dotages their stagger him," and others in Earle's gallery are amusing as well as thought-provoking. Fewer of the sallies in these Characters discover "occult resemblances" than do those in the shallower pieces; Earle's humor and insight are reward enough without conceits.

But there are signs that Earle and Donne were contemporaries. In the Characters as in Donne's work, analysis of human behavior penetrates insistently to motives and desires, and the psychological inspection is phrased imaginatively, colloquially, sometimes with an air of irritation. The famous metaphysical conceit, conspicuous in the poet for its logical complexity and surprise and its functional value, cannot be said to appear identically or often in Earle.[38] There are surprises, to be sure (though

[38] In attempting to place Earle in relation to the elusive concept "metaphysical," I have used ideas from Williamson's *The Donne Tradition* (pp. 90-98), W. B. Smith's "What is Metaphysical Poetry?" (*Sewanee Review*, XLII [1934], 261-272), Tuve's "Imagery and Logic," Brandenburg's "The Dynamic Image in Metaphysical Poetry," and a paper on English baroque literature read by Roy Daniells at the annual meeting of the Modern Language Association (General Topics IX), December, 1945.

in general Earle is less fantastic than Overbury): the Carrier "is the Vault in Gloster Church, that conveyes Whispers at a distance; for hee takes the sound out of your mouth at Yorke, and makes it bee heard as farre as London." The logical burden of such a metaphor is neither sufficiently intricate nor sufficiently important to the sense of the piece to suggest Donne's performances, even if one guesses that Donne would have relished the figure. Instead we here have "style," appliquéd in the manner of some of the Overbury Characters. In Earle too there is little of the "metaphysical shudder." As one must associate the extreme Lipsian style and Stoic idealism of Hall and the bitterness of Overbury with the Jacobean court and the temperamental intensities that produced the Civil Wars, so one may see in the greater openness of Earle's sentence-structure[39] and in the greater moderation of his attitudes the kind of man who could later appeal to Charles the Merry and, indeed, who may as tutor have been in part responsible for his shaping. Though far from simple, Earle appears less baroque than Donne, for his tensions and obscurities were more nearly resolved. But these witty clerics had a real affinity; it seems appropriate that Isaak Walton, the devoted biographer of Donne and Herbert, should also have spoken warmly of Earle—but in a Life of the reasonable Hooker.

One further aspect of Earle's style we may notice, his development of Hall's rhetorical ending. Sometimes Earle provided an effect of literary finality by suggesting the mortal end of the man. Thus the "Plain Country Fellow" concludes with the sentence, "For Death hee is never troubled, and if hee get in but his Harvest before, let it come when it wil he cares not."[40] The "Antiquary" and "A Child" demonstrate Earle's charming use

---

[39]See pp. 181-185.
[40]Stephens' "Farmer," mentioning the man's death in the penultimate assertion, had prevented the effect of finality by concluding in an extra figure.

of this device.[41] Often finality is achieved by a suggestion of the probable end of a type: the Young Gentleman of the University next will become an inns-of-court snob; the Young Raw Preacher may, with effort, attain to thirty pounds a year and a chamber-maid, "with whom wee leave him now in the bonds of Wedlocke. Next Sunday you shal have him againe." Whether with a pun or a modest hope of reform or a witty hint that each of us is merely one of a series, Earle always concluded a Character in a stylistic felicity.

4. FRANCIS LENTON

The first Character-book to be published after Earle's seems not to have been regarded with great admiration by its author nor to require much from us. Its title page reads *Micrologia. Characters, or Essayes, Of Persons, Trades, and Places, offered to the City and Country. By R. M.* (1629). In his "caveatory Epistle" the author explains that because men are "lesse offens-ively reprehended by a conceited iesting reproofe, then a serious" he has written Characters. But this hint of a moral aim is sub-stantiated only in "A Player," a Character which follows both Stephens' and Earle's on the same topic but adds a new, Puritan-ical note. The epistle also acknowledges that the author, being unequal to a "Cosmographicall or Chronologicall relation," has "not searched deeply into any mans matters" but only "touched their manners, and perhaps started their humors." The latter promise is the correct one; the book is shallow. Its emphasis is upon the occupational oddities, the professional humors of twelve "Trades" and the public aspects of four "Places." This emphasis we shall see persisting in later books, but it weakens the appeal

---

[41]The "Antiquary" ends: "His Grave do's not fright him, for he ha's been us'd to Sepulchers, and hee likes Death the better, because it gathers him to his Fathers." "A Child" ends thus: "Could hee put off his body with his little Coate, he had got eternitie without a burthen, and exchang'd but one Heaven for another."

of the Character; for as "R. M." declares in his epistle, "Charactery [comprises] the Natures, Arts, Humors, and dispositions of men." Yet he limits himself chiefly to the "Arts" of the toothdrawer, rope-maker, tailor, and the others, ignoring their "Natures" and "dispositions." As for the word *Essayes* in the title, if that signifies anything more than the publisher's consciousness that most Character-books somehow bore it on their title pages, it may allude to the essay-like ending of "Bethlem."

Although "R. M." took ideas from Stephens and Earle, he was even more indebted to the Overbury collection, especially to the punning descants on humble occupational types. He tells us, for example, that the "Smith" is "no lesse ingenuous then industrious; for he is still hammering on some subiect or other" and that the "Fiddler" "scrapes out a poore living." John Stephens, on the contrary, carries us beyond the fiddler's "arts" to deeper human relations when he writes that "*disquiet* is not all the danger he brings with him: for he can send his little spirit of Musick upon a ladder of Lute-strings, into your private chamber: and enforce you to picke your own pockets that he may depart contented"; fiddlers were at first "instruments of the warres; but now of ryot." The four Characters of places in *Micrologia* show that Earle's development of Dekker's idea was still considered a fresh one to exploit. But "R. M." was not sure of how to utilize the scheme; his "Bethlem" becomes a platitudinous essay, and his "Bridewell" shelters a twenty-four-line poem on "the new Law" as well as a description of a progress of rascals, "*Pampred Iades of Asia*," driven through the streets. Yet the latter sketch, though a poor Character, is interesting to read. The sentences of "R. M." are less Senecan than Stephens' but more flexible and expressive.

Neither "R. M." nor Francis Lenton, the next Characterwriter in our list, appears to have had any direct acquaintance

with the work of Theophrastus. But because of the unimaginative, relatively unembellished prose style and the pictorial, concrete method of Lenton's Characters, they are more Theophrastan in effect than those of "R. M." Lenton's book, containing
forty-one Characters, appeared in 1631 with the title *Characterismi: Or, Lentons Leasures. Expressed in Essayes and Characters, Never before written on.*[42] Readers familiar with the preceding Character-books would soon discover the misstatement
in the title page; for at least half of the types represented had
been treated before, some of them—the "Usurer," the "Jealous
Man," the "Constant Man"—many times. Lenton's "Elder
Brother" is Overbury's "Elder Brother" but older, married, and
overburdened with debts. His "Alderman's Daughter" is a
special variety of Overbury's "Very Woman." His "Country
Girl or Darling" is a coarse and foolish cousin of the famous
"Milkmaid." His "Gentleman Usher" had already walked about
in the theater.[43] There are, almost necessarily, resemblances
between Lenton's "Host" and Overbury's, between Lenton's
"Drunkard" and Earle's "Tavern." Occasionally one meets
a phrase or a detail that reminds one of Earle, Stephens, Overbury, or even Hall; but Lenton, though a wordly gentleman,
is less free with other men's verbal property than the professional
guardians of morality, Adams and Earle. Allowed by Henrietta
Maria to call himself the "Queen's Poet," Lenton might be
expected to have the courtier's bias as Earle had the don's. There
are two disapproving sketches of the "cit," one of the "cit's"
daughter, a series of sketches of the shady side of the life of
pleasure (one piece on the predicaments of the bachelor), and
two exposures of corruption in high place. The detailed assault

---

[42]Editions also in 1636, 1639, 1663. See Leota S. Willis, *Francis Lenton, Queen's Poet* (Philadelphia, 1931), pp. 95-96.

[43]See pp. 309-310.

upon the "Double-Beneficed Parson" is especially interesting. But Lenton's selection of topics is not narrow.

In addition to stock types Lenton presents some "Never before written on." Of course the search for new types meant the choice of rare types. The opening Character, "A State Politician" who has fallen from great place, may have been drawn from many examples, but the modern reader is likely to fit Bacon or Buckingham into the frame. The "Low Country Common Soldier" is at least as special a phenomenon as Overbury's "Drunken Dutchman Resident in England." The "Sempster Shopkeeper," the "Lawyer's Clerk," "A Gentleman Usher" (quoted below), and "An Alderman's Daughter" (who is not merely rich, vulgar, amorous, and socially calculating, but also ugly and possessed of a "splea foot") are all close to becoming portraits of individuals. But they offer more rewards to the reader than can be found in the Characters of such indisputable, traditional types as the "Bawd" and the "True Friend." Lenton paid his devoirs to the classical Character in several pieces, and he honored the moralistic theory of Casaubon and Hall in three idealistic sketches.[44] But both groups are unimpressive.

For Lenton was much more interested in his own scene than in universal man. The picturesque manners of certain people whom he had watched and the oddities of certain occupations and social situations absorbed more of his attention than did men's inner natures. Theophrastus observed how people behaved in order to identify and expose the human character beneath the conduct. Lenton, on the contrary, seems eager to catch the manners, the surface maneuvers, for their own sake. His "Chambermaid" has little individuality of character, but her life

---

[44] Of his 41 Characters, 3 are idealistic, and only 8 or 9 more are treated without caustic disapproval. Four of the Characters are strictly social or occupational in basis, 11 are moral or psychological, and the remaining 26 are compounded of social and moral features.

is made definite. His "Double-Beneficed Parson," his "Broken Citizen," his "Sempster Shopkeeper," and his "Host" are alike in being immoral and greedy for money, but how different their appearances! In these pieces Lenton is not the Characterist pursuing the essence of a type but a descriptive writer painting society.

The four Characters last mentioned are really exposures of the tricks of a trade, coney-catching studies on a higher social and artistic plane. When we turn back to Theophrastus to seek the authority for these Characters and others like them, beginning with the Overbury "Quacksalver" and "Host" and Dekker's prison types, we do not find it. Theophrastus gives us in "Wilful Disreputableness" a rascal who is shameless and unprincipled in business, at home, in the law courts. "Penuriousness" also has his particular tricks, but they are such as any man might be guilty of once or twice. Theophrastus does not give us the Dishonest Oil Vendor, the Sly Cobbler, the Immoral Wine Merchant. Always concerned with basic traits of character behind variety in behavior, he drew "Wilful Disreputableness" once and for all; the special and separate corruptions of an inn-keeper, a seamstress, a money-loving priest have the same, basic wilful disreputableness at their centers. When Lenton and Overbury presented current rascals, it is theoretically conceivable that they would do so in order to study the peculiar psychology of each kind of rascal. But actually in almost all cases they did not. What differentiates the types is not character but professional practices, and it is the latter which are described.

Satire, the literature of Estates, and a few other literary kinds could have taught writers how to extend the Character in the direction of pictures of trades and professions. And the extension was inevitable. Moral and psychological subdivision can go only so far, but business and social types will be multiplied or superseded perpetually as the economic and political world moves into new phases. These classes may occasionally have moral or mental characteristics; the professor of accounting or American history, the young welfare worker, the metropolitan newspaper reporter may be as recognizable in their points of view as in their professional behavior and hence could be presented in moral-psychological Characters. But ordinarily the social or occupational type must be distinguished chiefly by his outward methods and manners. Hall in his "Good Magistrate," Breton in his Estates Characters, as well as Overbury, Stephens, and Earle, contributed to the shift from moral to social bases of classification, and Lenton was by no means original. Yet he illustrates the newer kind of work very well. What makes his "Sempster Shopkeeper" so effective is not the pretty woman's greed nor her slack morals but her amusing way of appearing in the window among cobweb lawn and delicate needlework to surprise the passer-by into coming inside to do business. It is a delightful little picture of London life, a scene to suggest the glove-purchasing chapter in *A Sentimental Journey*. The artistic essence of such writing is not that of Theophrastus' Characters; it is, rather, that of Addison's essays and of the novel of manners.

Similarly individual, similarly ample as a picture of a social scene, similarly rudimentary as a study of a moral type is the following piece.

A Gentleman-usher,

Is a spruce fellow, belonging to a gay Lady, whose foot-step, in times of Yore, his Lady followed, for hee went before. But now hee is growne so familiar with her, that they goe arme in arme, the cause sometimes that he slights the Gentlewoman, and yet, upon better advice, pleaseth her in secret. Hee is a man whose goings and standings ought to bee upright, except his Lady be crooked, and then 'tis no matter though hee stoope a little to please her humour. His greatest vexation is going upon sleevelesse arrands, to know whether some Lady slept well last night, or how her Physick work'd i' th morning, things that savour not well with him; the reason that oft-times hee goes but to the next Taverne, and then very discreetly brings her home a tale of a Tubbe. Hee is still forc'd to stand bare, which would urge him to impatience, but for the hope of being covered, or rather the delight hee takes in shewing his new Crisp't hayre, which his Barber hath caus'd to stand like a print hedge, in equall proportion. He hath one Commendation amongst the rest, (A neat Carver) and will quaintly administer a Trencher in due season. His wages is not much, except his quality exceedes, but his vailes are great; insomuch that he totally possesseth the Gentlewoman, and commands the Chambermaid to starch him into the bargaine. The smallnesse of his legs bewrayes his profession, and feeds much upon Veale to encrease his Calfe. His greatest ease is hee may lye long in bed, and when hee's up, may call for his breakfast, and goe without it. A Twelve-moneth hath almost worne out his habit, which his annuall pension will scarcely supply. Yet if his Lady likes the Carriage of him, shee increaseth his Annuity. And though shee saves it out o'th Kitchin, she'l fill up her Closet.

Because Lenton's talents were for description, not psychological analysis, he often proves informative on other matters than human character. His "Young Schoolmaster," for example, tells us that a "new Commenc'd Bachelour" would, "with Lilly in's head, and Ramus in's hand," set himself up in a village to teach "infants." "Two pence a week, by the Rurals, is proffered him at his first entrance, for the literature of little Primmer Boyes, and foure pence a weeke for Accidences, besides his Sundayes dinner, by turne . . . [T]he greatest part of his Revenue, is the fees of tender mothers for sparing his Rod, and hating their Children." But this Character illustrates one of Lenton's weaknesses, his failure sometime to establish a point of view, a tone. Most of the time he is plainly sarcastic, though never as witheringly so as Overbury. But in a number of cases he neglects to make clear what he thinks of a type or what we should think of it. His young schoolmaster is certainly doing badly now and as certainly may do better in the future; we shall have to wait to know whether to laugh or applaud. His gawky country girl or "Darling" seems, on the whole, offensive. His "Carle," a miserable tenant farmer, though "somewhat of the nature of a Hogge," seems to deserve our pity rather than such scorn as Earle demanded for his slightly more prosperous "Plain Country Fellow." The wavering tone is perhaps one phase of Lenton's descriptive instinct. Perhaps it is in imitation of the neutral or uncertain style of some of John Stephens' sketches of rustic types. Again a comparison with Theophrastus will throw light. In his Characters—at least, in those that have come down to us—there are no explicit statements of scorn or mirth, nor are there any of the derogatory metaphors that perpetually point the seventeeth-century Characters. But since he chose only bad moral dispositions to draw, his attitude was always openly disapproving. But Stephens and Lenton in these pieces are concerned less with the basic cast of mind than with the manner of living. As descriptive sketches the pieces are delightful, but as Characters they have less flavor than we have learned to expect.

The subtitle, "Lentons Leasures," would be as good a label for the book as *Characterismi*. Lenton was not a sharp student of human character as Theophrastus was, nor had he the sparkle, the imagination, the pregnancy of phrase,[45] the famous seven-

---

[45]Not that he did not attempt stylistic ornamentation. One sees him following Breton's Euphistic manner when he says that the country girl is "her fathers hope, and her mothers happinesse, the Paragon of that Progeny, though the coursest in that Countrey." And in his dedicatory epistle he offers, if these Characters are well received, to write "more, and more merry," as if he sensed that something of brightness was lacking in his work.

teenth-century complexity of vision that occasionally did make Hall and Overbury and Earle memorable. Lenton profited from the compression of the Character. Actually, however, the Character served him as the familiar letter served Suckling and Fontenelle and Le Pays and Tom Brown later in the century; until the periodical essay developed, other prose forms, of classical origin, provided writers with vehicles for descriptive and analytical discussions of the social scene.

5. RICHARD BRATHWAITE

Richard Brathwaite's *Whimzies: Or, A New Cast of Characters* (1631)[46] appeared in the same year as Lenton's *Characterismi,* and though there is only the slightest evidence that either author was imitating the other, the books are sufficiently alike to suggest what the inevitable development of the Character was to be in the hands of writers of ordinary ability. There are twenty-four Characters, one for each letter of the alphabet, plus four more printed at the end with a separate title page (*A Cater-Character, throwne out of a Boxe. By an Experienc'd Gamester*). All but one of the Characters are of contemptible or ridiculous types, and all but a doubtful few of the types combine social and moral features. Though Brathwaite was a country gentleman of some education, he omitted university as well as court types. He drew a mildly flattering picture of his own class (a "Keeper" of a country house) and presented two or three other pictures of possibly good society. The remaining types Charactered are such as live humbly or contemptibly. *Whimzies* more than any other of the Character-books keeps us in the company of the lower

---

[46]The work was published anonymously. Although the attribution of it to Brathwaite was questioned by J. O. Halliwell in his edition (1859), Matthew W. Black (*Richard Brathwait, An Account of his Life and Works,* Philadelphia, 1928) follows the article on Brathwaite in the *Dictionary of National Biography* in assuming Brathwaite's authorship.

classes. It might be said to be a bridge from Overbury's sarcastic treatment of the vulgar to the more sympathetic studies made by various authors of Bunyan's day and Defoe's.

That the Overbury collection supplied topics goes without saying. At least ten of the types were probably suggested by Overbury's, and in certain of these—the "Almanac-maker," the "Apparator," the "Ostler," and the "Zealous Brother"—there is more than a general resemblance.[47] From Earle came suggestions for the "Ballad-maker" and "Neuter" (a cynical opportunist based upon Overbury's "Timist" as well as Earle's 'Skeptic in Religion"); from Stephens came hints for the "Forester" and "Piper," from Mynshul, for the "Jailor";[48] possibly from Lenton came ideas for the "Under-sheriff" and "Jealous Neighbor";[49] from *Bartholomew Fair* came matter for the "Zealous Brother." But Brathwaite's Characters are not slavish copies; he had his own ideas and his own attitudes, and in each sketch he wrote two or three times as much as his predecessors.

Richard Brathwaite's activities as a Character-writer appear to have extended over a longer period of time than those of anyone else. In 1614 in *The Schollers Medley* he had experimented with the analytical sketch somewhat after the manner of Hall; in *Essaies upon the Five Senses,* issued six years later, he adopted the sarcastic and graphic style of the Overburians; still other uses and misuses of the label and form of the Character can be seen in the two manners books which he was offering to

---

[47] See Overbury's "Almanac-maker," "Apparator," "Ostler," "Puritan," and "Precisian."

[48] Cf. *Essayes and Characters of a Prison,* pp. 8, 29-30.

[49] The resemblances between Lenton's "Jealous Man" and Brathwaite's "Jealous Neighbor" are perhaps inevitable. And it is possible that *Whimzies* appeared before *Characterismi* rather than, as I have guessed, after it. *Characterismi* was entered in the Stationers' Register (Arber's edition, IV, 252) April 29, 1631. Brathwaite's book seems not to have been registered at all.

the public in 1630 and 1631 and in other works published as late as 1665.[50] In view of the wide variation in his experiments with the Character one is glad to find extensive remarks on that literary form in the prefatory addresses in *Whimzies*. In the dedication he writes as follows:

> Many *Characters* . . . have beene published both in former times, when the ignorance of the age could scarcely render the ambiguitie of the word: as likewise in these more refined times of ours, wherein, as in habit and attyre, so in discourses of this nature, nothing but *rarities* (bee they never so light) can afford delight . . . they relished more of *Aphorisme* than *Character* . . . [W]hat else are *Characters* but *stampes* or *impressures*, noting such an especiall place, person, or office;[51] and leaving such a marke or cognizance upon it, as the conceit may neither taste of too much lightnesse; nor the cloze of so wittie an observance leave too much bitternesse, nor the whole . . . incline to too much dulnesse . . . *Strong lines* have beene in request; but they grew disrelishing, because they smelled too much of the Lampe and opinionate singularite. *Clinchings* likewise were held nimble flashes; but affectation spoyl'd all, and discovered their levitie.
>
> *Characterisme* holds good concurrence, and runnes with the smoothest current in this age; so it bee not wrapp'd up in too much ambiguitie. Hee writes best that *affects* least; and *effects* most . . . This hath beene ever my *maxime*, that *singularitie* and *affectation* are *Antypodes* to *Iudgement* and *Discretion* . . . [I] have preferred the *pith* before the *rinde* . . . My provision was how to furnish the

---

[50]See pp. 215, 300. Black, p. 96, says that the Characters in *The Captive-Captain* (1665) are "better written and generally more workmanlike" than those in *Whimzies* but lack the human details and the freshness of the latter. The sketches in *An Age for Apes* (printed with *The Honest Ghost*, 1658) show Brathwaite working backwards from the Character to verse satire.

[51]Cf. the title of *Micrologia. Characters . . . Of Persons, Trades, and Places.*

maine building: for other ornaments . . . they tendered themselves; they were not much sought after.

The Senecan mannerisms and compressions of Hall and Overbury do not appeal to Brathwaite's journalistic taste. In an address to the reader he observes that *"Characters in this age, may be properly resembled to. Squibbs or Crackers; they give a Cracke and a Flash, and so dye . . . Or to the growth of Mushrom's, who no sooner florish than perish . . . But here be fruits . . . of former setting, deeper rooting and longer promising."* Yet it may as well be revealed now that Brathwaite falls into something like "Clinchings" himself and that his Characters are not of a superfine flavor. But they seem to have good roots.

They can be arranged, in respect to method and aim, in three groups. There are six Characters—the "Keeper," the "Metal-man" or alchemist, the "Neuter," the "Traveler," the "Jealous Neighbor," and the "Zealous Brother" or Puritan—that picture the inner natures of moral or psychological types. Although much longer than Theophrastus' Characters and though developed in part by means of subjective analysis, these six sketches have the Theophrastan aim and even at times the Theophrastan method. The essence of the "Neuter" and "Metal-man" and "Zealous Brother" may seem to be largely an accumulation of mistaken ideas; but the same might be said of Theophrastus' "Superstitiousness." The serious alchemist with his wild hopes and the perverse, physical, hypocritical Puritan are especially interesting.

A larger group of the Characters delineate occupations and social situations, the "place . . . or office" rather than the "person." The "Post-master," the "Ruffian," the "Forester," the "Peddler" follow their originals in Overbury and Stephens with much material added. The "Corranto-coiner," on the contrary, and the "Quest-man," the "Launderer," and the "Painter" are new subjects, treated with such amplitude that the result is a picture of a trade or profession and its methods, clients, oddities, practitioners, and chances of success. The moral or psychological bent of the man who practices the trade receives hardly a word. The personal character of the "Launderer," being downright shoddy, is passed over in favor of her career, which begins in intimate services to "Collegiat Underbutlers, Punie Clarks in Innes of Chancery," and ends in a hasty marriage and suspicious prosperity. One of the most piquant sketches deals with the painter's livelihood, which consists of painting portraits (flattering, of course) of middle-class dignitaries, ale-house signs (whether a mermaid, as the ale-wife shrewdly suggests, or a lion, as he prefers), and strangely profane frescoes in country churches. Some of these Characters depict both the inner life of a type and the picturesque, tangible outward routines. Of this sort, the "Hospital-man" is remarkable both for its vividness as a scene and its faithfulness to the probable state of mind of such an unfortunate. In still other Characters the emphasis is put upon the dishonest practices of a trade. Such is the case in the "Decoy," the "Under-sheriff," the "Apparator," and the "Ostler"; the first is little more than a set of coney-catching anecdotes.

One tendency in this group of Characters of occupations should be noticed. It is the impulse, matching that of the Characterist of moral types, to talk about the subject instead of dramatizing it. For example, in "An Exchange-man" Brathwaite describes the tradesman's offerings and his treatment of a group of women customers. But he also deplores spending on trifles the money "which might support a needfull family. But the Age labours of this Epidemicall Error; too universall therefore is the Crime to admit of Censure." With an interest only somewhat less technical than Defoe might have, he considers why prices rise and how novelty catches the buyer. If this is a Character, it is a Character of the Exchange, not of the Ex-

change-keeper. It could without exaggeration be called an essay.
The same discursive and meditative propensity can be seen in "A
Gamester" and "A Traveler." The latter topic Brathwaite had
already considered in *The Schollers Medley* at the time that the
vivacious "Affected Traveler" of Overbury was newly in print.
Now, as then, Brathwaite went beyond mere description of such
showy and absurd folk to a rhetorical harangue on them. A man
of their kind may be affectedly complimental, lascivious, unreliable,
and mercenary, but what really upsets our author is his neglecting his unusual opportunity for learning something useful.

> *Merchants* of unvalued fortunes hath hee seene *split-
> ted*, while their *factors sported*; *ruin'd* while they *rioted*.
> *Curtizans* hee hath observed, their sumptuous state, the fuell
> of their maintenance, and how their Comick Scenes ever
> clozed with tragick Catastrophes. *Forraine favorites* hath
> hee marked, their projects, designes, events: What faire
> flourishes their first admittance to their Princes presence
> shewed; how soone those fading blossoms of vading glory
> were nipped. Stately and sumptuous *statues* of victorious
> Champions hath hee eyed, their inscriptions perused, and
> trampled upon those scattred ashes (the remaines of a
> greater worke) which sometimes were with the breath of
> fame enlivened.

But he is none the wiser; and what he would print in folio for
the profit's sake is undigested, its style foolishly "illaborate."
Brathwaite the essayist sits comfortably down beside Brathwaite
the Characterist in such work, and one hears both voices.

A third group in *Whimzies* are united by a conspicuous narrative tendency. One should not forget, in this connection, that
Theophrastus organized the material of his "Cowardice" in
chronological order. Furthermore, Casaubon regarded Lycon's
narrative description of a drunkard and also the story-like description of the pretender to wealth included in the *Rhetorica ad*

Herennium as good examples of the Character.[52] But it is clear that Theophrastus ordinarily and for good reasons chose rather to expose a moral nature by presenting it in several situations, not just in one nor in a connected, chronological series. It is a feature of the classical Character to present a man's heart and mind and yet to resist the impulses of story-telling and, hence, the temptations of both allegory and individual portraiture. But Brathwaite in his volubility and artistic carelessness frequently resorts to narrative. There is something of it in "A Launderer," "A Painter," "An Exchange-man." But "A Wine-soaker" is narrative undisguised. A marginal note labeling this "A Character upon a late occasion, truely expressed," and the epithet "true *Northerne Blade*" suggest that Brathwaite was describing a drunken ramble of some actual man. For though such a person could be any Northern drunkard, his fortunes are particular, and it is his fortunes that keep us attentive. Brathwaite liked to talk about drunkards.[53] Still more remarkable as a variation of the classical Character is "A Xantippean" which presents not one type but two, a shrew and a drunkard. The shrew is drawn in more or less traditional fashion; "she *spits* more than she *speakes* . . . She makes every place where shee comes, an *Enclosure* . . . *A Burre* about the *Moone* is not halfe so certaine a presage of a *tempest*, as her *Brow* is of a *storme* . . . It is wonder shee fell not fowle with the *Priest*, when shee was married." After two pages about her, Brathwaite writes: "Methinks I see the *creeping Snaile* her *husband*, blesse him, as if there were *Lightning*, when hee comes in her presence. Shee ha's either quite forgot his name, or else shee likes it not, which makes her *re-baptise* him with names of her owne. She accoasts him with such fresh but furious en-

---

[52]See pp. 22-26.

[53]See his most popular work, *Barnabee's Journey*, and the passage described in Chapter VI, p. 215.

counters, as he *sneakes* away from her like a *Truant* from his *Master*. Hee is never more *homely* used than at *home*: so as to comfort his cold stomach, and encourage him . . . against his next encounter, he hath challeng'd a *pot of Ale* to enter lists with him in a single combat. The challenge is entertained, the field pitched, the weapons provided." After a siege of drinking,

> Home hee would goe, if he could goe, but he must first learne to *stand* before hee *goe;* and so by *holds* till hee crawll home. Meane time, suppose him now drawing out his *Indentures* at length . . . and spending halfe the night and more in his short Iourney. Moone-light he needes not, for he hath a nose in *graine* to guide him . . . While his crazie vessell is rowling homeward, a sudden panicke feare suggests to his phantasie . . . the apparition of a *spirit* now approaching. Betwixt two wayes, perplexed with two mindes, he stands amazed . . . [T]hus hee encounters it, having first *blessed* him . . . *If thou beest a good spirit, thou wilt doe mee no harme, such is my affiance; and if the Divell himselfe, thou hast no reason to doe mee harme, for I married thy sister* . . . But this *Spirit* . . . is presently transform'd into some sheepe, so as his feare . . . is to reflect more on his *Spirit* at home . . . Hee findes her asleepe, but muttering words of revenge: which upon her awaking . . . shee makes shew of, by grinding her teeth, beating her fist . . . All this while, hee sleepes soundly without rocking, till an unseasonable correction awake him.

Then her rage becomes violent; he bears it as best he can, casting about in his mind for some way of escape—perhaps their marriage can be proved illegal; perhaps he can have her brought to the cucking-stool. But death alone rids him of her.

I have quoted this sketch at length partly to illustrate a generalization I offered concerning *Characterismi;* Brathwaite, like Lenton, crowds his material into something resembling the Character form not because of an especial liking at the moment for the Theophrastan genre but because it was handy and popular. Fifty years later he possibly would have chosen the letter instead as his vehicle. An interesting feature of "A Xantippean," in addition to the presenting of two types within the same sketch, is the combining of a static description of a type and a narrative in which the type takes a part. Brathwaite was anticipating one of the devices of La Bruyère, the embedding of a Character in an account of social manners and ideas; he was also anticipating Joseph Addison's adaptation of La Bruyère's method in *Spectator* Number 108, in which a Character of Will Wimble, a younger brother, precedes the appearance on the stage of Will himself "with two or three hazel twigs in his hand that he had cut in Sir Roger's woods."

The narrative tendency in Brathwaite's Characters was exaggerated by a modification he made of the custom, well established by 1631, of ending a sketch in such a curt phrase as "whence I leave him" or "it has been his practice to die bravely" or "His beginning is detestable . . . his end damnable." Earle had often ended both a Character and the life of the man represented in the same sentence. Brathwaite's innovation was to terminate almost every one of his Characters with a brief account of the last years or hours of the figure drawn. In some cases— the "Zealous Brother" most conspicuously—the device is used to good effect. But it is also true that some types seem less typical in their last moments. The terse enumeration of a limited number of revealing actions is the first rule in the Theophrastan methodology; the quick finishing-off of a man in an epigram or a withering phrase or two is the last rule for the English Character. Brathwaite deliberately broke both rules.

To be sure, he prepared us for amplitude if not volubility in his prefatory complaint that earlier Characters "relished" too much of aphorism. But Brathwaite was too fond of gossiping out a tale or making an individualized portrait. The common human habit of condemning in other people the faults a man possesses in himself was shared by Brathwaite; he scolded travelers for bringing back reports that were trivial and concerned only with the superficies of life, yet he built up his Characters with details about the way men live that are graphic and true and generously supplied but are neither profound nor fresh enough to be of real service. Dapper Dick, as he was called, journeyed among his alphabet of types with the eyes of a humorous, not a philosophic, traveler. He reported on the world sometimes as a satirist, sometimes as a raconteur, but one cannot believe that he devoted much thought to its political and social structure. In *Whimzies* there is little idealism, and it is the first of the main Character-books not to include at least one picture of the ideal Christian or Stoic-Christian. The only admirable type in the collection is the hospitable country gentleman, who being not "so precise as to admit of no pleasure . . . *keepes Horses, Hawkes, Hounds.*" I think it safe to say that Brathwaite felt no vast admiration for the "Stoicall Stocke,"[54] as he once labeled that favorite type of the Character tradition.

The very want of idealism and bitterness and reforming zeal in *Whimzies* makes possible its principal value—an interesting, lively, abundant panorama of the workaday world of the "mechanical" and commercial part of the population. The depiction lacks subtlety, for Brathwaite rarely penetrated to fine distinctions in behavior, and he expressed his opinions with a blunt plainness unthinkable in the more sophisticated writers. "See," he says in the "Neuter," "how this *grand Polititian* hath deluded himselfe." A cheerful observer of the surface pattern, Brathwaite tended to become the London Spy, not a Characterist.

His style matched his interests. Only in the Character of

---

[54]*Whimzies*, p. 51.

the pleasant country "Keeper" is there much of the compressed
formal sentence-structure that Hall originally attached to the
genre. For the most part, Brathwaite's style is of an unpreten-
tious, spontaneous sort such as his prefatory remarks on Character-
writing would justify. Of the major authors in our list he is
the most colloquial in vocabulary and construction. "By this
time," he writes, "with botches and old ends, this *Ballad-Bard*
ha's expressed the Quintessence of his *Genius,* extracted from the
muddie spirit of Bottle-Ale and froth. But all is one for that;
his *Trinkilo* must have it, if he will come to his *price,* yet before
hee have it, it must suffer the *Presse.* By this, *Nick Ballad* ha's
got him a Quarterne of his new Impression; with which hee
mounts *Holborne* as merry as a Carter." Here are the carelessness and facetiousness that one thinks of as belonging especially
to the journalists of the Restoration. The "ornaments or imbel-
lishments" which Brathwaite said had tendered themselves consist usually of puns and quibbles. The Painter makes "the ugliest
Hagge unlike her selfe, purposely to make her *like* her selfe."
He and his tavern hostess "*draw* both together, but not in like
nature; She in *ale,* hee in *oyle.*" The latter sort of sprung rhyme
charmed Brathwaite: the shrew "never *spits* but in *spite*"; the
laundress has helpers so that "The *sweate* is theirs; but the *sweete*
is hers." The meaningful sentence in the Overbury "Precision"
that he "hath nick-namde all the Prophets & Apostles with his
Sonnes, and begets nothing but *Vertues* for Daughters" is here
adulterated into "He baptizeth his Children with *Scripture-
names;* wherein onely hee shewes the depth of his reading.[55]
Wit has yielded to jokes and humor in *Whimzies.* By 1631
both the Theophrastan and the Senecan aspects of the English
Character seemed threatened with abandonment.

---

[55]"A Zealous Brother."

6. WYE SALTONSTALL

The third Character book of that year (1631), Wye Salton-stalls' *Picturæ Loquentes. Or Pictures Drawne forth in Characters,* carried a slightly different prophecy for the future of the genre. It was a thoroughly imitative volume, even to the extent of duplicating the format and tiny dimensions (less than five inches by three) of Lenton's and Brathwaite's books. What it suggests about the older variety of Character of moral types is that such things were still interesting and still possible but that they made heavier demands upon the author's originality than the descriptive Character of a phase of the current social scene.

Both varieties, and indeed almost every variety, are to be found among the twenty-six pieces in the first edition and the thirty-eight pieces in the second edition (1635).[56] Not much is known about Saltonstall's life beyond his having studied at Oxford and Gray's Inn and his having taught French and Latin at Oxford.[57] It is apparent that he was a close student of the work of others: *Picturæ Loquentes* is a compendious résumé of the previous development of the Character. In addition to the long poem "A Mayde," an imitation of Overbury's famous poem, there are eight Characters of laudable beings constructed after the manner of Joseph Hall,[58] one Character ("The World") copied from Breton's model, at least eight sketches visibly indebted to Overbury's work for topic, method, style, or details, and one piece, "A Farmer's Daughter," that throughout suggests Stephens' friendly pleasure in country bumpkins.[59] Salton-stall asserts his independence by taking a subject from one

---

[56] My quotations are from the second edition.

[57] Kathleen Lambley, *The Teaching and Cultivation of the French Language in England* (Manchester, 1920), p. 203.

[58] "A captain" is indebted in both manner and matter to Hall's "Valiant Man." "A Happy Man" echoes Hall's "He is a Happy Man."

[59] Saltonstall's picture of the "Townsman in Oxford" may have been indebted to Earle's "Mere Gull Citizen."

predecessor and treating it in the manner of another or in a mood not usually adopted for that topic. His "Country Bride" begins in the mood of Overbury's "Milkmaid" but ends in the realistic, amused spirit of Stephens' rustic sketches. "A Young Heir," a rather well-managed picture, reminds one of Overbury's "Elder Brother," Earle's "Young Gentleman of the University," Stephens' "Novice," and Lenton's "Prodigal."

One notices a pretty, idealistic, literary vein in Saltonstall that is perhaps the only individual feature of his collection. In the opening Character he laments that "To make love the foundation of marriage is contemn'd as befitting the Innocency of *Arcadian* Sheapheardes." The last sentence of his "True Lover" suggests that he had been reading Donne's "Canonization." There are wood-nymphs in the "Keeper's" woods. The "Country Bride," whose path is "pavd with strewings on which shee treads so lightly, that she hardly bruses a gentle flower," reminds one of Suckling's "Ballad upon a Wedding," which we may suppose Saltonstall liked; for he dedicated his translation of Ovid's *De Ponto* (1639) to Sir John in an epistle that implies no personal intimacy.[60] The "Plowman," "Shepherd," and "Mower" are made appealing, pictorial, pastoral.

I have called Saltonstall's prettiness "literary." The details are, if not bookish, at least conventional and antique. The figures are simplified; their motions and sentiments are immediately recognizable. There is an ornamental, theoretical decorum of design like what we have noticed in the lifeless figures of Sidney's *Arcadia*. From the *Arcadia*, indeed, these pieces may have been derived just as the Overbury "Milkmaid" was. The following Character will illustrate this part of Saltonstall's work.

---

[60]Hamlet's ghost is mentioned in "A Chamberlain." In "A Maid" Saltonstall may be echoing *The Comedy of Errors* (IV, ii, 27) and *Much Ado about Nothing* (III, i; II, i); in that piece also is a reference to the *Arcadia*.

A true Lover,

Is one whose Soule hath made choice of a mistres to serve and obey: and this service proceeds not from feare but love, and he loves her not for her beauty, but for her inward vertue, which shines through the coverings of her body, as gold worke shadowed under Lawne. His desires are so chast that if he thought enjoying would abate his love, he had rather stil love than injoy. In his visits he uses a plaine eloquence, as best becomming the truth of his affections, Telling her that he loves her, and then supplyes the rest with sighs. If she wish for any thing, her wishes are his commands, and he runnes to provide it for her. If his mistresse be wrong'd, hee makes his owne sword, the sword of justice to right her, and he thinkes injur'd love the fairest Quarrell. Hee loves her not for wealth or portion, but *per se* that is, for herselfe, and could be content to take her as *Adam* tooke *Eve*, though she were naked. When shee speakes hee thinkes he heares the Lute of *Orpheus,* and so stands amaz'd like a wondring statue, till the close of her speech dis-enchants him. If her answer be full of scorne and disdaine, he retires to some solitary place, breathing forth his complaint to Rocks & Mountains, where Eccho from her hollow dwelling replyes againe: and when he cryes she is cruell, Eccho cryes againe she is cruell too . . . If he take his Lute, hee quarrels with the strings, and cannot please himselfe in tuning it; when indeed the discord is in his owne thoughts. If at last shee vouchsafe to write to him, hee receives her letter with more adoration than a Sybils leafe, and having bestowed some kisses on the paper, opens it to know the blest contents, and in answering it spends much time, before he can resolve what to answer: yet at last love quickens his Invention, and fils his braine with choyse fancies, while he invokes no other Muse but his mistresse. Thus he lives like a man tost in Cupids blanket, and yet is so constant to his sufferings, that he could bee content to be Loves martyr, and dye in the flames of love, onely to have this Epitaph: Heere lyes the true Lover.

Saltonstall made greater use than any of his predecessors except Breton[61] of the idea of Charactering a place or institution or space of time. The Overbury volume had begun this sort of thing in Dekker's "A Prison." Earle followed with "A Tavern," "A Bowl-alley," "Paul's Walk," and another "Prison," and the author of *Micrologia* drew pictures of Bethlehem Hospital, Ludgate, Bridewell, and Newgate. Breton's Characters of the months, seasons, and the hours of the day belong to the same genus. Among these pieces one can distinguish those that really attempt to present the nature or essence of a place or time through its characteristic features and those that merely describe the place or time without attention to the philosophical or emotional or sociological cause, the kernel or control that gives the scene its unity. The former, of course, are true Characters; the latter, in strict language, are descriptions only. Dekker and Earle kept to the Character-idea by the use of metaphors and by emphasis upon the effect of the institution upon its parts. The abstract idea of prison or town should be the object of study in a Character quite as much as the particular behavior that happens to be visible in such a place. "R. M." in his pieces thought about the essence of his topic even if he also at times slipped into mere enumeration of visible details. Breton tended to write description; March may have a different essence than May and six o'clock than seven, but Breton was able only to differentiate the outer phenomena.

As for Saltonstall's work in this kind, the majority of the pieces are granular—accumulated, merely. The bright and

---

[61]Donald Lupton should perhaps be mentioned as an exception too, because the first edition of his *London and the Countrey Carbonadoed and Quartred into severall Characters*, which was almost entirely composed of sketches of places and times, appeared before Saltonstall issued the second edition of his *Picturae*. But the proportion of such sketches in Saltonstall's second edition is about the same as in the first edition.

humorous details of "A Petty Country Fair" he gives us, but what distinguishes this kind of fair from other kinds or what holds the meeting together as jealousy holds together the enumerated actions of a Jealous Man we cannot feel sure we know. Saltonstall's "Country Village" and "Horse Race" are likewise descriptions. But in his "Gentleman's House in the Country," "Alehouse," and "The Term" there is a more definite suggestion of the final cause, so to speak, as well as of the material cause of the phenomenon.[62] Earle tells us that a tavern is a broacher of news, a theater where men act themselves, a place of quick quarrels and friendships to interest the melancholy philosopher, a method of consuming unwanted time, and a useful place even if a sinful one. He makes us see what its function is as a social institution. Likewise Saltonstall clinches the points he has made in his "Gentleman's House in the Country" by a final string of metaphors (Earle also ended in this way): "To conclude, his house is the seate of hospitality, the poore mans Court of Iustice, the Curates Sunday ordinary, and the onely exchequer of Charity, where the poore goe away relieved, and cry, God blesse the founder."

A Character-writer who essays the social scene rather than the moral types should of course have a keen social sense, but Saltonstall lacked it. His best Characters are the bookish ones. He wanted an unequivocal standpoint from which to view his modern creations. Earle saw the world through the eyes of a philosophical, aristocratic don; Overbury and Lenton were courtiers; Brathwaite seems, as we read him, to have been a cheerful journalist with a good appetite for life, shams and crudities included. But Saltonstall, a teacher of languages in a small way, had not decided whether to pity his "Scholar in the

---

[62]Since the first of these was published before Lupton's volume appeared and the last afterward, it seems unsafe to argue an influence of Lupton's method.

University" for his poverty or to jeer at him for that and other inadequacies.[63] How are we, furthermore, to reconcile the fact that the Melancholy Man's passions are strong and violent, "not enduring on the suddaine any opposition of good counsell, but like a torrent beares [sic] downe all before it," and the next remark, "If he fall in love, he wooes more by letter than his own presence, and is not hasty in the desire of fruition"? In his dedicatory epistle Saltonstall acknowledged his failure to portray his subjects "with those lively and exact Lineaments, which are required in a Character." Whether he was referring to such apparent discrepancies as I have mentioned or to the generality of his pastoral sketches or to the merely accumulated pictures of institutions and social types I do not know. In any case his defense of his work— "it is not the nature of a Character to be as smooth as a bull-rush"—will not do. A successful Character, as the Overbury definition explained, must be heightened by shadowing; but Saltonstall too frequently had not decided from what direction his light should fall.

There is little to choose between Saltonstall and Lenton as stylists. More formal in vocabulary and idiom than Brathwaite, Saltonstall in his five unflattering pictures of women is also a degree less frank and suggestive in language.[64]. He puns and he tries conundrum-wit: if you drink with "An Arrant Knave," beware he doesn't "like Northerne cloath . . . shrinke away in the wetting, and leave you to pay all." But compared with

---

[63] The presence here of a parallel to Earle's sarcastic "Young Gentleman of the University" and of another to Earle's basically approving "Downright Scholar" may explain the contradictory tone of the sketch.

[64] The Overbury collection contained 4 Characters of ridiculous or contemptible feminine types; Stephens', 7; Lenton's, 8; Brathwaite's only 2. Saltonstall's moral carefulness shows in his failure to match Lenton's and Brathwaite's descriptions of the cuckold (real or suspected) and Lenton's of the bawd and pander. Lenton, on the other hand, would not have been equal to so prim a piece as Saltonstall's poem, "A Mayde."

Hall and Stephens and even Parrott, Saltonstall seems an un-
reflective author and writes himself out at length in loose, compound constructions, leaving little unsaid. Not the earlier
aphoristic manner but Earle's easier style is the model, yet without the baggage of meaning, the unexpected freshness and
pungency of opinion, that Earle managed gracefully to carry in
his open sentences. In the three Character-books of 1631 the
Senecan style of Hall has almost completely relaxed into casual-
ness just as Hall's serious ethical preoccupation has been mostly
pushed aside by a more trivial descriptive tendency. Of the
three volumes, Saltonstall's has the least vitality.

7. DONALD LUPTON

Donald Lupton's entrance into the field a year later meant
still further disintegration of the art of the Theophrastan Character, though there were compensations. For Lupton, who had
come back to England after serving as chaplain with the army
on the Continent, possessed fresher views and more vigor for
their expression than either Lenton or Saltonstall. There is a
breath of gunpowder in his title, *London and the Countrey
Carbonadoed and Quartred into severall Characters*, and the
book, Lupton plausibly said, was conceived and "perfected"
within ten days. But his boast that the "Subiect is new & Merry"
we need not take very seriously nor the commendatory lines of
one John Barker:

> *I wonder at thy strange device,*
> *That thus thou shouldst Characterize:*
> *And how alone that thou shouldst finde,*
> *These two new Subiects to thy minde.*
> *Brave* Overbury, Earle, *nay none*
> *Found out this Plot but thou alone.*

True, no previous Character-writer had proposed such an extensive and orderly tour of both town and country. Yet in 1629 "R. M." had called his *Micrologia* "Characters . . . Of Persons, Trades, and Places, offered to the City and Country." And once we start to visit Lupton's places and institutions we discover we have seen many of them before—Smithfield and Bridewell in *Micrologia*, the Charterhouse and Christ's Hospital in Brathwaite's "Hospital Man," and tenants-by-lease, country ushers, and alehouses in Lenton's "Carle," "Young Schoolmaster," and "Country Alewife." Though the debts are neither numerous nor important, they are there, and they justify one's impression that Lupton had observed many kinds of Characters but chose the least Theophrastan to imitate.

The table of contents leads one to expect a series of Characters of places in the manner of Earle, "R. M.," and Saltonstall. The opening sketch, of London, resembles Earle's "Paul's Walk" not merely in certain phrases but also in the effort to capture the essence of the whole thing and in the use of the same subject in most of the sentences. Numerous puns advance the discussion. But in the remaining pieces, places and institutions are personified (as in the attractive sketch of London Bridge) or described in their pictorial aspects (as in "Smithfield," which tells us about butchers, buyers, and animals) or presented only in pictures of their main residents (as of the master in "Fencing Schools") or variously analyzed in essays. No single phrase will fit all of Lupton's compositions, but most of them seem at least part of the time to be elementary essays in sociology rather than Characters or even descriptions.

Certain of the earlier writers we have considered, especially those treated in Chapter VII, resorted to an approximation of the Character in order to enforce their didactic and moral arguments. The Character-form they consciously adapted to their own purposes. Lupton, on the contrary, seems to have meant to offer a Character-book, but, blunderingly and with little literary self-consciousness, he turned instead to description and thence to undisguised analysis of social questions. Not one of his thirty-six sections constitutes a true Theophrastan Character. The nearest approach is perhaps "Fencing Schools," most of which exhibits the professional behavior of the fencing master, or "Apparators," which treats both the moral being and the professional, though in the plural. In "Country Chaplains" Lupton briefly sketches both good and bad varieties before expressing, in the first person, his own somewhat commonplace notions about both. "Country Schoolmasters" and "Country Ushers" are likewise part Character, part essay, the artistic effect being further demoralized by a pointless alternation between "he" and "they" in the Character parts. These two sketches and "Alehouses" are less unorthodox than most, however, because they were formed with an eye upon genuine Characters in Lenton's book. "Hospitality" presents a "true noble hearted fellow" who wavers between hospitality in the abstract and an actual hospitable country householder.

There is much in Lupton's book to recommend it. His essay on St. Paul's, in which he observes that formerly "the World was all Church, and now the Church is all World," contains other "dispersed meditations" of interest. His fanciful portrayal of "a long, broad, slippery Fellow" who is the Thames, his suggestions for the proper management and use of the Charterhouse and Christ's Hospital,[65] his picture of the actors and spectators in the playhouse, his deploring the urban movement of population ("Of the Country"), and his analysis of the effect of enclosures and of tenancy "by lease" and "at will"—all are worth reading. But social or sociological analysis, which is his

---

[65]His remarks, more constructive than those in Brathwaite's "Hospital Man," are only a faint foreshadowing of Samuel Pepys' later concern over the particular problems of Christ's Hospital. See Rudolf Kirk's *Mr. Pepys upon the State of Christ-Hospital* (Philadelphia, 1933).

forte, like mere description of a scene, will not provide the
pleasure of the Character. Neither will puns, in spite of the Overbury example of their use. Lupton says that in Cheapside it is
suspected that there "are not many sufficient able men, because
they would sell all: and but little honesty, for they show all, and
some think, more some time then their owne: they are very
affable, for they'le speak to most that passe by," and "they that
bring them money, seeme to bee used worst, for they are sure
to pay soundly." The ironic implications of these particular
quibbles justify them, but such writing grows tiresome. In the
latter sketches, including those suggested by Lenton's, Lupton
relinquished this mannerism. As for Senecan concentration of
thought and cadence in expression, they were beyond him. From
the technical angle, this is the poorest of the Character-books,
for neither the idea of the Character nor the best style associated
with it by the English writers of his period really captured Lupton's attention. Yet the form of the Character, especially that
of the later Character of institutions, assisted him to produce an
interesting sort of essay. The following piece will illustrate one
variety of it.

Tenants by Lease

There compasse ordinarily is three Prentishippes in
length, one and twenty yeares. Once in halfe a yeare they
must bee sure to prepare for payment. *New-yeares day*
must not passe over without a presentation of a gift: If the
Land-lord bee either rich, good, religious, or charitable,
hee feasts their bodies ere *Christmas* runne away. If they
see the Ladies or Gentlewomen, or my Ladies Parrat,
Babone, or Monkey, you may know what their talke is of
with wonder when they come home againe: many fill their
Tenants bodies once, but empty their purses all the yeare
long. They take it for no small grace, when the Groome,
or the Undercooke, or some such great Officer convay them
to the Buttery to drinke, they have done Knights service,

if they have drunke to the uppermost Gentlewoman: And it's 'a marvaile if they stand not up to performe this point of Service, or else blush a quarter of an houre after; they seeme merry, for most eate simpering: They dare not dislike any meate, nor scarce venter upon a dish that hath not lost the best face or piece before it come thither, many of them Suppe better at home, then they Dine here: It's their owne folly. He seemes to bee a Courtier compleate, that hath the witte or the face to call for Beere at the Table: their Land-lord fetches their Charges out of them ere halfe the year passe, by getting them to fetch Coale, Wood, or Stone, or other burthens to his House. The Land-lord, Bayly, and other Informers are so cunning, that the Tenants shall but live to keep Life and Soule together, if through Poverty and hard Rents they forfeit not their Leases. You may know where they live ordinarily, for Leases runne now with this clause usually in them, *they must not let or sell away their right to another*. Well, he that hath a good Land-lord, a firme Lease, and good ground, prayes for his owne life, and Landlords; and wishes hee had a longer time in his Lease.

In Lupton's transmutation of the Character into the analytical and descriptive essay on a mixture of economic, moral, and social matters we seem almost to have returned to one of our starting-points, the moralistic treatises and social pamphlets of the sixteenth century. Except for the full-fledged polemic Character and the valuable and delightful department in seventeenth-century prose. portrait-Character, the main variations of the Theophrastan form have been developed. Hall's witty and subjective precept-Characters, Overbury's quick and tart and vivid sketches of current classes, Dekker's Character of an institution, Earle's subtle revelations, Lenton's scene-paintings, Brathwaite's story-Characters, and Lupton's mixed essays taken together form a A few minor creations remain to be considered in the next chapter.

IX
OUTLYING TERRITORY:
LATE CHARACTERS,
BIOGRAPHY,
AND THE DRAMA

Ship-money, conformity, war, and regicide are ahead of us, and the "Noble Cavalier Caracterised" will be set against the "Rebellious Caviller Cauterised." Jesuits and bishops will be damned as well as "all Make-bates . . . whether they are Eves-dropping-newes-carriers, Murmurers, Complainers, Railers, Reproachers, Revilers, Repining Reformers, Fault-finders, Quarrell pickers, and Corn-creepers; with all the rabble of Brain-sicks, who are enemies to Old Englands Peace."[1] The course of true history, including literary history, will not run smooth, and our path at times may seem to go in a circle. The Character as a literary form was perfectly developed by 1632. Yet in 1642 the state of affairs bore a superficial resemblance to that of 1600: Theophrastus' kind of Character was known, but more common in new publications were looser type-satire in prose and verse, moralistic, discursive approximations, hortatory descriptions of model conduct, "humors," and the caustic representation of social eccentrics and enormities.

What we must notice first of all is that the Character-book reached its apogee in respect to numbers in the four years after the publication of Earle's little volume. The "fift" edition of the *Micro-cosmographie* in 1629 and the "sixth" in 1630 were accompanied by the "foureteenth Impression" of Overbury in 1630, a new edition of Stephens in 1631 as well as the initial publication of Lenton's, Brathwaite's, and Saltonstall's collections in that year. In 1632, besides Lupton's book, there were issues

---

[1] John Taylor and Richard Carter supplied these titles.

of Overbury's book and Lenton's.[2] Certainly the reader had no lack of Characters in these later years and, presumably, no lack of enthusiasm for the genre. But in the decade after 1632, though Characters of a traditional sort were written, the tendency visible in the few new Character-books published was either retrogressive or centrifugal. Inevitably the possibilities of the strict form had been exhausted, with the result that the most interesting phases of our study will not be the orthodox collections of Characters.

That these collections were derivative goes without saying. The set of ten Characters by Dudley, third Lord North, "Written about the yeare, 1625," and published in 1645,[3] took from Breton's *Good and the Badde* several hints for its more explicit statement of the duties of "A King," "A Good Counsellor," "A Divine," and other Estates. Reminiscences of Hall, of Bacon's instructive essays for courtiers, and a retort courteous to Overbury ("A Good Courtier") also appear. The most effective note in North is the urgent seriousness about conditions which Charles and "A Good Parliament-man" and the divine ("God's ordinary Ambassadour residing with us") either could not understand or could not remedy. The Senecan precept-Character here was moving in the direction of the argumentative pamphlet-Character. An earlier and more inert variety of the precept-Character was what William Habington attempted in the three Characters (of a mistress, a friend, a wife) which he added to *Castara* in the second edition (1635). The short cadence and epigrammatic propensities of Hall pleasantly reappear, accompanied by the weakness of Hall's method of creating visions of impossible excellence, all the figures being endowed with too many identical virtues.

---

[2]There were issues of Earle in 1633, Hall in 1634, Saltonstall in 1635, Lenton in 1636, and of Overbury, Earle, and Mynshul in 1638.

[3]In *A Forest of Varieties.*

Thomas Jordan enlivened his composite imitations of his predecessors in *Pictures of Passions, Fancies, & Affections* (1641)[4] by putting them into decasyllabic couplets. Breton's sort of accumulation of loose metaphors imitated in "A Rash Man" (also based upon Earle's "Rash Man") gains by the frank acceptance of meter and rhyme. The transversing of Overbury in "A Melancholy Man" is also agreeable. But a determination at this late date to treat such fundamental types as the "Complete Man" (Stephens' idea), the "Rustic," the "Complimental Man" (Earle's idea), the "Seaman" (Overbury's idea), the "Drunkard" and "Usurer" (everybody's idea), in spite of its loyalty to the classical theory of the genre, cannot, at least in Jordan's case, promise much. Equally familiar, though ranging out from moral types to social and abstract subjects, were the nineteen topics chosen by Humphrey Browne for treatment in *A Map of the Microcosme, or, A Morall Description of Man. Newly compiled into Essays* (1642). As the title page indicates, Browne was a discursive writer, and at least seven of the sections can only be called essays. Some others—"A Factious Hypocrite," "A Covetous Wretch," "A Good Woman," "A Brain-sick Man," "A Proud Woman"—are as definitely Characters, sometimes in Hall's manner, sometimes in Overbury's. In many pieces the mixture of singular and plural, Greek and Latin quotations, addresses to the reader, witty figures, and digressive generalization carries one back to the sermons of Thomas Adams, from which, indeed, Browne lifted more than one sentence (in "A Covetous Wretch" and "A Brain-sick Man"). Though lively and inventive often, the book is a retrogression artistically.

The current towards satiric painting of manners accounts

---

[4] This book I have been forced to judge on the basis of the description and selections given in Egerton Brydges' *Restituta*, II (1813), 171-176.

for the majority of a group of somewhat better Characters written just at the end of our period. Though they seem not to have been published, their author, Sir John Reresby the elder, prepared a manuscript of them that looks like copy for a printer. The manuscript has a title page reading as follows: "Characterismes of Errors & Abuses of these our times daylie acted by too many. Written (as a Parenthesis to my more troublesome occasions) to refresh myselfe, delight my friends & incite the Conscious Perusers too Reformation."[5] An epistle "To the Friendly Peruser," remarking that "the Nature of a Character (you know) is to Anatomize the secrets of the Heart," indicates again that Reresby proposed "by displaying the Uglines of Sinne in its proper Colour . . . [to] Beget a Loathing in the Spectators" and also to create an ambition to attain the opposite virtues. Thirty-one Latin epigrams are followed by eleven Characters, which as they correspond in subjects with the first eleven epigrams are perhaps only the surviving part of a longer collection.

Despite Reresby's professed moral intention, his writing tends toward the facetious and the gross. An exception among his pieces is "A Common Parasite," who is

> a Creature, moulded and made up, of all Pleasing Compositions that may bee. Hee is A What You Will, and what you Dislike, he seemes to Loath. If his next Encounter happen to be with a Man of a contrary Humour: there what he Hated in your Presence he highly loves and Admires. Indeed He is of a (Seeming) Singular Sweete Nature, for Hee'le not Crosse you in any thing. Though you Call him Knave, he will Take it modestly (or onely reply) he Hopes you have a better Opinion of him.

---

[5]MS Eng. 243.50 in the Houghton Library, Harvard University. The dedicatory epistle is dated January 1, 1642, but beneath the 2 the shadow of an erased 3 remains. Possibly the date was 1643 new style.

Nature never intended to make him a Schooleman, for he delighte's not in disputing Any thing. He will suffer words of Reproach, rather then Seeke to make his Friend a Lyer. If he be o' th' cunninger Crue; he Loves very much to Whisper: for in speaking Loude, he may Contradict himselfe by the Eares of Bystanders.

He hath commonly A Good Memory, or else he would Discover one Knave in every Company he comes in. He studies Controversy much, but not to Argue it, he loves not Opposition, though for Gods Sake. The Use he makes of it, is to Comply with every man in private Opinion: and h'as severall Arguments to Confirme their Beliefe. He ha's Vowed solemnly (to himselfe) never to Dye a Martyr: for of all Deaths, he ha's no Conceipt of it; He holds him a Simplician that will willingly Change a knowne happy Life for an Uncertainty.

He knowes all the Occurrence and Newes in the Country where he lives: and All he Heares, he will not Bate you an Ase, in his Delivery, but rather give some Addition of his Owne. If you question him for it, his Answere is, He Tell's you what hee Heard, but Beleves not a Sillable, and rather then Displease You, hee'le Confirme it by oath.

(It may be truely said of Him, as one did of a periur'd Lyer) he is Valiant to God, but a Coward to man. In a word, he is an Ubiquetarian where, when, and what you'le have Him.

Except for the sarcasm and the subjective analysis and the self-conscious prose—a sizeable exception, to be sure—this piece might have been modeled upon the work of Theophrastus and is, therefore, remarkable in this late period. The other Characters borrowed ideas and phrases from Overbury, Earle, Lenton, and Saltonstall[6] and kept the same pattern of figurative amplification,

---

[6] For example, the "Wandering Fiddler," like Saltonstall's "Wander-Rogue," is an "Individuum Vagum," and the "Religious Counterfeit" appears to echo the Overbury "Puritan" and Earle's "She Precise Hypocrite."

puns, irony, topical allusion, the startling first sentence. Like the later writers, Reresby inclined to avoid the obvious but fundamental sort of material and to choose a class more interesting for its habits and manners than for its character. Though they lack fresh insight and the felicitous phrase, these sketches are workmanlike.

The value of new matter and a new approach shows in *A Strange Metamorphosis of Man, transformed into a Wildernesse. Deciphered in Characters* (1634).[7] Like certain of Lupton's pieces and like Breton's *Fantasticks*, this is a work of imagination; similarly, too, though it pleases the reader by a stylized description of behavior and the effects of behavior, the subjects are not men and the real charm is in the fantasy.

Perhaps the hint for this original book came from Lupton. But the author went much farther than his predecessor, lighting upon animals, birds, plants, fish, the lake, mines in the earth, and even the echo for pretty personification and Charactering.[8] The preface hardly needs to tell us that we are still dealing with the different appetites of men and that we must look for tongues in trees, books in the running brooks, and sermons in stones. The sweetness of the town crab apple contrasted with the boorishness of the country crab, the beneficence of the rock and its valor against all buffetings, the admirable loyalty of the moss

---

[7] Sometimes attributed to R. Brathwaite. The printer was responsible for printing three of Brathwaite's works between 1635 and 1641. In his *Survey of History* (1638) Brathwaite discussed the usefulness of natural history in moral instruction (p. 160) and praised the pretty inventions of the "witty Emblematist," showing how several fish, plants, and animals (some identical with those treated in *A Strange Metamorphosis*) might teach us valuable human lessons. But like Black (*Richard Brathwaite*, p. 98) I find myself doubting that forthright Richard Brathwaite was the author of this fanciful volume.

[8] Caussin's *Eloquentiæ*, which I have discussed p. 45, in the eleventh book (lvii-xcii) offered "epidictici characteres" of animals, birds, plants that also may have stimulated the imagination of the author.

to the thing it loves, the killing kindness of the ivy ambitiously attaching itself to the ancientest houses all speak for themselves.

The method is perpetually amusing because, except for the fundamental novelty of the non-human subjects personified, it is always Character-like, even to the fillip at the end. Here is a fair sample.

The Mustard-Seed

Seemes to be a thing of nothing. It is even the dwarfe among the rest of seeds; and yet is a Giant if you deale with him. Hee is very snappish, for if you meddle with him, he will strait take you by the nose. He is full of his jests, which are so quick and sharpe, as you will not know how to relish them, for they bite shrewdly. Hee hath a strange manner with him, while hee will touch you by the tongue, and tickle you in the nose, and so tyrannize upon you, as he will make you put finger in the eye. He is alone but a common souldier, but if they gather together, and make a muster, there is no hoe with them, especially when they take their liquor well, for then they will assault the stoutest man of the guard. Poore Iohn were but a poore thing, were it not for him, and a Ioule of Ling, a fit companion for the best mans table, will blush to appeare without his company, when they will never lin calling for him, where is the Mustard? yea, a Surloyn of Beefe, as surly as he lookes, after he hath bin well soused in a brinish sea, and come safely off with a powder, and be never so well larded within with fat on his sides, yet if he have not this case of Pistols by his side, no man will reguard him. Hee is hot and firy of nature, which makes him mount up to the brain . . . where he keepes such a bustling, as hee turnes all the liquors thence out of the glasse windowes. . . He is but little in himselfe, but growes to be an Oak among the rest of herbs; upon whose boughes, the chanting birds take pleasure to warble out their descants, and who knows whether to the honour of this miracle of seeds. He feares not the Muster master so much . . . as the Mustard

293

maker, who puts him into Bridewell, as it were, to pound in a Mortar. If he be of the right stamp, and a true Tewxbury man, he is a cholericke gentleman, and will beare no coales; but will himselfe strike any man into a heat . . . though indeed he will easily bee pacified againe with a crust of bread, and so long I hold him to bee no such perillous Companion.

We are told of the Echo that "She is no *Ciceronian*, nor apt for fluent stiles; but a *Lipsian* right, and fitter for a briefe manner of speech Dialogue wise." Like her, our author keeps to the Lipsian manner, though for a different reason.

So far the writers we have been discussing have used the form and label of the Character knowingly and respectfully. Now we must turn to those books and plays in which all sorts of adumbrations, adulterations, and reflections of the Theophrastan genre appear, often in only a half light. We must not be misled by the word *character*, which seems to have grown more common as the decades advanced and to have had varying connotations. The only meanings given for the word in Bullokar's *English Expositor* of "hard words" (1616; 1641) are "the forme of a letter" and a "marke, signe, or stampe made in any thing." It is the latter sense of the word that we meet ordinarily in Shakespeare. It is this also that we have in Francis Bacon's "Characters of a Believing Christian, in Paradoxes, and seeming Contradictions."[9] Each of the thirty-four numbered paragraphs gives one sign or "character," usually an article of belief, by which to know the Christian. The cumulative effect, however, is that of a somewhat amorphous Character. The other main non-technical use of the word—for the "aggregate of distinctive qualities belonging to an individual or race," as *Webster's Collegiate Dictionary* defines it—was also growing familiar. For example, a character

---

[9] *The Remaines of the Right Honorable Francis Lord Verulam* (1648), pp. 88-94.

in Glapthorne's *Wit in a Constable* (1640) after hearing a ten-line description of a witty and lovable lady, exclaims: "You give her a brave Character."[10]

The word was further extended to mean an account of the aggregate of qualities in someone's nature. Thomas Heywood used the word thus when he wrote of the comedian Greene that there was not an actor "in his time of better ability in performance of what he undertook; more applaudent by the Audience, of greater grace at the Court, or of more general love in the Citty, and so with this briefe character of his memory, I commit him to his rest."[11] Finally, the word could mean an account not only of a person's nature but also of the special circumstances of his life. Such was Jonson's use of it in the list of dramatis personae before *The New Inn* and John Shirley's in his list before *The Politician* (1655). For Albina, for example, Shirley's "small Character" reads: "wife to Gotharus a vertuous but suffering Lady, under the tyranny of an imperious, and disloyal husband."[12] It is this sort of *character* that we have—more highly developed, to be sure—in the portrait-Character, of which more will be said presently. The word could be stretched to apply to the most discursive description and analysis. The publisher of *Panacea: or, Select Aphorisms* (1630) included in his book "A Characterisme of the Foure Cardinall Vertues" which, as a note explains, would not "to sparkling Wits. . . sute. . . point

---

[10]Page 179. Artlesse in Glapthorne's *Hollander* (1640), meeting Sconce, says: "With licence sir, let me desire your character, I long to know you." See also Glapthorne's *Argalus and Parthenia* (1639), II, i.

Dates given for plays in this chapter unless otherwise explained are those of the first printed texts.

[11]Prefatory epistle by Heywood for John Cooke's play, *Greene's Tu quoque* (1614). For similar employment of the word see John Sylvester, *Panthea* (1630), the last page; Thomas Heywood, *The English Traveller* (1633), sig. B₁.

[12]See also the anonymous *Lady Alimony* (1659), II, ii.

blanke with Theophrastus his superlative Idea" but is, in fact, four separate essays on prudence, fortitude, temperance, and justice. One Thomas Trescot could refer to a whole sermon, consequently, as "a lively Character of a Zealous Magistrate."[13] "Analytical and allegorical characterization" is the nearest modern paraphrase for the word "Character" as it is used in the headings of the essays on the history, climate, topography, social and moral disposition of the people, and so forth, of various European nations set forth by James Howell in ΔΕΝΔΡΟΛΟΓΙΑ. *Dodona's Grove* (1640). When the word has gone this far it is broad enough to cover the expository and argumentative essay that is generally labeled the pamphlet-Character. Not one of these quoted uses can fairly be equated with the technical use for the Theophrastan sketch. Yet the latter use unquestionably accounts for the rapid popularization of the others.

Now that the English Character was firmly established, it influenced literature as well as language, shoring up many a flaccid description, concentrating the animus of the satirist, putting pictures in the harangues of the didactic, and beguiling the people in current plays to stop to talk—dryly or admiringly or fantastically but ever descriptively—about each other and the rest of society. Perhaps, too, it induced the poet Milton to make more comprehensive his somewhat theoretical and fancy accounts of the Pensive Man and the Cheerful man.[14]

Where the school of Theophrastus, that "ancient Master of Moralitie," would most naturally exert its influence—in the moralistic and didactic department of literature—there had been

---

[13]See the beginning of his "Assize Sermon," *The Zealous Magistrate* (1642).

[14]As Lawrence Babb pointed out in "The Background of 'Il Penseroso,'" *Studies in Philology*, XXXVII (1940), 257-273, Milton's melancholy man, like Saltonstall's, presents the more flattering interpretation of the "humor."

character sketches from the beginning, and they helped shape the style and tone of Hall and Overbury. But now the current runs in the opposite direction. A long allegorical composition by Richard Bernard called *The Isle of Man: or, The Legall Proceeding in Man-Shire against Sinne* (1627) vivified certain of its half-symbolic, half-typical figures by borrowing the Character-writer's device of revealing a man through his behavior. The figure usually remains only part of a man or a shadow of a man, but the first one, "Mr. *Out-side*," a "carnall Securitan," is well drawn in the manner of a Character and poses the question whether a similar work, *The Pilgrim's Progress*, was also aided by the Theophrastan tradition. Built-in and recognizable Characters can be seen here and there in other sober volumes. A witty sketch of a gamester brightens *A Timely Advice. Or, a Treatise of Play and Gaming* (1640).[15] More original in function, the "short Character" of the "Courteous Reader" with which David Person ingratiatingly prefaced his handbook on science, *Varieties: or, A Surveigh of Rare and Excellent Matters* (1635), is preceptual and too plainly instructive to be artistic.[16] But its appearance, as well as that of a more nearly Overburian picture of "the carping Reader" accompanying it, suggests an unexploited possibility, the Character as propitiatory prologue.

It is the fragmentary Character in the Overbury manner or, complete, the hortatory precept-Character that one meets most often in moralistic literature. When Brathwaite expanded his earlier *Schollers Medley*, offering it in 1638 as *A Survey of History: Or, A Nursery for Gentry*, he introduced various kinds of descriptive and illustrative material to which he applied the label "Character" as freely as he had done elsewhere. The plan adopted by John Gaule for his *Distractions, or The Holy Mad-*

---

[15]Page 119.
[16]I owe notice of these Characters to Paul H. Kocher.

nesse. Fervently (not Furiously) inraged against Evill Men (1629) is more interesting. He intended, apparently, to write three long Characters, or perhaps several Characters, of the proud, the angry, and the covetous, which he would interrupt, as his holy madness seized him, with expostulations and commentary, the latter to be printed in italics to mark their separate function. But fervor and volubility prevented his accomplishing so exacting a task. Sometimes the turbulent prose reads like old-fashioned type-satire, but sometimes it reminds one of the Vices of Hall,[17] of the graphic scorn of Overbury,[18] or the analysis of Earle; in treating the covetous,[19] Gaule like Burton may have gone straight to Theophrastus. What *Distractions* would have been, exactly, without the aid of the Character it would be rash to say, but probably nothing so entertaining.[20]

The employment of the Character to present the admirable or ideal types of human nature is difficult, as I have pointed out. Joseph Hall managed, by going down to the deepest desires and principles of such men, to make them credible and relatively likelike. When subsequent writers followed his pattern they had a measure of success too. Hall was judicious enough to try to sustain the illusion that he was describing real men,

---

[17]See pp. 114-118, 333-334.

[18]See pp. 90-95, 231-233, 361-364.

[19]See pp. 336-350.

[20]One might anticipate that when *The Man in the Moon* of 1609 was reworked in 1640 (as *The Wandering Jew telling Fortunes to Englishmen*) there would be even greater resemblance to a Character-book than originally (see p. 169 n. 27). There are some modifications in that direction, such as the reduction of the descriptions from three divisions to two, the addition of nine new types all familiar in the Character tradition, and the appearance of two moderately successful Characters (the "description" of the honest citizen's wife, the "Character of the Glutton"). But there are compensating losses. The reviser, though familiar with the Character, was not sufficiently impressed with it to remake the book in that pattern.

omitting *ought* and *should* and the future tense as being too
patently the devices of the preacher and teacher. But many
writers let this phase of the art of the Character go. Thomas
Fuller belongs to this group. His *Holy State* and *Profane State*
(published as one book in 1642) were composed, as Walter E.
Houghton, Jr., has pointed out in an excellent analysis,[21] not
to study character in actual, representative men but rather to
set forth rules of outward behavior according to "callings," to
teach conservative, middle-class decorum (for example, how
the widow is to face not herself but the world). The con-
tributing literary forms were the conduct-book, casuistry, the
literature of Estates and of private economy, the aphorism,
biography, such schoolbooks as Reusner's *Symbola Heroica*,[22]
all in addition to the Character; so neither the tone nor the
procedure is usually right for the latter. Of the five books (four
"Holy," one "Profane") one consists entirely of essays on
abstract subjects; the other four comprise forty-eight sections
describing "states" and thirty-two biographies illustrating them.
The division into good and bad along with the prominence of
Estates suggests Breton's influence.

Fuller ordinarily opens the descriptive sections with a paragraph or two introducing the subject, perhaps conversationally
or by a division of the material or, often, in a definition, even a
conceited one (the Good Widow "is a woman whose head hath
been quite cut off, and yet she liveth, and hath the second part
of virginity"). Then a set of paragraphs follows, each paragraph labeled "Maxime" and opened by an important, general
remark about the type of person under consideration. This

---

[21] *The Formation of Thomas Fuller's "Holy and Profane States"* (Cambridge, Mass., 1938).

[22] See J. Croft's review of Houghton's book and M. G. Walten's edition
in *Modern Language Review*, XXXIV (1939), 437-440. Houghton also
considers the possible influence of Caussin's Characters.

opening sentence, in italics, is more commonly followed by exegesis or examples from history than by the accumulation of revealing actions and ideas and speeches that the genuine Character would supply. Digression and commentary bulk as large as in Gaule's *Distractions,* but the intervening delineation of types is not so concrete or lively. Wit and Senecan cadence are only intermittent. Fuller talks down to his reader as neither Hall (who may talk above the reader) nor Overbury would ever do, and he introduces, practically for the first time in the Character tradition, a sympathetic understanding of the tactics of the climbing classes, those frequent objects of Overbury's and Earle's and Lenton's mirth. No perfectly sustained, complete Characters can be found in the *States*—the "Degenerous Gentleman" is perhaps the nearest approach—but like other didactic and educational writers of these decades Fuller found a plan in the Character-book and gave force if not wings to his ideas by borrowing something of its technique.

That the Character should begin to pay its debt to the conduct-book is not surprising. The repayment was begun in two books that declared much more frankly than Fuller's what their purpose was—*The English Gentleman: Containing Sundry excellent Rules . . . tending to Direction of every Gentleman . . . How to demeane . . . himselfe in the manage of publike or private affaires* (1630) and *The English Gentlewoman* (1631), both by Richard Brathwaite. Characters of many kinds, complete and fragmentary, appear in these books. The general, abstract Character of an admirable moral type is used at the very end of the former volume as a sort of elegant peroration. It is labeled "Character" and headed "A Gentleman." In the second volume Brathwaite employed this sort of sketch, but with more of the precept showing, in the dedicatory epistle and in the epistle "To the Gentlewoman Reader"; he also used it for a statement about modesty[23] (perhaps reflecting Breton's Characters of essays), for an account of the noblewoman[24] (in which Euphuistic constructions accentuate the old-fashioned appearance), and for a summary at the end.[25] It is testimony to Brathwaite's enthusiasm for his subject that he could develop the same topic so often; the weakness in these passages is not repetitiousness but too much didacticism, too little suggestion that a real person is before us. That weakness vanished when he wrote his humorous, journalistic sort of sketch, as in the report on "Roarers"[26] and, tucked away in a misnamed supplement bound with only some copies of *The English Gentleman*, the following passage (of what use in forming the gentleman I am not sure I know):

> He that is *Married*, is a man of another world, he hath bid all good fellowship adue, and now playes the Mould-warpe. . . He hath learned by this to man his wife to Church and Market . . . he carries nothing with better grace, or more willingnesse, than his wives Misset, fisting-dog, or fan. . . His pocket is still farced with *memorandums;* as *Item* for Sope and Candles; *Item* for Garlicke and Onions . . . he begins to looke asquint, having one eye on his businesse, the other on his wives favourites . . . hee admires the *good carriage* of his wife, though in that he erres, for it is too *common;* he is much addicted to commend his wives vertues, and so he may, for they are *rare;* hee begins to have a spice of the *Syatica,* or hip gout, and therefore goes furr'd like an Alderman. . . [H]ee is no sooner in bed than he sleepes, but his wife complaines that his sleepes are *too long.* He can play huswife for a need, and he is sometimes put to it; he cannot endure to

---

[23]Pages 168-169.
[24]Pages 202-204.
[25]Seven unnumbered pages, beginning sig. Ff$_4$.
[26]*The English Gentleman*, pp. 41-42.

heare a baudie tale in his wives presence, lest it corrupt her manners . . . he is now out of all young Gentlewomens favour . . . he is flat opposite to the *Puritan,* for the *spirit* seldome moves him . . . when he lookes on the *May-pole, Morice,* and *Summering,* hee fetcheth a great sigh, adding no more than *Bacons* brazen head, *Time was:* his judgement growes subordinate, having ever dependance on his wives watchword. . . He much delights to be slovenly, with a fashionless beard, a drivelling mouth, and a sniveling nose. . . In briefe, his life is a Labyrinth of vexation, whence it is impossible for him to be free, till the threed of his life be shreaded. Where (Sir) I leave you.

This wry piece, obviously a Character, is not so labeled; but elsewhere in the book—in marginal notes, supplement, and table of contents—Brathwaite uses "Character" to mean anything from "aggregate of qualities" to "essay."[27]

How the Character could penetrate the book that aimed to shape certain kinds of people is obvious enough. But how it got into biographical and historical writing, writing that studies individualities, is not quite so simple. One cause was the extenson of the word *character* to mean the sum of all the qualities of a person, then a written or spoken account of that aggregate. Both these significations were intended, perhaps, in the label given to the droll sketch which Ben Jonson wrote as a sort of preface for *Coryat's Crudities* (1611)[28]—"The Character of the Famous Odcombian . . . Traveller . . . Done by a charitable Friend, That thinks . . . you should understand the Maker, as well as the worke." "He is an Engine," Jonson begins, "wholly consisting of extremes, a Head, Fingers, and Toes. For what his industrious Toes have trod, his ready Fingers have written, his subtle head dictating." A good many biographical

---

[27]A Latin quotation attributed to "Theophrast" appears not in a Character but in an essay (*The English Gentleman,* p. 267).

[28]I have used the three-volume edition of 1776.

details are followed by more characterizing: "The word Travaile affects him in a Waine-Oxe, or a Pack-horse. A Carrier will carry him from any company that hath not been abroad, because he is a Species of a Traveller. But a Dutch-Post doth ravish him. . . And at seeing the word Frankford or Venice, tho but on the title of a Booke, he is readie to breake doublet, cracke elbowes, and overflowe the roome with his murmure." After much more comic description of Coryat's idiosyncrasies Jonson concludes by saying that at a table Coryat would "rather be served in as a Dish" than sit as a guest and that he is much more of a man than a mere author. All of this is to present Coryat as the oddest species of traveler, the scribbling variety. In the portrait of the individual are the tone, attitude, and style that Overbury was to adopt for his portraits of types.

By the time[29] Sir Henry Wotton penned his "Characters of some Kings of England," Character-literature was well known. But the meaning of Wotton's word is still not the technical one; rather, he means "signs" or descriptions of the physical and mental constituents of a man in addition to a summary of his political and economic policies. "It has beene a custome of old Historians," wrote Thomas May in 1633,[30] "when they record the actions of great Princes, to deliver also some Characters of their persons and peculiar dispositions." He and Wotton and Bacon in his book on the reign of Henry VII and Lord Herbert of Cherbury in his *Life and Raigne* of Henry VIII all followed classical historiography in composing such summaries of the facts about men's natures and lives. The compact summary at the end of Bacon's history, coherently organized with a fre-

---

[29]Before 1639. The "Characters" were printed in *Reliquiæ Wottonianæ* (1651).

[30]*The Reigne Of King Henry the Second* (1633), "The Description of King Henry the Second" printed at the end of the volume.

quent return to *he* as the subject in his sentences, is perhaps as
nearly like a Character in method as the similar passage early
in May's statement about Henry II. But both summaries are
very long; they run over into the history of the country; and
they, of course, treat individuals, not types. At this point historical writing can hardly be proved to have felt more than a
faint pressure from our genre. The next step would be to
compose a description of a character and a career with greater
economy, more artful selectiveness, and brighter phrasing—to
put the character-account into the Character-pattern. Additional
influences—the French portrait, Clarendon's personal acquaintance with the author of *Micro-cosmographie,* a new classical
feeling for design—would help. But the portrait-Character, in
a sense a contradiction in terms, came to its finest flower outside our period, in the hands of Clarendon, Dryden, and Halifax.

In the department of the epigram the influence of the Character had exerted itself so plainly already that we need not re-
examine the subject. The only pieces after Earle that need a
word are John Milton's two epitaphs on the University carrier,
Hobson. Here is the longer one. Presumably written at the
time of Hobson's death in 1631, it was first published in Arm-
strong's *Banquet of Jests* (1640).

> Here lieth one who did most truly prove,
> That he could never die while he could move,
> So hung his destiny never to rot
> While he might still jogg on, and keep his trot,
> Made of sphear-metal, never to decay
> Untill his revolution was at stay.
> Time numbers motion, yet (without a crime
> 'Gainst old truth) motion number'd out his time:
> And like an Engin mov'd with wheel and waight,
> His principles being ceast, he ended strait,
> Rest that gives all men life, gave him his death,
> And too much breathing put him out of breath;

Nor were it contradiction to affirm
Too long vacation hastned on his term.
Meerly to drive the time away he sickn'd,
Fainted, and died, nor would with Ale be quickn'd;
Nay, quoth he, on his swooning bed outstretch'd,
If I may not carry, sure Ile ne're be fetch'd,
But vow though the cross Doctors all stood hearers,
For one Carrier put down to make six bearers.
Ease was his chief disease, and to judge right,
He di'd for heavines that his Cart went light,
His leasure told him that his time was com,
And lack of load, made his life burdensom,
That even to his last breath (ther be that say't)
As he were prest to death, he cry'd more waight;
But had his doings lasted as they were,
He had bin an immortal Carrier.
Obedient to the Moon he spent his date
In cours reciprocal, and had his fate
Linkt to the mutual flowing of the Seas,
Yet (strange to think) his wain was his increase:
His Letters are deliver'd all and gon,
Onely remains this superscription.[31]

Hobson's type had been described, with similar scorn and punning, in John Earle's "Carrier," and Brathwaite in the year of
Hobson's death brought him and *decorum* together in his account
of a "Painter," who could "accommodate his portraiture with a
true garb; *Hobson* the Carrier must have his picture, with his
hand in his bag to designe his Condition." Whether young Milton needed Earle and Brathwaite to guide him is not worth heavy
thought. But we are licensed to round out our image of the
great poet with the supposition that he shared one more interest
with his contemporaries—sarcastic portraiture of the commercial
classes.

---

[31]*The Student's Milton*, edited by F. A. Patterson (New York, 1930),
pp. 22-23. Cf. also Overbury's "Footman."

Humorous literature of the more popular variety could not be expected to make much use of the shapely character. John Taylor, the "Water-poet," duplicated the harsh and figurative jocularity of the Overbury portrayals of low types in several portions of his pamphlet, *A Bawd. A vertuous Bawd, a modest Bawd* (1635) and adulterated the epigram and Character in *A most Horrible, Terrible, Tollerable . . . Satyre* (1635). Brathwaite put a "sprung" Character of a gentleman-usher among the anecdotes, salty and risqué, that he gave to the knowing reader under the caption, *Ar't asleepe Husband? A Boulster Lecture* (1640).

It is in the drama that one finds the most interesting connections with the Character, connections that in some instances defy definition but that, taken all together, imply a tangible influence and in "humors" comedy a real enforcement. The sort of casual, momentary depiction of types that Hamlet and Portia and Maria indulged in becomes less casual. The habits of the usurer, pander, and bawd, of the "wits of the town . . . whose jeers are all authentic,"[32] of some innocent country girl whose life makes a fine lady laugh,[33] the activities of "a sprig of the nobility . . . that loves clean napery [a "lady of pleasure"]"[34] or of the serving-man, "a fellow which scalds his mouth with another mans porridge, brings up meat for other mens bellies, and carries away the bones for his own, changes his cleane trencher for a fowle one, and is glad of it"[35]—these matters, always important to the social satirist, were well tended to in many plays written between 1610 and 1642. Whether Plautus and Jonson or Overbury and his sort encouraged their authors one cannot say.

---

[32]Shirley, *The Lady of Pleasure* (1637), III, ii.
[33]Massinger, *The City Madam* (licensed 1632, printed 1658), II, ii.
[34]Shirley, *Hyde Park* (1637), I, i.
[35]John Cooke, *Greene's Tu quoque* (1614), sig. D_2. See also Shirley's *Love's Tricks* (1631), III, v; Rowley's *All's Lost by Lust* (1633), V, iii.

Then there is the more pretentious type-satire, carried out by a summary of the habits that signify character. Once more Jonson must be taken into account. In his late play, *The Magnetic Lady* (1640), he reverted to the device employed in his early "humors" comedies of offering vivid characterizations of his people before they have a chance to reveal themselves. It was probably the "humors" tradition that Shackerley Marmion meant to follow in his *Fine Companion* (1633). But the graphic descriptions of the typical behavior of citizens' widows, of a virago, of a quarrelsome, extravagant young gallant, of Captain Whibble (a new blend of Thraso and Gnatho), of a libidinous wife, and of a rich gentleman-turned-country-stinkard are offered not at the outset in Act I but rather in Acts II, III, and IV and serve a different purpose than Jonson's. Cleverly woven into the dialogue, they are almost more essential to the effect of the play than the plot, for *A Fine Companion*, like *Characterismi* and *Whimzies* (both printed two years earlier), is chiefly concerned with manners.

Some of the descriptive sketches in the dramas of these decades present folk who seem to be escaping from the type into individualities of their own. Once more we see a starting-point in Jonson. Morose in *Epicoene* is too unusual a figure, too special a phase of unsociableness, for Theophrastus to draw; "Surliness," his nearest approach, is more familiar. Morose is, then, an individual, but in the wonderful flow of description and anecdote assigned to Truewit and Clerimont in the first act of the play Jonson devotedly builds Morose into a heroic representative of a class of which he is the only member. Very likely Jonson needed no help from the Character-books in such work; and it was probably Jonson who taught his former servant, Richard Brome, to paint a small picture in vivid colors of the behavior of prurient,

ushers Grammer" returned in a long dialogue on the subject in Brome's *Northern Lasse* (acted in 1629, printed in 1632, in which year *The Turke* was reprinted). To the previous data Howdee and Squelch add many details, such as the usher's being probably a tailor. "[P]runing his haire," clean linen, "ruffling his Bootes, or ordring his shooe-tyes," neatness in "Chamber-work" about his mistress's person, dexterity in carving are all part of the job, as well as being able to remember "how this Ladies tooth does; and tother Ladies toe. How this Ladies Milk does; and how tothers Doctor lik'd her last water: how this Ladies husband; and how tother Ladies dogge slept last night: how this childe, that Monkey." The reward is "at boord and at bed: by good bits, and the love of the Chambermayd."[42] Here is plentiful material for a Character. The topic, we notice, is not a "humor" but an occupation, as was often the case in the 1631 Character-books. There are signs that Lenton had heard this dialogue before he composed the regular Character of a gentleman-usher that I quoted in the previous chapter. There again the sleeveless errand and the skill in carving are specified. A much shorter description of an usher spoken sarcastically in Thomas Nabbes' *Covent Garden* (V, vi; acted the next year, printed in 1638) echoes Brome's suggestion that the fellow would be a tailor. Brathwaite's contribution to the subject, announced in 1628, appeared in 1640[43]—a long, graphic, tangy Character in the manner of those in *Whimzies*. Friendship with skinkers

---

[42]IV, i.

[43]Entered in the Stationers' Register in June (Arber's reprint, IV, 199), it was first printed, seemingly, in *Ar't asleepe Husband*, pp. 161-166. That Brome had heard of Brathwaite's Character or seen it is possible, though he emphasized different matters. But Brathwaite's remark that though the usher's "*revenues* be but small, his *vailes* are great" was matched by a nearly identical statement in Lenton's Character, so that one is forced to suppose either that Lenton had seen Brathwaite's manuscript or that Brathwaite's sketch was remade in imitation of Lenton's.

and personal conceit are additional marks of the trade in this piece. They are carried over into the largely derivative Character of a gentleman-usher included in Reresby's manuscript. A more exact accounting in this long commerce between comedy and Character need not be made; it would probably put comedy in the position of creditor.

Thus far it is the sarcastic, graphic description of reprehensible types that we have been noticing. Comedy could utilize a good deal of that sort of writing in spite of the latter's being static and, since compact, expensive. The preceptual delineation of admirable types of men also had its place as Jonson demonstrated when he gave a debate on valor[44] momentary eloquence by interrupting it with a panegyric on the valiant man. But Shirley gained first an elevating effect and then a comic one when he had a lady[45] keep her rival lovers (a courtier, a soldier, a scholar) breathless while she described in turn the ideal exemplar of the group to which each belonged. The lady's impromptu vein had perhaps been enriched by a previous reading in Breton's *Good and the Badde*.

We must look into the allegorical play also. In Nabbes' *Microcosmus* (1637) the abstraction "Tasting" reveals himself in a way that reminds one of the Charactering of the Thames and the Bridge in Lupton's book and of the Characters of inanimate things in *A Strange Metamorphosis*. In Thomas Randolph's *Muse's Looking-Glass* (acted about 1632, printed in 1638) the people of the play are chiefly the pairs of opposed moral qualities in Aristotle's *Ethics*, personified and set to talking about their own natures and especially about the faults of their opposites. Their speeches cannot be called Characters, particularly as they are in the first person; but it is hard to believe that the

---

[44]*The New Inn*, IV, iii. Acted 1629, printed 1631.
[45]Honoria in *Honoria and Mammon* (1659), II, ii.

311

vogue of the Character was not one source of Randolph's courage in planning such a play. As for John Day's masque-like work, *The Parliament of Bees* (1641), its pattern of monologues in which several kinds of bees expose their (human) natures could have been derived from classical satire. Yet the appearance of the word "Character" at the head of each scene and in many of the little explanatory quatrains supplies adequate evidence of another influence. But only the prejudiced could thank the Character for fostering these strange compositions.

There is one more thing the Character-books could do for the drama—give breath and locomotion to one of their figures and send it on to the stage. The Overbury-Webster "Fair and Happy Milkmaid" and Earle's "Antiquary" had the honor of this sort of life after life, the former in Nabbes' *Totenham Court* (acted in 1632), the latter in Marmion's comedy, *The Antiquary* (1641). If we were to judge Cicely, who is the milkmaid in Nabbes' play, merely by her own conduct we would not recognize her as Webster's sweet innocent, for though chaste and fair, she possesses a surprising knowledge of various forms of misconduct in high and low life that she glibly shares with others and she indulges a taste for free speech and practical joking for which Webster did not prepare us. It is in Frank's description (II, i) that we first learn of her origin.

She is faire:
Upon her person all the graces waite,
And dance in rings about her. Her bright eye
Is Loves chiefe mansion where he keepes his Court.
. . . . .
Her white and red she borrow's not from any
Cosmetique drugs; nor puzzles the invention
Of learn'd practitioners for oyle of Talxe
To blanch an Ethiops skin.

Her innocence he and she insist upon, and her soul "is guarded

with so many vertues Temptations cannot batter it." Her courage is remarkable; "no deluding spirits can abuse" her,

> nor imperfect moone-light
> Mock with false shadowes.   Danger frights not me.

Webster's charming picture of the maid at her milking is given
a new use:

> My father oft hath told me when my fingers
> Prest the Cowes dugges, and from their fulnesse drew
> Aboundance of white streames, that Nature meant not
> These limbs for labour (IV, i).

And he was right: Cicely is proved to be of noble birth. The
power of locomotion and the modes of Caroline comedy have
permitted Cicely to come a long way from the "Milkmaid's"
haycock and merry wheel.

   In bringing Earle's "Antiquary" on to the stage Shackerley
Marmion kept much closer to his original.   Like Earle he made
the fellow ill-judging and contemptible.   Sometimes it is the
antiquary himself who utilizes Earle's phrases, sometimes it is
someone else speaking about him.   One turn in the action comes
from a sentence in the Character (Lionell gets money which
he needs by selling to the antiquary two books falsely offered
as "of the old Roman binding" and in "Marcus Tullius Cicero's
own handwriting").[46]   It is worth remarking how much less
interesting—at least, in the reading—the ridiculous fellow is in
his appearances in the play than he is in *Micro-cosmographie.*
Relinquishing the concentration of the Character, Marmion

---

[46]Earle writes it thus: "He would give all the Bookes in his Study
(which are rarities all) for one of the old Romane binding, or sixe
lines of *Tully* in his owne hand."   The echoes of Earle's wording appear pp. 210, 228-229, 251-252 *(Dramatic Works of Shackerley Marmion).*

seems not to have had enough dramatic invention or enough wit to preserve the literary charm of the original.

But it must have been easy for Nabbes and Marmion to make characters out of Characters. The surprising thing is that there were not more transformations of this sort. Quite possibly I have missed some. If, as we have seen, the gentleman-usher gained clarity as a static figure by the standardizing of the descriptive detail accumulating in plays and Character-books, so, no doubt, other figures became more immediately recognizable through the same kind of mutual assistance. Certainly comedy and Character abetted each other in the pursuit of types and especially in the emphasis upon manners. For the genuine "humor" cannot be delineated again and again without monotony, whereas the changing forms and costumes and careers of society can be so freshly presented as to conceal the tedious sameness of the men beneath the forms. And the shift from moral classes to current modes had more than a literary cause. In the first half of the century in England it was as much a social self-consciousness as a moral one that was developing and splitting the nation into factions. There were Good Divines and Cowards in all parties, of course, but a man would recognize virtue and vice according to the lights of his present party, and the distinguishing features would be local, dialectical, in an absolute sense superficial. New Presbyter is perhaps but Old Priest writ large, but a Milton was needed to point that out. Meanwhile the followers of Theophrastus and Plautus turned to the conspicuous absurdities of the new day. Appropriately, too, the Character, which had learned something about style from Ben Jonson at the beginning of the century, now helped sustain the popularity of the sort of comedy from which it had taken lessons. As Jonson was now retiring from active writing, such support was of value. Character-writers could show, if the demonstration were needed, how the "humors" technique might be applied to the merely picturesque.

The theater, shut up in 1642, had evil associations for the Puritans and so, no doubt, had the Character, for it was usually written from the Royalist and Anglican point of view, and one of its butts had been the zealot. But on the other hand, Characters of Virtues, of an unquestioned fervor even if inaugurated by a future bishop, had also become a recognized part of the repertoire, and the rational, half classical ideal of conduct there advanced could not have been altogether unpleasing to the better-educated Puritans. In addition, from Casaubon to Reresby there was always the doctrine (no matter how scatological the illustrative detail) that Theophrastus and his school should "incite the Conscious Perusers too Reformation." The practical sense of the Puritans eventually impelled them to adopt so convenient a form of writing. Yet the party that employed the epithet "Formalist" as one of their milder forms of abuse might be expected to compose Characters that sprawled. Only when the regular Character had started to degenerate into the pamphlet did the Puritans use it very much.

The pamphlet-Character, which after 1640 like a rank weed nearly choked out the cultivated species, lies outside the limits of this book. Before we close, however, it will be interesting to notice the weed, which had already begun to grow. Its origin was in old-fashioned satire upon types, especially types working against Church and state. The Character-writers took over the attack, but as the dangers to be inveighed against were concealed and insidious, the objective technique of Theophrastus would not do, at least not alone. The hypocrite and the superstitious that Theophrastus portrayed are always with us, but they are not the parochial varieties that caused alarm in the early seventeenth century. It is, rather "A Precisian" (a "faire object to the eye," with the most shocking principles) and "A Jesuit" whom the Overbury writers unmasked and analyzed. Here and in the excellent depiction of "the selfe-opinion'd *Puritan*" in Thomas Heywood's *Troia Britanica* (1609)[47] outward conduct, picturesque as it may be, will need supplementing with a clear and hostile statement of the man's theories and slogans. As the enemy grows more threatening, a more explicit statement and more sarcasm will be needed[48] and, eventually, personalities and argument. Something of the shapeliness of the Character, a little of its exposure of a man's nature through his actions, and much of its irony could at first be kept, as one sees in *The True Character of an Untrue Bishop* (1611) or in *The Iesuits Character, Or, A Description of the wonderfull Birth, wicked Life, and wretched Death, of a Iesuite* (1642). The shift of emphasis from what a man is to what he believes and at last to what he (horribly) does can be noticed, along with the tendency of these pieces to become catalogues of errors, in the eleven-page Character of "A Projector" in Thomas Heywood's pamphlet, *Machiavel* (1641). The next step, a resort to implied argument and free vilification, came in *The Character of an Oxford Incendiary* (1643?), which begins in the more or less traditional way ("An *Oxford Incendiary* is a Court Salamander, whose proper element is Fire: An *English*-man, yet lives by *Anti-peristasis* to his native *Climate*") but which on the second page admits all those who blew up Scotland, on the third page a whole train of bishops, and, before the

---

[47]Canto IV, stanzas 50-53.

[48]How an ordinary Character-book could be twisted into serving a faction is well illustrated in *England's Selected Characters* (1643), which consists of twenty-eight Characters from Breton's *Good and the Badde*, re-labeled and just slightly reworded to make them hostile to the Royalist party. Breton's "Unquiet Woman" becomes "An Unworthy Queen or woman," his "Reprobate" becomes "A Jesuit reprobated," and his "Coward" becomes "A Cowardly Cavalier"!

eight pages are finished, personal attacks on Henrietta Maria, Newcastle, and others of the Royalists. Were not this a Roundhead piece, we should say that now all the stops were pulled out to let the organ roar.[49]

In times like these, the small, polished, and lucid sketch in the manner of Theophrastus was irrelevant. Never intended for use in battle, it might aid in early propaganda, but with the flight of Charles in 1642 it too had to retire. Its principle of killing many birds with one stone might still serve, as could its habit of collecting vivid samples of revealing behavior. But in the battle of the books in Civil War days, the word *Character* became hardly more than a phrase for the title page, a mere design to paint on the upper armor. The strength of the pamphlet was elsewhere. Until another neo-classicism should revive it, the Theophrastan Character languished.

---

[49]That the Puritans did not always roar can be seen in the interesting and deceptive irony of a verse Character of a so-called Puritan appended to a Mar-prelate pamphlet, *A Dialogue Wherein Is Plainly Layd Open the Tyrannicall Dealing of Lord Bishops . . . Reprinted . . . 1640.*

INDEX

Adams, Thomas, Characters in his sermons, 200-208; 209, 240n., 289

Addison, Joseph, 232, 273

Aldington, Richard, *Book of Characters*, 71, 108

Ancren Riwle, 55

Aphthonius, 28-29

Ariston, 19

Aristotle, influence on Theophrastus, 13-16; logic, 153-156, 163, 245-246; *Ethics*, 11-15; *Rhetoric*, 11-16, 41; 164, 219, 227

Arte of English Poesie, 46

Ascham, Roger, 41, 52n., 76

Bacon, Francis, 41, 81-83, 164, 174n., 184-185, 190-192, 253n., 294, 303; on need of "Probative" character-studies, 173-175

Baker, E. A., *History of English Novel*, 71n.

Baldwin, C. S., *Medieval Rhetoric and Poetic*, 21n.

Baldwin, E. C., 71n., 101n., 106n., 125n.

Barclay, A., *Ship of Fools*, 62-63

Barclay, J., *Icon Animorum*, 75

Barnes, B., *Four Bookes of Offices*, 127

Bartholomew, *Batman uppon Bartholome*, 75

Baskervill, C. R., *English Elements in Jonson's Early Comedy*, 66n.

Beaumont, F., and J. Fletcher, *Woman Hater*, 116n.

Bellasys, Margaret, 206n.

Benedicti, Jean, 72-74

Benson, A. C., on Earle, 188, 238n.

Bernard, R., *Isle of Man*, 297

Bible, 66n., 83, 191-193; near-Characters, 55-57

Biographical sketches, 84-85; see also Character: tendencies toward portrait-Character

Black, M. W., *Richard Brathwait*, 265n.

Blount, T., *Academy of Eloquence*, 51

Brandenburg, Alice, "Dynamic Image in Metaphysical Poetry," 144n.

Brathwaite, Richard, *Ar't asleepe Husband*, 306, 310; *English Gentleman*, 300-302; *English Gentlewoman*, 300; epigrams, 171-172; *Essaies*, 197; *Schollers Medley*, 199, 209, 297; *Solemne Ioviall Disputation*, 215-216; *Whimzies*, 265-275, 305; 292.

Breton, Nicholas, *Characters upon Essaies*, 190-194, 220n.; *Fantasticks*, 111n., 234-235; *Good and the Badde*, 216, 221, 228-234, 311, 316n.; 88, 93-94, 181, 185, 190n.

Brewer, T., *Knot of Fooles*, 171

Brinsley, J., *Ludus Literarius*, 41, 45, 161n.

Brome, R., *Northern Lasse*, 310

Browne, H., *Map of Microcosme*, 289

Bryskett, L., *Discourse of Civill Life*, 219

Bullein, William, 66n.

Bunyan, John, 69

Burton, R., *Anatomy of Melancholy*, 195-197

Bush, D., *English Literature in Earlier Seventeenth Century*, 194n.

Butler, Charles, *Rhetoricae Libri Duo*, 48

Casaubon, Isaac, his edition of Theophrastus, 23, 36, 37, 44; definition of Character, 44; 53, 122, 160, 240

Castelvetro, L., 47, 49n., 50

Caussin, Nicholas, 45, 292n., 299n.

Cavendish, Sir William, 194, 199

Chapman, George, 94n., 114-115

Character, defined, 3, 19, 151, 152, 160, 177, 191, 267-268, 271;

319

INDEX